Asian Container Ports

Books are to be returned on or before
the last date below.

Asian Container Ports

Development, Competition and Co-operation

Edited by

Kevin Cullinane and Dong-Wook Song

First published 2007 by
PALGRAVE MACMILLAN
Houndmills, Basingstoke, Hampshire RG21 6XS and
175 Fifth Avenue, New York, N.Y. 10010
Companies and representatives throughout the world

PALGRAVE MACMILLAN is the global academic imprint of the Palgrave
Macmillan division of St. Martin's Press, LLC and of Palgrave Macmillan Ltd.
Macmillan® is a registered trademark in the United States, United Kingdom
and other countries. Palgrave is a registered trademark in the European
Union and other countries.

ISBN-13: 978–0–230–00195–4 hardback
ISBN-10: 0–230–00195–5 hardback

This book is printed on paper suitable for recycling and made from fully
managed and sustained forest sources.

A catalogue record for this book is available from the British Library.

Library of Congress Cataloging-in-Publication Data

Asian container ports: development, competition and co-operation / edited by
          Kevin Cullinane and Dong-Wook Song.
        p. cm.
    Includes bibliographical references.
    ISBN 0-230-00195-5
    1. Container ports—East Asia—Cost effectiveness. 2. Container ports—
Southeast Asia–Cost effectiveness. I. Cullinane, Kevin. II. Song, Dong-Wook.

HE551.A76 2007
387.1'53095—dc22   2006047457

10 9 8 7 6 5 4 3 2 1
16 15 14 13 12 11 10 09 08 07

Printed and bound in Great Britain by
Antony Rowe Ltd, Chippenham and Eastbourne

This book is dedicated to Tan Sri Frank W. K. Tsao, Chairman of the IMC Group, for his generous support and wise counsel during the five years I spent in Hong Kong.

Prof. Kevin Cullinane

This book is dedicated to port professionals in Asia for their contribution to the industry, to his beloved family members, Sung-Hee, Jee-Young and Jee-Hoon, for their love evermore and to the Lord for the good.

Dr Dong-Wook Song

Contents

List of Figures

List of Tables

Acknowledgements

The authors are grateful to all the contributors for their unstinting efforts in bringing this book to fruition. We also take this opportunity to thank the many staff at Palgrave Macmillan that helped see the book to press. In particular, Rebecca Pash and Jacky Kippenberger exhibited immense reserves of patience in awaiting the final manuscript. Finally, we should also voice our appreciation of the patience shown by our long-suffering wives, Sharon and Sung-Hee.

All efforts have been made to contact copyright holders. If any have inadvertently been overlooked, the publishers will be pleased to make suitable arrangements at the first opportunity.

Professor Kevin Cullinane
Dr Dong-Wook Song

Notes on Contributors

Dr Tao Chen
Associate Professor
Department of Shipping and
  Logistics Management
Kai Nan University
No. 1 Kainan Road, Taoyuan
  County 338
Taiwan, ROC
Tel: (8863) 341 2500
E-mail: chentao@mail.knu.edu.tw

Dr Sam-Hyun Cho
Research Fellow
Busan Development Institute
Water Authority Building 273-20
Yangjung 2-dong, Busanjin-gu
Busan 614-052
Korea
Tel: (8251) 860 8822
E-mail: shcho@bdi.re.kr

Professor Kevin Cullinane
Chair in Marine Transport and
  Management
School of Marine Science and
  Technology
University of Newcastle
Armstrong Building
Newcastle upon Tyne NE1 7RU
United Kingdom
Tel: (44191) 222 6218
E-mail: kevin.cullinane@ncl.ac.uk

Dr Yun-Su Hur
Research Fellow
Busan Development Institute
Water Authority Building 273-20
Yangjung 2-dong, Busanjin-gu
Busan 614-052

Korea
Tel: (8251) 860 8821
E-mail: logiyun@bdi.re.kr

Professor Hajime Inamura
Department of Civil Engineering
Graduate School of Information
  Sciences
Tohoku University
Aoba 06, Aoba-ku, Sendai 980-8579
Japan
Tel: (8122) 217 7492
E-mail: h-inamura@
plan.civil.tohoku.ac.jp

Dr Kazuhiko Ishiguro
Assistant Professor
Faculty of Maritime Sciences
Kobe University
Higahinada, Kobe 658-0022
Japan
Tel: (8178) 431 6314
E-mail: ishiguro@maritime.kobe-
u.ac.jp

Dr Choon Heng Leong
Associate Professor
Malaysia University of Science and
  Technology
17 Jalan SS7/26, 47301 Petaling Jaya
Selangor
Malaysia
Tel: (603) 7880 1777
E-mail: chleong@must.edu.my

Mr Daniel Olivier
PhD Researcher
Department of Geography
The University of Hong Kong

Pokfulam Road
Hong Kong
Tel: (852) 2859 2828
E-mail: olivied@hkusua.hku.hk

Dr Dong-Keun Ryoo
Assistant Professor
Division of Shipping Management
Korea Maritime University
1 Dongsam-dong, Yeongdo-ku
Busan 606-791
Korea
Tel: (8251) 410 4381
· E-mail: dkryoo@hhu.ac.kr

Dr Ryuichi Shibasaki
Researcher
National Institute for Land and
   Infrastructure Management
Ministry of Land, Infrastructure and
   Transport
Nagase 3-1-1, Yokosuka-shi
Kanagawa-ken 239-0826
Japan
Tel: (81468) 44 5028
E-mail: shibasaki-r92y2@ysk.nilim.
go.jp

Professor Bing-Liang Song
School of Economics and
   Management
Shanghai Maritime University
1550 Pudong Avenue
Shanghai 200135
China
Tel: (8621) 5885 5200
E-mail: blsong@cct.shmtu.edu.cn

Dr Dong-Wook Song
Associate Professor
Centre of Urban Planning and
   Environmental Management
The University of Hong Kong
Pokfulam Road

Hong Kong
Tel: (852) 2241 5554
E-mail: dsong@hkucc.hku.hk

Dr Jose Tongzon
Associate Professor
Department Economics
National University of Singapore
1 Arts Link, AS2 Level 6
Singapore 117570
Tel: (65) 6874 6258
E-mail: ecsjt@nus.edu.sg

Dr James Wang
Associate Professor
Department of Geography
The University of Hong Kong
Pokfulam Road
Hong Kong
Tel: (852) 2859 7026
E-mail: jwang@hkucc.hku.hk

Mr Peter Wong
Lecturer
Department of Logistics
The Hong Kong Polytechnic
   University
Hung Hom Kowloon
Hong Kong
Tel: (852) 2766 7921
E-mail: lgtpwong@polyu.edu.hk

Dr Gi-Tae Yeo
Researcher
International Shipping and
   Logistics Division
University of Plymouth Business
   School
Drake Circus
Plymouth PL4 8AA
United Kingdom
Tel: (441752) 23 2412
E-mail: gi-tae.yeo@plymouth.ac.uk

Part I
Introduction

1
Introduction

Kevin Cullinane and Dong-Wook Song

1.1 Background

Globalisation has been an emergent trend in many industries over recent years and the port industry is no exception. The globalisation of the port business is the natural corollary of a geographical diversification strategy on the part of the operators of what were previously significant, but localised, port businesses. As a consequence of this strategy, the leading port operators have extended the boundaries of their interests to encompass the regional and/or global scale; to such an extent that many of today's major port operators have evolved to the level of multinational corporations. Indeed, as one of the defining characteristics of this globalisation process, the management of port operations has become increasingly concentrated into the hands of just a few large port operating groups, such as Hutchison Port Holdings (Hong Kong), PSA Corporation (Singapore) and DP World (Dubai).

With the globalisation of production and consumption, it is imperative that worldwide distribution channels operate efficiently within a reliable multimodal system. This has led to an era where *logistics* and *supply chain management* have become critical concepts that impact directly upon the business success of any commercial operation. Given its pivotal role in both logistics and supply chain management, the whole transportation industry – but most especially the maritime sector – has had to respond accordingly.

As an integral element of the change in management perception and system orientation that this shift in emphasis has pre-empted, the role of ports has evolved. In the past, they were perceived to provide merely the required interface for transferring cargoes between the sea and other transport modes. Now they constitute an important node within global logistics networks (Robinson, 2002; Notteboom and Winkelmans, 2001). In consequence, whereas ports have traditionally been considered to provide a component function within a logistics system as the point of convergence between intermodal transportation and both gateway and transhipment traffic, they have become increasingly considered as important logistics platforms. As a result, the level of development and growth of transport logistics within a port exerts a substantial influence over the perception of a port's quality.

Although ports have a significant role to play within this newly evolved system, because of the development and continuous improvement of globally extended supply chains (Christopher, 1998) ports no longer enjoy a natural monopoly over their hinterlands as was the case in the past. Within such an environment, it is inevitable that ports will face new levels and forms of much more intense competition. In order to be successful, therefore, they will need to identify their true market and adopt a customer-oriented stance towards that market to secure their positions within global distribution networks. They also need to accept and incorporate everything that this might entail: a change in corporate culture, greater levels of efficiency, a different pricing strategy, a lean and agile approach (Marlow and Paixao, 2004; Paixao and Marlow, 2003) and even a certain level of co-operation (either implicit or explicit) at the national, regional and international level, with entities that may ostensibly be direct competitors.

As the major user of the services that ports offer, it is vitally important to address the situation of the shipping industry. In this respect, containerisation continues to have a major influence over international transportation.

The globalisation of manufacturing industry and the associated growth in containerised trade have created a demand for the delivery of global service networks on the part of container shipping (liner) companies. In order to properly satisfy this demand, the liner shipping industry has adopted a range of strategies, some of which rely upon some form of co-operation between what are substantive industry competitors. For more than a century, the traditional forum for co-operation within the liner shipping industry has taken the form of unidirectional route-specific conference arrangements. This has been followed by the establishment of rate stabilisation agreements on certain routes. However, in recent years, the container shipping industry has entered a period of considerable rationalisation of its operations, in response not only to ever-mounting regulatory pressure but also to other changes in the business environment. This is manifest in both a commitment to the deployment of ever-larger container ships and to the implementation of operational network structures based on the hub-and-spoke concept (Cullinane and Khanna, 1999, 2000). As a corollary of the operational changes that have been implemented in order to fulfil modern market needs, there has also been a rationalisation of industrial structure. This has evolved as the product of significant merger and acquisition activity, as well as from the formation of strategic alliances among most of the largest shipping companies. The greater industrial concentration that has ensued has been a necessary prerequisite for the consolidation of the leading role in the market played by the major container shipping companies (Heaver et al., 2000) and, specifically, for the maximisation of market share and minimisation of costs (Cullinane and Khanna, 1999). In responding to the demands of shippers, shipping companies do now duly provide worldwide networks, whereby one mega-carrier or an alliance can move goods freely around a global market.

Increased concentration and co-operation in the container shipping industry has led to much greater market power for shipping companies and alliances in their negotiations with the ports that handle their cargoes. Operational constraints inevitably continue to exist and, in many instances, impinge upon port choice decisions more onerously than previously was the case. However, operational rationalisation and infrastructure development have together combined to give international shipping lines greater choice than they would otherwise possess as to which ports they call at. This has had the effect of even further enhancing the bargaining position of the container shipping industry vis-à-vis the ports sector.

Several shipping lines are able to collectively negotiate with port or terminal operators for favourable charges and service conditions. In an extreme case, the loss of an alliance customer leads to substantial damage to a port operator in terms of throughput and sales revenue. For example, in 2000 and 2001 respectively, Maersk Sealand and Evergreen moved the hub for their Southeast Asian operations from Singapore to their neighbouring competitor, the Port of Tanjung Pelepas (PTP), situated just across the border in Malaysia (Cullinane et al., 2006).

Competitive pressure need not be felt solely at a local level when attempting to secure hinterland cargoes. Intense rivalry between ports exists even within a very wide international arena. This is largely because of the many operational and strategic developments and influences that have already been alluded to above and which have led to the transformation of some feeder ports into regional hub ports or vice versa. As a consequence, ports not only compete locally, but also regionally, against other ports; even some that may be very distant from each other indeed, although still serving the same shared hinterland. A good example of this is provided by North America, where the efficiency and effectiveness of the landbridge across the continent is such that the whole of North America now constitutes a shared hinterland for ports on both the east and west coasts (McCalla, 1999). While almost inevitably facing severe port competition both locally and regionally, port operators have sought a new approach in order to gain mutual benefits from and with their competitors (Culpan, 1993). Instead of succumbing to the vagaries of the intense competition they face, container ports are increasingly implementing what they regard as a win-win strategy of forming strategic alliances with their competitors. In this respect, *co-opetition* among ports has become an obvious strategic option that a port might successfully pursue in this highly intense competitive business environment (Song, 2003).

This kind of business pattern is one which is particularly evident amongst Asian container ports. As such, this book brings together a number of contributions that present and discuss recent and prospective port developments, national port policy and the strategic responses of major players in the Asian container port market.

1.2 Ports analysed

The container ports that are analysed within this volume have been chosen on the basis of their impact on regional and international trade. In this respect, a world league table of annual cargo throughput provides a solid starting point for the selection. Clustering the geographic locations of the Asian container ports with the largest throughputs has resulted in the identification of three sub-regions: Northern, Central and Southern Asia, as illustrated in Figure 1.1.

In the Northern region, Shanghai, Busan, Kobe and Yokohama have been selected for inclusion, while in the Central region Kaohsiung, Shenzhen and Hong Kong are chosen. Singapore and its Malaysian rival, the Port of Tanjung Pelepas (PTP) have also been chosen for analysis as representatives of the Southern Asia region.

1.3 Structure

Parts II–IV are dedicated to a region-by-region analysis of national and/or municipal policies on port development and current and prospective development plans, with some insights provided into: the administrative and

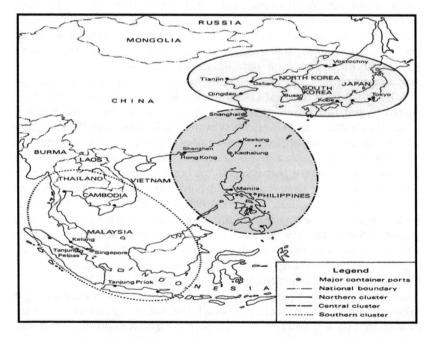

Figure 1.1: Major container ports in Asia
Source: Modified from Loo and Hook (2002: 223).

ownership structures of the ports considered; the business strategies pursued by terminal operators, regardless of their ownership; the financing of these developments (e.g. private, public, joint or some other form); and the competitiveness of the port within the region.

To this end, Part II looks at the set of individual ports in the northern region of Asia. This is begun by Bing-Liang Song, who provides an analysis of the Port of Shanghai that focuses most particularly on its position and future development in the light of ongoing problems and improvements in inland infrastructure. In Chapter 3, Dong-Keun Ryoo and Yun-Su Hur provide an explanation of Busan's development as Korea's primary container port and focus on the changes in governance structure that have been linked to the port's development as a national and regional hub. In Chapters 4 and 5, Hajime Inamura, Ryuichi Shibasaki and Kazuhiko Ishiguro provide detailed explanations of the physical development of the Ports of Kobe and Yokohama respectively. In so doing, they focus on the required capacity and strategic response to predictions of future demand for container port throughput in Japan and highlight the main policy issues that need to be addressed.

Part III of the book focuses on container ports in the central Asian region and begins with Tao Chen's analysis of Kaohsiung. This looks at the highly advantageous position of the port as a potential regional transhipment hub for Chinese and other cargoes. It provides an in-depth analysis of the political situation in the region, especially with respect to shipping relations with mainland China, and points to ongoing physical and political developments that, it is intended, will lead to an enhanced role for the port in the future. In Chapter 7, Peter Wong presents the situation in Hong Kong. His focus rests very much on: the physical development of the port – both historic and prospective; the governance structure which underpins port policy and operations; the financing of the port; and the intense competition that exists with the neighbouring Port of Shenzhen, located just across the border in mainland China. Emphasis is placed upon how and why Hong Kong can maintain its competitive position in the light of the intense competition it faces in its immediate hinterland.

Part IV of the book is devoted to the situation in the southern Asian region. In Chapter 8, Jose Tongzon analyses the role played by Singapore's port in contributing to the economic growth of the nation. As well as providing a detailed inventory of the port's physical characteristics, the major thread running through this contribution is a justification of how and why Singapore can indeed compete, both operationally and strategically, with an intense rival located just across the border in Malaysia. In Chapter 9, we gain another perspective on this same intense rivalry in a contribution from Choon Heng Leong that analyses the situation of the Port of Tanjung Pelepas (PTP). The work provides a detailed vision of how and why the port came into being and the strategic thinking and political issues which surrounded its inauguration and further development. In all of this, its relationship to and with the Port of Singapore is clearly a significant one.

Following these chapters, Part V is dedicated to the analysis of the interrelationships that exist between certain pairs of adjacent ports. As such, the various individual chapters all focus on the level and form of competition between the ports under scrutiny and any co-operation and/or co-opetition that exists within the geographic locale. To this end, competitive–co-operative relationships are explored in relation to the port pairings of: Shanghai and Ningbo (by James Wang and Daniel Olivier, Chapter 10); Hong Kong and Shenzhen (by James Wang and Daniel Olivier, Chapter 11); Singapore and PTP (by Jose Tongzon, Chapter 12); and Busan and Gwangyang (by Gi-Tae Yeo and Sam-Hyun Cho, Chapter 13).

References

Christopher, M. L. (1998) *Logistics and Supply Chain Management: Strategies for Reducing Cost and Improving Service* (2nd edn), New York: Financial Times–Prentice Hall Books.

Cullinane, K. P. B. and Khanna, M. (1999) 'Economies of Scale in Large Container Ships', *Journal of Transport Economics and Policy*, 33(2): 185–208.

Cullinane, K. P. B. and Khanna, M. (2000) 'Economies of Scale in Large Containerships: Optimal Size and Geographical Implications', *Journal of Transport Geography*, 8: 181–95.

Cullinane, K. P. B., Yap, W. Y. and Lam, J. S. L. (2006) 'The Port of Singapore and its Governance Structure', in M. R. Brooks and K. P. B. Cullinane (eds), *Port Governance and Performance*, Research in Transportation Economics, Vol. XIV, Amsterdam: Elsevier, (forthcoming).

Culpan, R. (1993) 'Multinational Competition and Co-operation: Theory and Practice', in R. Culpan (ed.), *Multinational Strategic Alliances*, New York: International Business Press, 13–32.

Heaver, T., Meersman, H., Moglia, F. and Van De Voorde, E. (2000) 'Do Mergers and Alliances Influence European Shipping and Port Competition?', *Maritime Policy and Management*, 27(4): 363–73.

Loo, B. and Hook, B. (2002) 'Interplay of International, National and Local Factors in Shaping Container Port Development: a Case Study of Hong Kong', *Transport Reviews*, 22(2): 219–45.

Marlow, P. B. and Paixao, A. C. (2004) 'Measuring Lean Ports' Performance', *International Journal of Transport Management*, 1(4): 189–202.

McCalla, R. (1999) 'Global Change, Local Pain: Intermodal Seaport Terminals and their Service Areas', *Journal of Transport Geography*, 7: 247–54.

Notteboom, T. E. and Winkelmans, W. (2001) 'Structural Changes in Logistics: How Will Port Authorities Face the Challenge?', *Maritime Policy and Management*, 28(1): 78–91.

Paixao, A. C. and Marlow, P. B. (2003) 'Fourth Generation Ports – a Question of Agility', *International Journal of Physical Distribution and Logistics Management*, 33(4): 355–76.

Robinson, R. (2002) 'Ports as Elements in Value-Driven Chain Systems: the New Paradigm', *Maritime Policy and Management*, 29(3): 241–55.

Song, D.-W. (2003) 'Port Co-opetition in Concept and Practice', *Maritime Policy and Management*, 30(1): 29–44.

Part II
Ports in Northern Asia

2
Shanghai: a Newly and Rapidly Developing Hub Port

Bing-Liang Song

2.1 Introduction

Over the past decade shipping in the Far East has proved an exceptional generator of container traffic. Foreign investment in the Chinese mainland – and in particular the Yangtze River Delta – by countries like Japan, the United States, South Korea and Singapore has produced extraordinary growth in international shipping services and trade volume (Figure 2.1). Spearheading these developments is Shanghai port, at once the centre of Chinese coastal shipping, Yangtze River traffic, ocean shipping and a water-rail intermodal junction. It is a comprehensive, multipurpose commercial port and one of China's principal foreign trade ports.

Shanghai has a highly developed economy, with 99 per cent of its foreign-trade goods handled by the port. Shanghai has established trade relations with about 160 countries and regions throughout the world and is served by all the top 20 international shipping lines. The cargo volume, foreign trade volume and container throughput of the Port of Shanghai reached an all-time high in 2003 (Figure 2.2). The port handled a total of 316 million tonnes of cargo, an increase of 19.9 per cent over 2002 and attained the rank of third in the world. Foreign trade cargo volume amounted to 130 million tonnes, a rise of 22.2 per cent over 2002, maintaining the number one position among mainland Chinese ports.

The port's rapid development has increasingly attracted Chinese and overseas shipping lines and agencies. By the end of 2003, there were 460 domestic shipping enterprises, including 71 for coastal shipping and 111 for inland river shipping. There were 36 international shipping enterprises, 48 ocean shipping agencies, 11 international ship-managing firms, and 328 non-vessel carriers. Up to 175 foreign-trading offices were registered in Shanghai, including 24 wholly foreign-funded shipping lines.

High levels of Chinese seaborne trade growth have given rise to functional and operational complications in ports, in port-linked inland transport networks, in shipping and in related institutions. Economies of scale are of great

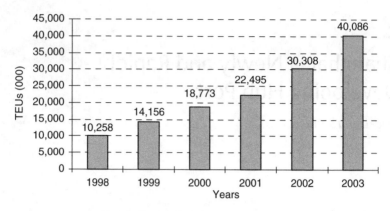

Figure 2.1:   Total container throughputs of the top 10 mainland ports

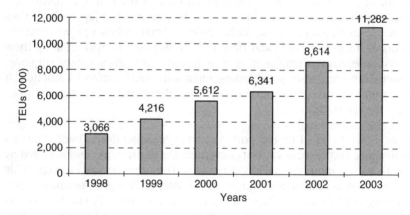

Figure 2.2:   Shanghai port container throughput

importance on the sea-leg, since ship size is only constrained by market demand and at times by a lag effect in berth provision. The consortium system was invented to allow operators to achieve a greater scale of operations by sharing vessel capacity without sacrificing frequency of service. Improvements in the way schedules are designed, whether by multistring services, round the world services, for post-panamax vessels or as pendulum services, have enhanced the quality of the basic port-to-port service, while costs have been reduced.

Shanghai and some Chinese eastern coastal ports such as Ningbo and Qingdao have been integrated into networks that serve the needs of their alliances. These ports have exceeded previous volume thresholds. For all but Shanghai, the new generation of container liners, with, say, 8,000-TEU slots, has been a boon. But for those giant vessels, access to the Port of Shanghai is restricted due to its limited depth and insufficient berths. Even with dredging of the Yangtze River entrance, there may be difficulties in accommodating 6,000-TEU ships.

Although Shanghai has made significant progress with its port infrastructure, container-handling capacity has failed to meet the fast-growing demand. According to the report of the Shanghai Municipal Port Administration Bureau (2004), container numbers passing through Shanghai port have grown by an average of 27 per cent annually over the past decade. This increase is based on the rapid development of foreign trade in the Yangtze River Delta area as well as the vast hinterland. Imports and exports through the Shanghai port grew in value by 41.2 per cent in 2003, to a record 201.2 billion US dollars, accounting for about a quarter of China's foreign trade.

On the other hand, Shanghai's container-handling facilities remain inadequate. Shanghai port is not only short of large deep-water berths, but also weak in modern logistics of the sort that can provide quick, reliable, flexible and comprehensive services. The Huangpu River – the mother river of Shanghai – is narrow and shallow, with a depth of only about seven metres, preventing container ships of 1,400 TEUs or more from entering the port. Large ships must wait for high tides to enter and leave Shanghai port, severely hindering the competitiveness of the port in the global market.

This chapter seeks to specifically explore the rapidly developing hub port status of Shanghai and the main challenges and opportunities it faces by analysing the current port infrastructure, the economic impact of the port industry and the inland accessibility of the port to its hinterland. What emerges is that the huge potential of Shanghai port rests with the improvement of both the hardware and software of its infrastructure and operations. To this end, the Port of Shanghai has done a lot to upgrade its services in quantity and quality through increased investment and accelerated structural reform.

The contents of this chapter are arranged as follows: Section 2.1 presents an overview of the performance of Shanghai port and the economies related to it. In addition, the objective of the chapter is briefly mentioned. Section 2.2 outlines the historical evolution of the efforts made by Shanghai to fulfil the blueprint of becoming a world-class hub port. Section 2.3 introduces the huge project of Yangshan Terminal, an offshore deep-water container terminal. Section 2.4 analyses the economic impact of Shanghai's water transportation industry (including the port industry) by evaluating its direct and indirect contributions to the Gross Regional Product (GRP) and local employment. Section 2.5 explores the inland access to Shanghai port by comparing the generalised transport costs for the available freight traffic routes between the main eastern coastal ports and their hinterlands in China's northwestern region. This is followed by the conclusion.

2.2   Fulfilling the blueprint

In the 1990s, Shanghai was brought to the forefront of China's economic development to conform to the trend of economic globalisation. The central government required that Shanghai spearhead economic development along the Yangtze Valley and become a centre of international economy, finance and trade as quickly as possible. To achieve this strategic goal, the construction of Shanghai International Shipping Centre was necessary. In January 1996, a meeting attended by both central and regional officials launched the construction of the Shanghai International Shipping Centre with Shanghai as the centre of this venture and neighbouring Zhejiang and Jiangsu provinces as its wings.

Since 1996, the construction of the Shanghai International Shipping Centre has been progressing in a number of stages:

1. Strengthening the leadership. In May 1996, the Shanghai Municipal Government founded the Shanghai International Shipping Centre with the Shanghai Regional Leading Group assigned to co-ordinate the project.
2. Enhancing the quality of shipping services. In November 1996, China's Ministry of Communications and the Shanghai Municipal Government jointly inaugurated the Shanghai Shipping Exchange, which carried out policy research, information release, tariff filing, tariff co-ordination and a one-stop customs declaration.
3. Strengthening co-ordination among the ports of Jiangsu Province, Zhejiang Province and Shanghai Municipality to pool together for the construction of the Shanghai International Shipping Centre. In September 1997, the Ministry of Communications with Jiangsu, Zhejiang and Shanghai provinces jointly established the Shanghai United Ports Administration to exercise unified administration and co-ordination over the deep-water shoreline of the container berths already completed and those planned on the Yangtze River downstream from the Yangtze River Bridge at Nanjing, and on the water areas of Ningbo and Zhoushan.
4. Accelerating the construction of the container terminals to expand container handling capacity and meet the increasing needs of container shipping. During the period from 1997 to 2003, phases one, two, three and four of container terminal construction were completed in Waigaoqiao, and the construction of phase-five multipurpose terminals in Waigaoqiao was begun.
5. Starting the Yangtze estuary channel-deepening project and the deep-water terminal construction which is aimed at putting an end to the bottleneck restricting the development of the Shanghai International Shipping Centre. The first phase of the channel-deepening project at the mouth of the Yangtze River began in 1998 and was completed in 2000, and the second phase is now underway, with a designed water-depth of 12.5 metres. In

June 2002, the first-phase construction of the Yangshan deep-water terminal was launched.

6. Accommodating more maritime activities. Shanghai made efforts to attract container lines, international shipping agencies and international freight forwarders to establish branches in the city and increase shipping services and sailings. Leading Chinese ocean carriers such as China Shipping (Group) Co. Ltd., COSCO Container Lines Co. Ltd., Sinotrans Container Lines Co. Ltd., etc. were stationed in Shanghai to support the Centre.

7. Initiating the reform of 'one-stop customs declaration' to improve the port environment. At the end of 2002, the goal of 'one-stop customs declaration' was realised ahead of schedule. In 2003, with the support of the China Customs Administration, the integrated operation between the Waigaoqiao Free Trade Zone Logistics Park and the port was inaugurated on a trial basis.

8. Restructuring the port system. In January 2003, the administrative system of the port underwent a significant reform. The Shanghai Municipal Port Administration Bureau was founded in accordance with the principle of 'separating government from enterprise functions'. The former Shanghai Port Authority was reorganised into the Shanghai International Port (Group) Co. Ltd., which pushed ahead with its internal reform.

Over the past five years, the Shanghai Municipal Government has kept the goal of developing its port and shipping industry in mind and has undergone a series of reforms to provide a good foundation for the future development of the Centre. Shanghai port has been the primary container port on the Chinese mainland, and its infrastructure, container throughput and economic importance surpass all other ports on the Chinese mainland. Up until the end of 2003, Shanghai port had built 24 specialised berths for container liners with a 6,787-metre-long shoreline. In 2003, the container throughput of Shanghai port reached 11.282 million TEUs, far beyond its annual designed handling capacity of 8.5 million TEUs.

At present it operates more than 20 international container liner services and over 100 feeder service routes across China. The port receives an average of 1,494 containership calls per month and has the capacity to handle fourth-generation container vessels of 4,600 TEUs. The developments in Shanghai's port industry in recent years were:

1. Shanghai Container Terminal Ltd.: a joint venture between Shanghai Port Authority, Hutchison Whampoa Group and COSCO Pacific (share ratio 5:4:1). Ten berths were built on the banks of the Huangpu River with an annual capacity of 1.7 million TEUs.

2. Phase 1 of Waigaoqiao Container Terminal: the total berth length measures 900 metres long, covers an open yard of 500,000 square metres and is backed up by three berths designed for 35,000-tonne vessels. The

designed annual capacity is 450,000 TEUs. In March 2000, the Shanghai Port Authority, Hutchison Whampoa Group, COSCO Pacific and Shanghai Industrial Investment reached a joint venture agreement (share ratio 4:3:2:1) on the management of Phase 1 of the Waigaoqiao Terminal under the Shanghai Pudong International Container Terminal Ltd.

3. Phase 2 of Waigaoqiao Container Terminal: Phase 2 commenced operation in September 1999. The terminal is equipped with three berthing spaces designed for 35,000-tonne vessels. It is 900 metres long with one million square metres of container yard and an annual capacity of 600,000 TEUs.

4. Phase 3 of Waigaoqiao Container Terminal: Phase 3 started its service in January 2002. The terminal has a designed annual handling capacity of 400,000 TEUs, with a 680 metre-long coastline, two berths to accommodate 35,000-tonne vessels, and a container yard of 500,000–700,000 square metres.

5. Phase 4 of Waigaoqiao Container Terminal: completed at the end of 2002, Phase 4 began to serve container liners in February 2003. The terminal has four berths with an overall length of 1,250 metres. Designed to handle 1.8 million TEUs annually, Phase 4 was jointly invested by Shanghai International Port Group (SIPG) and the world number one container carrier, i.e. Maersk Sealand Group (share ratio 51:49 per cent).

6. Phase 5 of Waigaoqiao Container Terminal: with a designed annual handling capacity of two million TEUs, the four-berth container terminal at Shanghai port is operated by Shanghai Mindong Container Terminal Ltd. – a 50–50 joint venture founded by Hutchison Port Holding (HPH) of Hong Kong and Shanghai International Port Group (SIPG). Spread over 1.6 million square metres, the new facility features 1,100 metres of quayside with a depth of 12.8 metres alongside, and began to accommodate ship calls on a trial basis in December 2004.

2.3   A deep-water port under construction

2.3.1   Context

Driven by strong foreign trade, container throughput in Chinese ports in 2003 exceeded 40 million TEU or 2.6 billion tonnes of cargo – the highest volume in the world. Eight of mainland China's ports had throughputs exceeding 100 million tonnes in 2003. Shanghai and Shenzhen handled more than 10 million TEUs each, becoming the world's third and fourth busiest ports, following only Hong Kong and Singapore.

China continues investing vigorously in port infrastructure to boost handling capacity. It is expected that by the end of 2005, the total number of berths in coastal ports will increase from 800 to 820. Chinese investment in seaports reached RMB 20.6 billion in 2003, a significant 48.8 per cent increase over the previous year. The new projects included 127 berths for medium-size ships and 45 berths for ships of over 10,000 tonnes. All these will equip the country with a further 82.2 million TEUs handling capacity.

Among mainland Chinese coastal ports, Shanghai is probably the most active in port infrastructure development. The Waigaoqiao terminal project, launched in 1993, is one of the largest port construction projects in Shanghai. The goal of the project is to create more than a dozen berths with a depth of 13 metres, capable of accommodating 4,000-TEU container ships. A question remains, however, over the feasibility of maintaining a 13-metre depth due to the silting of the river.

Under these circumstances, the construction of a mega-deep-water port became a 'must' for Shanghai, providing a long-term solution to fulfil the city's ambitious goals to become a major shipping hub in the world. The planned deep-water port includes three main parts: the offshore Yangshan Deep-water Terminal, the Donghai Bridge linking it with the mainland, and the seaboard Luchaogang New Harbour City.

2.3.2   Yangshan island: a reluctant choice

Shanghai has no suitable place in its immediate area to meet the demands of a deep-water harbour. After six years of feasibility studies, the islands of Xiao Yangshan and Da Yangshan in Hangzhou Bay, 25.7 kilometres from Shanghai's southern coast, and under the jurisdiction of the neighbouring province of Zhejiang, were chosen as the site of Shanghai's deep-water port. The project enjoys strong backing from central government. The average water depth in the area of the islands is over 15 metres. A comparison of today's sea charts with those of 100 years ago shows the geographic and geological structure is stable. However, this project requires a tremendous scale of investment and its operation will be affected more heavily by frequent typhoons in summer and autumn, compared with the neighbouring coastal ports.

The first phase of the Yangshan Deep-water Terminal construction started in the middle of 2002. It was completed in 2005. A land area of 1.53 square kilometres, equipped with a storage yard of 720,000 square metres and 15 container cranes was built in the first phase. This phase will also see the first five container berths from Xiao Yangshan island to Huogaitang isle with a 1,600-metre waterfront. The designed water-depth of the channels will be about 15.5 metres, capable of accommodating the fifth and sixth generation of container ships. Each berth was designed to handle 440,000 TEUs per year. The total annual handling capacity will therefore reach 2.2 million TEUs, which should meet the fast-growing demands of Shanghai port in the mid-term future.

According to the master plan, the whole project will be completed by 2020. At that time, the man-made area will increase to 18 square kilometres, and the deep-water coastal line will reach 22 kilometres. More than 50 container berths, capable of handling fifth and sixth generation container ships (5,000–6,000 TEU) will be built. The annual handling capacity of the deep-water port will increase to around 25 million TEUs, probably making it the biggest – and busiest – container terminal in the world.

The budget for the first phase was approved at RMB 14.31 billion (USD 1.73 billion), but no final budgetary target has been announced for the whole project. The developer of the port is the Shanghai Tongsheng Investment (Group) Co. Ltd., which is owned jointly by the Shanghai International Group Co. Ltd. (52 per cent), the Shanghai Port Administration and the Shanghai State-owned Assets Operation Co. In June 2002, the Shanghai Tongsheng Investment (Group) Co. Ltd. was offered RMB 7.5 billion (USD 907 million) in loans for the first-phase construction by a consortium of five domestic banks (China Construction Bank, the State Development Bank, the Bank of China, the Industrial and Commercial Bank of China, and the Shanghai Pudong Development Bank). A larger consortium made up of these five banks and five other lending institutions also signed a deal in June 2002, providing a credit line of RMB 17 billion (USD 2.06 billion) for port construction up to 2020.

In principle, foreign investors are allowed to own stakes of as much as 75 per cent in port projects, according to China's agreement with the World Trade Organisation (WTO). Hutchison International Ports Ltd., PSA Corp. of Singapore, P&O Nedlloyd Container Lines Ltd., Modern Terminal Ports Ltd. (controlled by Wharf Holdings Ltd.) and other international companies have shown an interest in joining the port project. The Shanghai Municipal Government, however, has not made any decisions regarding membership.

Port policy-makers seem to want to rely on themselves at first for the basic work of port construction. In the later phases, they will probably seek partners to attract more capital and the most advanced techniques and management for handling the port. This consideration is not only due to optimistic marketing estimates, but also to the strategic importance of the project for the national economy of China.

The long bridge to be built in the northern part of Hangzhou Bay and linking the deep-water terminal with the mainland has been named 'Donghai Bridge'. Bridge construction has already begun on the underwater foundations and should be finished by 2005, during the first phase of the port project. Services like container distribution, water and power supply and communications to the island terminal will be provided through this bridge. According to the plan, the bridge will be 31.3 kilometres long and 31.5 metres wide, with six highway lanes. The bridge has one main span (a box girder cable-stayed bridge with two towers) with a 40-metre clearance for 5,000-ton vessels, one side span for 1,000-ton vessels and two side spans for 500-ton vessels. The annual navigable capacity under the bridge will be over 5 million TEUs.

2.3.3   Luchaogang New Harbour City: a maritime cluster

Designed as one of the eleven satellite towns in the new round of Shanghai's urban planning, Luchaogang New Harbour City is situated in the southeast corner of Nanhui District, about 30 kilometres away from Yangshan island, 55 kilometres from downtown Shanghai, 30 kilometres from Pudong International Airport and 10 kilometres from Shanghai's outer expressway. Luchaogang Harbour City will be built to a high standard as a world-class modern harbour city. Based on the Master Plan by architects Von Gerkan, Marg and partners and adopted by Shanghai Municipal Government, it will be a combination of European and Shanghai styles and bear the characteristics of a southern Chinese town. The design defined the city as a coastal region with a maritime culture. In the centre of the New Harbour City, there will be a large circular lake with a diameter of almost 2.5 kilometres. The city extends radially from this freshwater lake and concentrically into a coastal area penetrated by canals.

The plan for Luchaogang Harbour City includes three urban rings. The first ring around the lake will be a belt of administrative, commercial and cultural facilities. The second ring is a green corridor decorated by flowers and trees. The outer ring is planned as a residential area complemented with shops, restaurants, clinics and an educational park including the relocated Shanghai Maritime University. Outside the outer ring, a modern traffic system will link the New Harbour City with the expressway network of Shanghai.

The New Harbour City will be the administrative centre of Nanhui District and the rear base of the deep-water port, encompassing comprehensive functions like container distribution and storage, offshore processing, shipping market, logistic centre, residence, financial and commercial services and tourism. A yacht club and a series of large cultural facilities including a theatre, maritime museum, aquarium, etc. will be established on the two islands in the lake.

The first phase of the city construction began in 2003 and will be finished by 2005. The number of inhabitants in the city at that time was expected to be 80,000–100,000. In about twenty years the city will host a population of 300,000 inhabitants. The Shanghai New Harbour City Investment & Development Co. Ltd. was founded jointly by the Shanghai Tongsheng Investment (Group) Co. Ltd. and Nanhui Land Reservation Centre in April 2002, with a registered capital of 1.3 billion RMB (157 million USD) and responsibility for the development of the Harbour City.

These projects, together with the existing Pudong International Airport and the forthcoming highway, railway and maglev train, present a vision of a huge logistics centre in the near future on the east wing of Shanghai, reflecting the city's dynamic growth and its initiative in a world economy in which China is going to play an ever-more important role.

2.4 Economic impact of Shanghai port

The operation of a port generates income and employment for the local community. All levels of government receive revenue from taxes and other charges on these activities. Along with growing enthusiasm for the new port projects in Shanghai, there have been lingering doubts about the management of such huge investments.

Port economic impact studies are contributing to a balanced assessment of the role of ports and to informed consideration of issues such as port planning and port investment. Port impact is mainly measured in terms of output, value added (the sum of payroll, tax revenue, profits and accounting depreciation) and employment. The studies aim to measure the economic impact of port and port-related activity, which is usually defined as the activity undertaken by firms and organisations in moving cargo through the port and in providing goods and services to directly facilitate the movement of cargo through the port. According to the US Maritime Administration guidelines, when estimating the primary economic impact of a port, the focus should be on the role of required and attracted industries.

2.4.1   Identification of port-related industries

Required industries are defined as the businesses necessary to the movement of waterborne commerce, including activities such as freight forwarding, port terminal operations, stevedoring, vessel supply, pilotage, towage, container servicing and a host of other functions necessary to the movement of cargo. Attracted and induced industries are firms which have been able to maintain or expand their markets by exporting/importing through a port or benefiting from reduced transport costs due to the existence of the port. All payroll, tax revenues, profits and employment from these industries are linked to the port because in its absence firms would fail to develop properly or simply locate elsewhere.

It is often assumed that economic activity within the area of the port is included in the port's primary impact. This assumption arises in the absence of a thorough investigation of the degree of dependency of those activities upon the port. Obviously, such rough conclusions would generate an overestimate of the port's impact. To evaluate a port's impact accurately, research institutions consider it important to identify the degree of port dependency in a logical way.

It appears that the only solution is a survey of firms and government institutions to ascertain the proportion of their workforce that is devoted to the movement of cargo. However, because employees within the same industry are not equally productive, the degree of port dependency based upon a proportion of their workforce might be inappropriate. Theoretically, there are several ways available to measure port dependency: one is a linkage coefficient between a port and its related industries.

Such linkage coefficients are divided into two categories: forward linkage coefficients and backward linkage coefficients. The former includes a cargo linkage coefficient (CLC), an expense linkage coefficient (ELC) and a labour linkage coefficient (LLC). A backward linkage coefficient measures the proportion of the product supplied by an industry and consumed by a port or waterway transport industry with respect to the total output of the selling industry. The functional expressions are:

1. Cargo linkage coefficient (CLC) = cargo volume handled by the port or waterway industry/total cargo volume generated from a particular sector.
2. Expense linkage coefficient (ELC) = expenditure by an industry for the port (or waterway transportation) service/total cost of inputs required by it.
3. Labour linkage coefficient (LLC) = employment attributed to the port (or waterway transportation) service/total employment of an industry.

2.4.2   Application of the Shanghai input–output model

In conducting an economic impact analysis of Shanghai port, the use of an input–output (I-O) model is simple if the model contains identifiable interindustry sectors and information on relative sector outputs. However, the use of the I-O model to determine the Shanghai port impact is normally complicated by the lack of a comprehensive sector that includes all direct port economic activities. That is, I-O models do not typically treat the port industry as a specific component of the interindustry mix.

According to the Standard Industrial Classification Codes of China (2002), port activities are included in SIC Code F54 (Waterway Transportation), which comprises F541 (Waterway Transportation of Passengers), F542 (Waterway Transportation of Freight) and F543 (Waterway Transportation Services, not elsewhere classified). Obviously, port activities fall into the category of F543, of which the individual economic performance cannot precisely be determined due to the lack of detailed information revealed by the current I-O table for Shanghai City. As a compromise, we can estimate the whole economic impact of Shanghai waterway transportation and deduce the contribution made by Shanghai port from a relationship between waterway transportation and port activities. Based on the results of research carried out jointly by the Shanghai Municipal Statistics Bureau and the Regional Leading Office of Shanghai International Shipping Centre in 1998, Shanghai port's contribution to the total value added of the waterway transport industry was approximately 61.41 per cent. Although such shares might change slightly, when evaluating the impact of the Shanghai port industry, it can be assumed that the relationship between these two sectors was constant in the following years.

2.4.2.1   *Waterway transportation's forward linkage coefficients*

With the application of Shanghai's input–output table, it is convenient to select either the direct input coefficients or total input coefficients to serve as forward linkage coefficients. In Table 2.1, the direct input coefficients for Shanghai's waterway transportation show the input value of services purchased from local industries that are needed to produce one basic unit of Chinese currency (RMB) of output by a given industry. For example, the sales

Table 2.1:   Input coefficients for Shanghai's waterway transportation in 2002

Selected purchasing industries	Direct input coefficients	Total input coefficients
Agriculture	0.007737	0.034741
Petroleum refinery	0.026209	0.064568
Basic chemicals	0.003330	0.030530
Steel manufacturing	0.013558	0.039089
Automobiles	0.010533	0.043832
Electrical machinery	0.003943	0.039674
New construction	0.012363	0.054513
Wholesale and retail trade	0.024096	0.045177
Warehousing	0.000334	0.010095
Exhibition and conference hosting	0.000018	0.011680
Tourism	0.000219	0.019939

Note: All the figures are either quoted or derived from the 2002 Input–Output Table for Shanghai Municipality published by Shanghai Municipal Statistics Bureau (2004) (based on the author's analysis, Song, 2003).

of waterway transport services to agriculture, RMB 75.2117 million, when divided by RMB 9,720.88 million (the total inputs required by agriculture) gives 0.007737. Similarly, every RMB of output from the steel manufacturing industry uses waterway transport to the value of RMB 0.013558 (total output equals total input).

On the other hand, total input coefficients attempt to estimate all subsequent rounds of local spending resulting from the production per RMB of output of a given industry. The listed total input coefficients reflect the combination of direct and indirect coefficients of the initial RMB of final demand for the output of some key industries such as agriculture, chemicals, automobile, wholesale and retail trade, etc. For example, to satisfy an RMB of final demand for Shanghai-made automobiles will require directly and indirectly the input of waterway transportation summing to RMB 0.043832. So, the total input coefficient is a major indicator of the technical-economic ties and interdependence between sectors of the national economy. The matrix of total input coefficients (B) is obtained by calculating the formula of 'B = $(I - A)^{-1} - I$', where I and A represent a unity matrix and the matrix of the direct input coefficients, respectively.

2.4.2.2   Waterway transportation's backward linkage coefficients

The backward linkage coefficients of Shanghai waterway transportation are the ratios derived by dividing the value of intermediate goods and services (inputs) that waterway transportation purchases from other sectors with the total production of these sectors (cf. Table 2.2).

For example, the backward linkage coefficient of Shanghai's waterway to the petroleum industry in Table 2.2 shows that every RMB of output from

Table 2.2: Backward linkage coefficients of Shanghai's waterway transportation in 2002

Selected selling industries	Inputs required by water transportation (mn. RMB)	Corresponding outputs (mn RMB)	B. Linkage coefficients
Petroleum	10,143.2954	24,320.9008	0.4171
Shipbuilding	2,715.7214	10,727.1889	0.2532
Rubber manufacturing	362.6275	9,419.3743	0.0385
Metal products	556.2874	44,034.5079	0.0126
Electronics	145.4342	31,229.6141	0.0047
Railway freight	13.4912	2,141.5869	0.0063
Road transportation	812.9443	599,829.09	0.1355
Warehousing	1,330.3946	2,992.1012	0.4446

Note: All the figures are either quoted or derived from the 2002 Input–Output Table for Shanghai Municipality published by Shanghai Municipal Statistics Bureau (2004) (based on the author's analysis, Song, 2003).

Shanghai's petroleum industry needs RMB 0.4171 of demand for its products from the waterway transport industry.

2.4.3 Estimate of the effects of Shanghai port

Our analysis quantifies the direct effects of Shanghai port, which are those caused directly by port operation, including the employment and value added generated at the port or by the businesses closely connected with the port, such as stevedoring, bunkering, shipping, cargo forwarding, etc. In other words, the direct effects of Shanghai port can be measured in terms of the total value added by Shanghai's waterway transportation sector.

Compared with other transport activities, including road, air cargo and even urban mass transportation, waterway transportation contributed much more value added, but the proportion of its value added to total output, at 16.52 per cent, remained the smallest among all the transport sectors and far below the average level of that for the whole of Shanghai's economy (32.29 per cent). This implies that Shanghai's waterway transportation, including the port service, is a typical intermediate-input-consuming industry, with its productivity in urgent need of improvement.

We also estimated indirect effects (forward-related sectors), which are value-generating capabilities supported by port operations or its broader coverage – waterway transportation. Indirect effects include a part of payroll, tax payment, depreciation and profits of the local port users, which can be attributed to the port service or the whole waterway transportation of Shanghai on the basis of the relevant forward linkage coefficients (direct input coefficients for Shanghai's waterway transportation). The calculation of indirect effects is given by: the value added of indirect port-users, attributed to the port = Σ (forward linkage coefficient) × (value added gained by the corresponding industry).

Table 2.3:   The values added and their composition in 2002

Item	Payroll	Taxes	Depreciation	Profits	Sum (million RMB)
Value 1	4,117.4163	1,524.9619	1,971.1421	1,508.8926	9,122.4129
Value 2	1,106.8647	1,334.6856	536.9600	812.3080	3,790.8183
Value 3	3,081.9347	2,681.2851	1,841.7567	3,749.6688	11,354.6453
Total	8,306.2157	5,540.9326	4,349.8588	6,070.8694	24,267.8765

Notes:
1. Value 1, 2 and 3 stand respectively for the value added for Shanghai's waterway transportation, the values added for the forward-related industries and the induced industries attributed to Shanghai Port.
2. All the figures are either quoted or derived from the 2002 Input–Output Table for Shanghai Municipality published by Shanghai Municipal Statistics Bureau in 2004 (based on the author's analysis, Song, 2003).

Induced effects are additional economic activities induced by expanded economic activity at the port or in Shanghai's water transportation sector. The development of a port industrial park around Shanghai port itself or the expansion of the Shanghai-based commercial fleets would generate opportunities for backward-linked businesses, such as petroleum, metals, shipbuilding, road transportation, etc. The calculation of induced effects is given by: the value added of induced industries attributed to the port = Σ (backward linkage coefficient) × (value added gained by the corresponding industry). The quantified results of these multi-effect estimates are provided in Table 2.3.

The whole economic impact of Shanghai port in terms of the value added can be demonstrated by the sum of the direct, indirect and induced effects, amounting to a total value of RMB 24,267.8765 million. According to a report by Shanghai Municipal Statistics Bureau (2003), Shanghai's total employment reached 7.9204 million jobs at the end of 2002, with a GRP of RMB 540.876 billion. On average, an increase of RMB 68,289 in the GRP is needed to create an additional job. With the total value added attributed to Shanghai port standing at RMB 24,267.8765 million, its contribution to local employment can be estimated as the creation of about 355.4 thousand jobs. However, employment in transportation, storage, postal and telecommunication occupations was reported to be only 323.4 thousand jobs. Therefore, the indirect and induced effects of Shanghai port in the creation of new jobs are significant.

Theoretically, other flow-on effects of Shanghai port cannot be ignored. The flow-on effects mainly include consumption-induced effects and production-induced effects (mentioned above). Consumption-induced effects are those brought about by household expenditures, while production-induced effects are generated by the direct purchases of local goods and services by firms in the sector. Considering the consumption-induced effects from the perspective of a Keynesian multiplier, the extended economic impact of Shanghai port might be much bigger and remains for us to study further.

2.5 Inland access to Shanghai port

Many different definitions of accessibility and many ways to measure it can be found in the literature (Pirie, 1979; Martellato et al., 1998). The basic concept of a location's accessibility has two aspects. First, any location offers possibilities in its surroundings to those who have chosen it. Secondly, to fulfil these possibilities efforts have to be made to bridge distance. Both aspects, opportunity and effort, related to bridging a distance, are key ingredients of accessibility.

A port's inland accessibility not only differs between logistic chains, but also changes due to fundamental developments in technology, economy and society, which have an impact on shippers' demands for transhipment as well as on generalised transport costs. Shippers' demands for transhipment to/from the hinterland are exogenous to the port. Different port performances might, however, exert different influences on transport costs. For example, a successful lobby for new infrastructure (e.g. the widening of the expressway linking Shanghai and Nanjing, Jiangsu from 4 lanes to 8 lanes) or the promotion of new transport services can improve accessibility to Shanghai or the Yangtze River Delta. Therefore, generalised transport costs can be considered as a tool for the Port of Shanghai to improve landside accessibility and to enlarge its hinterland.

2.5.1 The current transport network for Shanghai port

Although water transportation by the Yangtze River and the Huangpu River is of prime importance, there are rail connections with Nanjing and Hangzhou, the capital cities of the two neighbouring provinces, with links through those cities to northern and southern China. Highways, including Numbers 204, 312, 318 and 320 China National Highways radiate outwards from Shanghai. Along these routes remote areas like Yunnan, Tibet and Xinjiang can be reached over roads longer than 3,700 km. Within a decade, the city has built half a dozen orbital ring roads: a grid of elevated motorways, tunnels, highways and cross-harbour bridges.

The links between the port of Shanghai and its hinterland are served by one or more transport systems, consisting of infrastructure and transport services. Transport systems can generate both economies and diseconomies of scale. Ports with a higher transhipment volume have gained scale advantages over ports with less transhipment. The inland accessibility of the main hub ports around the world varies in terms of transport modes, generalised transport costs and spatial scope. That implies that with an equal effort (for instance in time or monetary costs), a different range of destinations can be

Table 2.4:   Modal split in landside transportation (%)

Port	Road	Rail	Inland waterway
Shanghai[1]	92.72	0	7.18
Hong Kong[2]	32.52	2.29	65.19
Rotterdam[3]	15	6	79
Hamburg[4]	52	33	15

Notes:
[1] Exported container cargoes from the hinterland to Shanghai port in 1997: Ministry of Communication of China (1999), the Annual Report on China Shipping Development in 1998, Beijing: China Communication Press, 115.
[2] Exported cargoes from the Chinese mainland to Hong Kong port in 1996/ Hong Kong Port Cargo Forecasts 1997/98 Appendices, 1998.
[3,4] All cargoes in 1996, inbound and outbound.
Source: Klink (1998: 5).

reached from two or more seaports. The variety in inland access becomes apparent in the modal split of the inland transport from the Ports of Shanghai, Hong Kong, Hamburg and Rotterdam (see Table 2.4).

Table 2.4 shows the modal split of all cargoes via Hong Kong, Rotterdam and Hamburg. If only containers are taken into consideration, the truck share may be much higher. These differences in the statistics might result in some misunderstanding. Still, we can conclude from the data listed that compared with other hub ports, inland access to Shanghai port relies more heavily on road transportation. Obviously, the roles of railways and inland waterways in the transport networks linking Shanghai port with its hinterlands are not effectively exploited. Several reasons can be given to explain why a comprehensive utilisation of the non-highway transport modes falls short: firstly, Chinese railways, due to their national monopoly, respond reluctantly to the fast-growing demand for intermodal container transport. Secondly, the current hinterland lies within a relatively narrow area: i.e. the Yangtze River Delta and Shanghai generate by themselves half of the inbound and outbound cargoes through the hub. Accordingly, trucks are a more convenient and efficient means of providing the feeder freight service for short distances. Thirdly, railway congestion and ill-planned bridges and dams hinder attempts to exploit the comparative advantages of railway and inland waterway transportation in this region.

2.5.2   New hinterlands and generalised transport costs

Economic theory holds that the costs and benefits of reaching a certain place are combined and expressed as the potential function, first identified by Stewart (1947). The potential function examines the attractiveness of a location in terms of its accessibility to relevant location factors in its surroundings.

This expression is called a location potential. A location potential is the sum of the location characteristics in all places j around a certain location i, weighted with generalised transport costs from i to j. Instead of direct monetary costs, generalised transport costs are used because costs related to risks and time also determine the efforts of bridging distance.

Since containerisation began three decades ago, the hinterlands of seaports have become more mutually intersected. The competitiveness of seaports to attract cargo flows from their hinterlands largely depends on the generalised transport costs of each shipment. By definition, generalised transport cost includes monetary costs such as the freight collected and other expenses charged by all related inland transport modes, port sectors for transhipment and consignment, second leg carriers (ocean-going container liners), and implicit costs related to time wasted, opportunities forgone and risks encountered. These elements vary, of course, with different traffic routes or different ports for transhipment.

The Chinese State Council (2000) issued a circular on 27 December 2000, granting preferential policies to western China with respect to investment, banking and credit support, taxation, land and natural resources. Foreign investment in the region is encouraged, as more projects will be opened to foreign investors than they would find elsewhere. These policies are granted for as long as ten years, effective 1 January 2001. The west, by the government's definition, consists of the provinces of Sichuan, Gansu, Guizhou, Yunnan, Qinghai and Shanxi, the municipality of Chongqing, and three autonomous provinces, including Ningxia, Xinjiang and Tibet. To expedite its 'Go West' campaign, the government has emphasised that priorities should be given to (1) improving infrastructure; (2) protecting the environment; (3) strengthening agricultural development; (4) adjusting the rural economic structure; and (5) developing science, technology and education. The government is aiming for a breakthrough in these areas over the next five to ten years to allow the west to catch up with the rest of the country.

To follow the national policy of 'Go West', Chinese railways have started to offer specialised container shuttle services along some east–west freight routes, including Shanghai to Xi'an and Shanghai to Chengdu, Sichuan. Central and western China is to become Shanghai port's new hinterland with a huge potential. The western provinces along the Yangtze River have a long-standing close relationship with Shanghai port. It is therefore appropriate for Zhengzhou and Xi'an, landlocked cities in the central and northwestern regions respectively, to represent new markets for development (see the locations shown in Figure 2.3). It seems likely that goods produced in these two nodes and bound for North America, Japan, Western Europe, etc., will travel to one of the most convenient eastern coastal ports (Shanghai and Qingdao – two major ports, or to Lianyungang – a promising middle-sized seaport connected to the new Asia-Europe land-bridge) by railway or highway for the first leg, and then be shipped to their final destinations by sea.

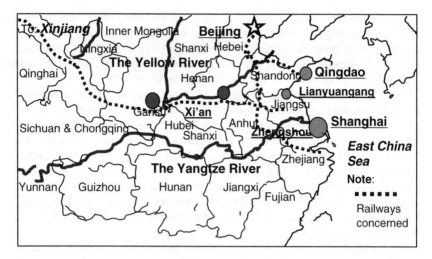

Figure 2.3:   The location of eastern ports and their hinterlands

2.5.2.1   *Inland transport costs*

Highway transport charges vary with geographic locations because of different toll rates or a different number of bridges and so forth. Based on the data for container haulage in the Yangtze River Delta collected in December 2002, we obtained the following haulage (RMB) function by a simple linear regression, with the relevant distance (d – measured in terms of kilometres) as its sole independent variable: $C_1 = 6.804d + 99$ (RMB/TEU).

Referring to the railway transport charges between the inland cities and the coastal ports, these were obtained from the Ministry of Railway Transport in early 2003. Calculations of basic freights and surcharges are listed in Table 2.5.

2.5.2.2   *Estimates of time costs*

Time costs divide into two parts: first, compensation to equipment owners for the use of containers or depot facilities; secondly, opportunity costs of idle capital (value of commodities in containers) in transit. In the early years of this century, a container detention fee was charged at the rate of USD 4.00 (or RMB 33.2) per TEU-day, and the average cargo value per unit load was estimated as USD 27,394 equivalent to RMB 227,370. For simplicity, we selected the interest rate of a one-year bank loan at 5.31 per cent p.a., effective from February 2002 to October 2004, to measure the time value of the cargoes in transit. Taking into account the traffic speeds of two modes and other daily equipment detention fees, we found the linear relationships between the total time costs (C_3 and C_4) and the distances (d) as follows:

Highway transport: $C_3 = 70.28 + 0.1107d$ (RMB/TEU)
Railway transport: $C_4 = 762.8 + 0.0855d$ (RMB/TEU)

Table 2.5: The particulars of highway and railway container cargoes

Transport mode	Description of the costs	Freight rate (RMB per TEU)
Highway transport	Freight charged = fixed component + freight rate × distance (d)	$C_1 = 6.804d + 99$
Railway transport	Basic freight rate	$0.7128d + 161$
	International container service charge (shipper owned container)	100
	Rental of container (carrier owned container)	100 (within 500 km); 10 per additional 100 km (beyond 500 km)
	Charges of container transloading between rail and highway modes at both an origin and a destination	2×195
	Truck haulage for a short distance	90
	Fee shared for newly built railways	$0.0176d$
	Contribution to the fund of railway construction	$0.528d$
	Total:	$C_2 = 1.2584d + 741$

Source: Ministry of Railway Transport (2003).

2.5.2.3 Generalised costs for inland transportation

Summing up the functions of ordinary freight charges and time costs, we find generalised transport costs for inland cargo flows from the hinterlands to the coastal ports mentioned above as:

Highway transport: $C_5 = C_1 + C_3 = 6.9147d + 169.28$ (RMB/TEU)
Railway transport: $C_6 = C_2 + C_4 = 1.3439d + 1,503.8$ (RMB/TEU)

Comparing these two equations, we see that the highway and railway have a cost advantage within and beyond 240 km. The hinterlands represented by Zhengzhou and Xi'an are located much more than 240 km away from the coastal ports, so the railway is preferred in principle. The distances between the hinterlands and the eastern coastal ports and the generalised freight costs (monetary expense plus time costs) are shown in Table 2.6.

2.5.2.4 Ocean freight routes and others

Ocean freight rates for container cargoes shipped from Shanghai, Qingdao and Lianyungang to the overseas destinations were quoted by the Shanghai Shipping Exchange, the Qingdao Office of Mediterranean Shipping Co. Ltd. (Hong Kong), and the Lianyungang Administration of Port and Transport at the end of 2002. For detailed information concerning ocean freight, surcharges and the time needed for the voyages, see Table 2.7.

Table 2.6:   Inland transportation distances and costs

Route	Distance (km)	Costs by rail (RMB/TEU)
Zhengzhou–Shanghai	1,000	2,847.7
Xi'an–Shanghai	1,511	3,534.4
Zhengzhou–Lianyungang	572	2,272.5
Xi'an–Lianyungang	1,083	2,959.2
Zhengzhou–Qingdao	1,059	2,927.0
Xi'an–Qingdao	1,570	3,613.7

Notes:
1. Kilometres are derived from the Traffic Map of China, published by Chengdu Cartography Publishing House in Nov. 2000, pp. 7–8.
2. Costs are calculated by the author based on distances and freight rates (Song, 2003).

Table 2.7:   Most cost-effective ocean routes and generalised costs

Ocean shipping route	Freight rate (USD/TEU)	THC (RMB/TEU)	Days in transit	Days at port	Total expense (RMB/TEU)
Shanghai–Japan	200.0	370.0	3	2	2,361.5
Shanghai–W. Europe	1,100.0	370.0	27	2	11,422.7
Qingdao–N. America	1,350.0	370.0	16	2	12,768.4
Lianyungang–S. Korea	170.0	370.0	2	3	2,112.5

Notes:
1. The four destinations mentioned here are represented by Yokohama, Rotterdam, Los Angeles and Busan.
2. THC is an abbreviation for terminal handling charges.
3. Information about the days in transit and at port was obtained from the cargo forwarders concerned.

2.5.3   Container cargo flow and inland accessibility

The rise of intermodal services brought changes in the pattern of freight transport and port competition in an overlapping hinterland. Stimulated by the policy of 'Go West', the growing interaction among regions, the threat of traffic gridlock in metropolitan areas and the enlarged scale of the transport industry, intermodal services are expected to gain a larger market share. Intermodal services – combined transport by truck, rail or vessel – will affect the spatial–economic structure of the transport industry in general and the position of nodes in central and western China. In particular, Zhengzhou and Xi'an can be served by the ports of Shanghai, Lianyungang or Qingdao. In theory, those places served by a port cheaper than other ports belong to the port's hinterland. In practice, however, direct monetary costs and geographic distances alone do not determine the competitiveness of the port towards an inland market.

Table 2.8:   The selection of traffic paths and their respective flow shares

Origin	Destination	1st best path	Min overall generalised transport costs (RMB)*	Flow shares among 1st best/2nd best/ worst paths
Zhengzhou	North America	via Qingdao	15,695.4	48.57:31.90:19.53
	Japan	via Shanghai	5,209.2	49.42:37.56:13.02
	South Korea	via Lianyungang	4,385.0	56.72:25.24:18.04
	Western Europe	via Shanghai	14,270.4	40.83:37.35:21.82
Xi'an	North America	via Qingdao	16,382.1	47.93:32.04:20.03
	Japan	via Shanghai	5,895.9	47.79:37.51:14.70
	South Korea	via Lianyungang	5,071.7	53.54:26.58:19.88
	Western Europe	via Shanghai	14,957.1	40.51:37.21:22.28

Notes:
* Overall generalised transport costs are measured in terms of RMB per TEU, covering the journeys from Chinese inland cities to overseas destinations. All the results are calculated based on the author's analysis (Song, 2003).

Delimiting a port's hinterland on the basis of generalised transport costs indicates the spatial dimensions of the hinterland. But to estimate the demand for transhipment generated by this area, the characteristics of the market – in terms of import and export volumes – should also be included. In the spatial–economic literature, the concept of location potential has been developed to determine the attractiveness of a location. In this section, the hinterland potential of a seaport is defined as the demand for transhipment in terms of imports and exports to and from a set of places weighted with generalised transport costs between them. The density of container cargo flow from the hinterlands to the eastern coastal ports is likely to follow the probability traffic flow model:

$$p_{ki} = \frac{\exp(-\theta \cdot t_{ki}/t_{li})}{\sum\limits_{k \in W} \exp(-\theta \cdot t_{ki}/t_{li})}$$

Here, p_{ki}: the share of the ith O-D cargo flow via the kth path; t_{ki}: the generalised transport costs of the ith O-D cargo flow via the kth path; t_{li}: the minimum generalised transport costs of the most efficient path (l) for the ith O-D cargo flow; θ: the parameter of flow distribution, set at 6; W: all paths available to cargo flows. By calculating the generalised transport cost and using the probability traffic flow model, we have derived the theoretic distribution of cargo flows originating in Zhengzhou and Xi'an among three paths as shown in Table 2.8.

Needless to say, the cargo volume to each final destination is different due to its uniqueness in the trade structure. Without the relevant information,

Table 2.9: Accessibility indices from the eastern ports to central and western China

Inland city	Seaport		
	Shanghai	*Qingdao*	*Lianyungang*
Zhengzhou	100	79.4	79.0
Xi'an	100	81.6	79.3

Note: 100 is the maximum value of the index.

we can use only the data based on Chinese foreign trade as a whole in terms of value. In 2001, the mutual proportions of Chinese exports and imports to and from Japan, South Korea, Western Europe and North America were 31.5 per cent, 12.9 per cent, 24.1 per cent and 31.5 per cent, respectively. So, taking the cargo flow shares and the corresponding size of trade into consideration, the weighted accessibility indices measuring the different inland potential of the three seaports can be calculated as in Table 2.9.

Shanghai port scores better, thanks to its efficient infrastructure and scale economies of cargo handling. Although Shanghai wins in general, Qingdao and Lianyungang are more competitive in forwarding cargoes to North America and South Korea. Moreover, the railways linking Shanghai, Zhengzhou and Xi'an have been overburdened for a long time. With the economy overheated, rail congestion is worsening. Fortunately, based on China's new five-year plan, the expansion of key railways such as the Beijing–Shanghai route is on the agenda.

However, fundamental developments undermine the role of infrastructure in inland accessibility. First, it cannot keep up with rapidly changing patterns of transport and logistic demand. Secondly, under the influence of congestion and the social awareness of environmental protection, scale economies from infrastructure seem to be diminishing. In the future, a sound infrastructure will be necessary to optimise a port's market reach. Shanghai port should look beyond infrastructure and give more value to intangible aspects of accessibility. To achieve this aim, development of the knowledge and human power concerned is a prerequisite.

2.6   Conclusion

This chapter has discussed the development of Shanghai port and the main Chinese mainland ports as a whole. The strategic forces behind the rapid emergence of Shanghai as an international hub port are revealed as the fast-growing Chinese economy generates a great volume of seaborne trade. The historical process of building an international shipping centre has been identified. This has included the construction of the container terminals, accommodating more maritime activities by the effective attraction of more foreign investments, and pushing ahead with deeper reforms. To break through the deadlock imposed by its poor natural conditions, Shanghai is rapidly building its deep-water container terminal on Yangshan island. In addition to the five container berths in the first phase, the construction of the Donghai Bridge connecting the island with the mainland was to be completed in 2005.

With regard to the benefits of these developments, an evaluation of the economic impact of Shanghai port conducted by the author shows that both its direct and indirect contributions to the Gross Regional Product and local employment are significant but that the overall operations of Shanghai's waterway transportation prove to be very costly and therefore need improving further. Finally, the chapter examined the extent and form of the inland access to Shanghai port. Compared with other main eastern coastal ports, Shanghai port enjoys a comparative advantage in serving the central and northwestern provinces. To enhance its competitiveness in both the domestic and international freight markets, it is of great importance for Shanghai port to strengthen its inland accessibility to the hinterland by all means to reduce the generalised transport costs of cargo flows as much as possible.

References

Chinese State Council (2000) Circular concerning the relevant policies and measures in favour of a great development of Chinese western region, *The People's Daily*, 28 December.

Klink, H. A. (1998) *Land Access to Seaports*, Working Paper of the European Conference of Ministers of Transport, October.

Martellato, D., Nijkamp, P. and Reggiani, A. (1998) *Measurement and Measures of Network Accessibility: Economic Perspectives*, Cheltenham: Edward Elgar.

Ministry of Communications of China (1999) *Annual Report on China's Shipping Development 1998*, Beijing: China Communication Press.

Ministry of Communications of China (2004) *Annual Report on China's Shipping Development 2003*, Beijing: China Communication Press.

Ministry of Railway Transport (2003) *Freight Department, the People's Republic of China*, January.

Pirie, G. H. (1979) 'Measuring Accessibility: a Review and Proposal', *Environment & Planning A*, 11(2): 299–312.

Shanghai Municipal Port Administration Bureau (2004) *Report on the Port and Shipping Development of Shanghai in 2003*, Shanghai: Shanghai People's Publishing House, April.

Shanghai Municipal Statistics Bureau (2003) *Statistical Yearbook of Shanghai*, Beijing: China Statistics Press, May.

Shanghai Municipal Statistics Bureau (2004) 'The Statistical Report on Shanghai's Economy and Social Development in 2003', *Jiefang Daily*, 31 January.

Song, B. L. (2003) *Dynamic Study of Port Cities' Development*, Dalian: Dalian Maritime University Press, 200–6.

Stewart, J. Q. (1947) 'Empirical Mathematical Rules Concerning the Distribution and Equilibrium of Population', *Geographical Review*, 37: 461–86.

Standard Industrial Classification Codes of China (2002) Codes for Chinese Economy (GB/T4754-2002)', www.csj.sh.gov.cn/wsbs/download_fagui/gnfldm.htm., October.

3
Busan: the Future Logistics Hub of Northeast Asia

Dong-Keun Ryoo and Yun-Su Hur

3.1 Introduction

Northeast Asia has emerged as one of the three most important trade zones along with the EU and NAFTA. Over the last decade, seaborne trades in this economic region have been rapidly growing due to the economic development in Korea, China and Japan and also the increase in the international trades of these countries. Its share in total global cargo is expected to increase from 26 per cent to 32 per cent by 2011. In particular, as globalisation continues and China joins the WTO, Northeast Asia will emerge as one of the most energetic markets with the rapid growth of the Chinese economy contributing to a sharp increase of container cargoes in the region. This has created business opportunities for major container ports in Korea and China.

The Port of Busan, the vital gateway to the Korean peninsula, has shown a steady growth of 10 per cent each year in container traffic over the past decade and has maintained its status as one of the world's top ports handling over 10 million TEUs in 2003. The increase of its container throughput is attributed to the growth of container trades in the Asian region, its advantageous geographical location and lower port charges compared with neighbouring ports. Busan has made great strides as a hub port in Northeast Asia, with transhipment cargoes accounting for 41 per cent of total container throughput in 2003. This situation provides the port with a reasonable opportunity for advancing as a logistics hub for Northeast Asia.

However, dramatic changes surrounding container ports, such as the advent of large size container ships and the hub-and-spoke concept, have led to keen competition among the ports in Northeast Asia. Today, Busan port is threatened by competitors and this competition to become a hub port in Northeast Asia is growing. The competing ports are concentrating on setting up marketing strategies to attract transhipment cargoes by reducing port charges and offering greater incentives for ships exceeding a fixed volume. Also, they are planning to build a large number of new container terminals. For instance, Shanghai is driving hard with the 'Yangshan project' to build 52 berths by

2020. Kaohsiung is establishing an international logistics complex. Recently, Kobe lowered its port dues by 30 per cent to attract more vessels.

Busan is now preparing for the next phase of development and modernisation to become a logistics centre in Northeast Asia. This chapter discusses its competitive positioning and the business strategies it has adopted to become a hub port. The first part of the chapter reviews the Korean economy and the growth in its container trade. This is followed by an analysis of the development of Busan port and its administrative structures. Also, port policy and financing for port development projects are discussed. Finally, there is a detailed discussion about the competitiveness of the port and the business strategies it is pursuing to become a logistics hub.

3.2   Overview of the Korean economy and the Port of Busan

3.2.1   Korea's economy and its container trades

Located in the heart of Northeast Asia and between two of the world's largest economies – Japan and China – South Korea serves as the gateway to the massive markets of Northeast Asia, which currently accounts for 22 per cent of global GDP. Korea recorded a GDP of $476.6 billion in 2002 and its 6.3 per cent real GDP growth rate for the same year attests to the dazzling growth potential of this rapidly expanding economy. In 2002, Korea's GDP was composed of 4 per cent agriculture, 41 per cent manufacturing and 55 per cent services (see Table 3.1).

Korea's GDP growth is expected to far exceed that of Japan, and its forecast real GDP growth rate of 4.3 per cent in 2003 is expected to be the highest among the OECD member countries. This record is especially impressive during the recent worldwide economic slowdown. As the world's thirteenth-largest trading country, Korea is one of the main players in Asia, along with Japan and China. Korea's brisk trade reflects the openness of the Korean economy.

Table 3.1:   Main socio-economic indicators in 2002

Population (millions)	48
National GDP (USD billions)	476.6
(% of GDP)	
Agriculture	4.0
Manufacturing	41.0
Services	55.0
FDI (USD billions)*	
Inward direct investment	34.8
Outward direct investment	20.9

* The figures represent the total amount from 1999 to 2002.
Source: Ministry of Commerce, Industry and Energy (2004).

In 2002, Korea racked up $314.6 billion in total trade, with $162.5 billion in exports and $152.1 billion in imports (MOCIE, 2004).

Korea is expected to maintain 5 per cent annual growth until 2010, thanks to ten major growth-leading industries with great market potential and employment opportunities. Korea offers a fast-growing and dynamic market, providing a wealth of opportunities for foreign investors. Inward direct investment was $34.8 billion and outward direct investment was $20.9 billion between 1999 and 2002. Korea is the ideal staging ground for launching a marketing offensive to tap into the vast Asian market with its total population of two billion, including 500 million in ASEAN countries (MOCIE, 2002).

Northeast Asia has recently emerged as one of the three most important trade zones along with the EU and NAFTA, and its share in total global cargoes is expected to increase from 26 per cent to 32 per cent by 2011. In the 1990s, China's economy grew by an average of 10.1 per cent per year and continued to grow by as much as 8 per cent per year in the late 1990s. The Chinese economy has been the biggest export market for Korea since the early 2000s. In addition, China's rate of growth in exports reached 30 per cent in 2002, and 47 per cent in the first half of 2003 as compared with the corresponding period of last year.

As can be seen in Figure 3.1, the country is maintaining a higher growth rate for its container business than the average of 9.75 per cent around the globe. Its average growth rate was recorded at 14.1 per cent between 1991 and 2001, whereas Taiwan was 6.2 per cent and Japan was 4.7 per cent respectively (MOMAF, 2004).

The growth of container traffic and transhipment cargoes in Korea is appealing as an attractive investment opportunity to a number of foreign port operators. For example, Hutchison Port Holdings, CSX World Terminals (since

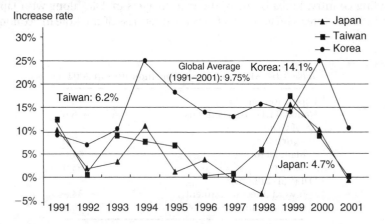

Figure 3.1:   Growth trend in container traffic
Source: MOMAF (2004).

acquired by Dubai Ports International) and PSA have already invested in Gwangyang port, Busan New Port and Incheon port respectively. P&O Ports and China Merchants Holdings are also working on securing facilities.

3.2.2   The growth of Busan port

Located at the southeastern end of the Korean peninsular, Busan port serves the role as a gateway connecting the Pacific Ocean and the continent of Asia. Located adjacent to one of the three international arterial routes as well, Busan port is endowed with natural advantages in terms of the requirements of a port.

Busan consists of four ports including North port, South port, Gamcheon port and Dadaepo port and six container terminals (see Figure 3.2). Five container terminals are located at North port and Gamcheon container terminal operated by Hanjin Shipping Company is located at Gamcheon port. Nearly 2,800 people are employed at the terminals (see Table 3.2).

Currently, Busan port has the capacity to process 91 million tons of cargoes annually, together with 26.8 km of quayside enabling simultaneous servicing of 169 vessels. As the foremost port in Korea, Busan processes 40 per cent of total marine export cargoes and 81 per cent of container cargoes in Korea as well as 42 per cent of marine products domestically produced (Busan Regional Maritime Affairs and Fisheries Office, 2004).

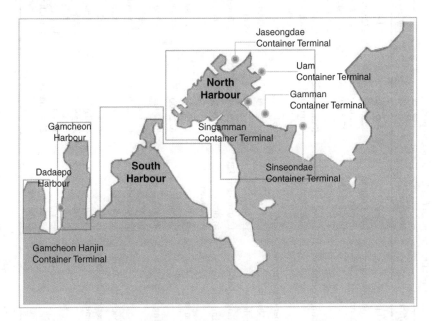

Figure 3.2:   Container terminals at the Port of Busan
Source: Busan Regional Maritime Affairs and Fisheries Office (2004).

Table 3.2: Container terminal facilities at Busan port

Classification	Jasungdae (1, 2)	Shinsundae (3)	Gamman (4)	Sin Gamman	Uam	Gamcheon
Project period	'74–'96	'85–'97	'91–'97	'95–2001	'95–'99	'88–'97
Total construction cost (won)	108.4 billion (Feeder: 16.6 billion)	222.6 billion (1 more berth: 37.2 billion)	472.4 billion (KCTA: 329.3 Government: 143.1 billion)	178.1 billion	53.5 billion	97.3 billion
Operating company	Korea Hutchison Co.	Shinsundae Terminal	Hanjin, Hutchison, Global Korea Express	Busan East Terminal Co.	Uam Terminal Co.	Hanjin Shipping
Number of employees	648	661	706	324	210	186
Quay length	1,447 m	1,200 m	1,400 m	826 m	500 m	600 m
Water depth	12.5 m	14–15 m	15 m	12–15 m	11 m	13 m
Handling capacity	1.20 million TEU	1.20 million TEU	1.20 million TEU	650,000 TEU	270,000 TEU	340,000 TEU
Berthing capacity	50,000dwt × 4 10,000dwt × 1	50,000dwt × 4	50,000dwt × 4	50,000dwt × 2 5,000dwt × 1	20,000dwt × 1 5,000dwt × 2	50,000dwt × 2
Total area	647,000	1,039,000	731,000	308,000	184,000	148,000
CY	394,000	672,000	336,000	153,000	156,000	105,000
Building floor space	38,000	28,000	16,000	12,000	5,000	4,000
CFS	26,000 (3 buildings)	11,000 (1 building)	8,400 (1 building)	5,500 (1 building)	–	–
Approached railroad	980 m	925 m	1,032 m	–	–	–
Number of handling equipment	12 C/C 31 T/C 14 S/C 4 R/S 65 Y/T 17 F/L 249 Chassis	11 C/C 32 T/C 19 R/S 61 Y/T 10 F/L 230 Chassis	14 C/C 37 T/C 9 R/S 73 Y/T 11 F/L 186 Chassis	7 C/C 15 T/C 2 R/S 36 Y/T 6 F/L 69 Chassis	4 C/C 10 T/C 3 R/S 20 Y/T 2 F/L 35 Chassis	4 C/C 10 T/C 1 R/S 19 Y/T 38 Chassis

Source: KCTA (2004).

The Port of Busan has developed rapidly since first opening in 1876. In 1978, the first Korean container terminal – Jaseongdae terminal – was constructed and since then has quickly grown to become one of the world's leading container ports with an annual growth rate of over 10 per cent. In 1975, Busan did not rank among the top 30 ports in container traffic. In 1985, the port had moved up to number 12 in total container traffic, driven by industrialisation within Korea and the growth of its consumer base. In 1990, it ranked as the sixth largest container port in the world because of its proximity to major shipping routes and the rapid growth of international trades.

Through the 1990s, Busan maintained its strong position, ranking fifth in the world in 1995. It was able to grow its container business because of its central location with respect to markets in north China, Japan and eastern Russia. With the growth in transhipment container cargoes and international trade, the port ranked as the third largest container port in the world in 2000, handling 7.50 million TEUs. As can be seen in Figure 3.3, in 2003 the Port of Busan achieved success by handling over 10 million TEUs, a 10 per cent improvement in container volume over the previous year (Ryu, 2003). The volume of transhipment cargoes has increased dramatically, recently constituting 41 per cent of total container throughput. As illustrated in Figure 3.4, most transhipment cargoes are originating primarily from, or are destined for, China, the USA and Japan. In particular, 60 per cent of Chinese transhipment cargoes originated in or were destined for Shanghai, Dalian, Tianjin and Qingdao in 2000 (Moon et al., 2003).

3.2.3 Administrative and ownership structures

The Port of Busan is administered and managed by several organisations such as the Busan Regional Maritime Affairs and Fisheries Office, the Korea Container Terminal Authority (KCTA), terminal operating companies and the

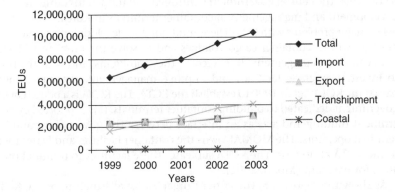

Figure 3.3: Growth of container traffic at Busan port
Source: KCTA (2004).

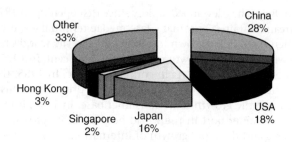

Figure 3.4:   Origin and destination of transhipment container cargo at Busan in 2003
(TEUs)
Source: KCTA (2004).

Busan Port Authority (BPA). This section discusses the administrative and ownership structures that apply to the port and the function of each organisation.

3.2.3.1   *Busan Regional Maritime Affairs and Fisheries Office*

The Busan Regional Maritime Affairs and Fisheries Office, one of the regional
offices of the Ministry of Maritime Affairs and Fisheries (MOMAF), is responsible for the daily operations of Busan port. It is mainly responsible for the
safety of shipping, protection of the marine environment, operating or leasing
of port infrastructure, securing port safety, dredging approach channels and
initiating port developments.

Since the establishment of the Korea Container Terminal Authority (KCTA)
in 1990 the responsibility for container terminal construction and leasing the
facilities to private terminal operators has been transferred to the KCTA.

3.2.3.2   *Korea Container Terminal Authority*

Before 1990 the central government controlled and funded investment in the
development and management of container terminals in Korea. This system
led to major problems with insufficient funds for port developments to meet the
rapid growth of container cargo volumes and to solve the problem of inefficiency in port management. To overcome these problems, and with the need
to invest to upgrade facilities and improve management, the government
passed the KCTA Act in 1990 to establish the KCTA. The KCTA is a branch of the
government dedicated to building container terminals. It is supported by government funding and acts as an interface between the government and the
terminal operators. The MOMAF owns the container facilities and leases them
to the KCTA at no cost. The KCTA subleases these facilities to terminal operators for payment (Moon, 2001).

As shown in Figure 3.5, the current organisational structure of the KCTA
consists of two headquarters, six teams and one business centre with a total
of 89 employees. The main objectives of the KCTA are to effectively develop,

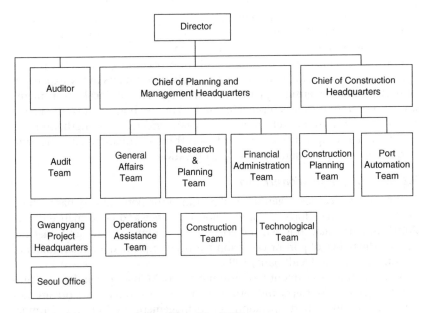

Figure 3.5: Organisational structure of the KCTA
Source: KCTA (2004).

control and manage container terminals, thus accelerating the smooth movement of container cargo and hence contributing to the sound development of the national economy. Major business areas of the KCTA include:

- Development, management and operation of container terminals;
- Investment in container terminal facilities and terminal management and operation;
- Development, management and operation of inland container depot (ICD) and traffic facilities for the promotion of inland container cargo movement;
- Administering port stevedoring services in accordance with the Port Transport Act;
- Dispensing government-entrusted duties related to development, management and the operation of port facilities; and
- Other duties entrusted to the KCTA by national or regional government or approved by the Minister of Maritime Affairs and Fisheries.

3.2.3.3 Busan Port Authority

In 2003, the Korean government enacted the Port Authority Act to reform the current management system of container terminals at Busan port and established the Busan Port Authority (BPA). The role of the management and operation of container terminals, previously falling under the responsibility of the KCTA, is now undertaken by the BPA. Independent from central or local governments, the BPA conducts port management, operation and development autonomously in accordance with corporate accounting methods.

With the establishment of the BPA it is now becoming relatively easier to finance port development and to make timely investments in the expansion of port facilities by ensuring participation of the relevant local governments and port users in the decision-making process of port policies. It is anticipated that this organisational reform will contribute greatly to strengthening the international competitiveness of Busan port through enhanced efficiency and performance in port management and operation.

3.2.3.4   *Port privatisation in Korea*

In the last few decades, organisational reform of the port industry has proliferated as part of the efforts to improve port efficiency and performance (Baird, 2001). In particular, to lessen the government's administrative and financial burden the policy of port privatisation has been implemented in a number of countries (Song and Cullinane, 1999).

In Korea, the government has introduced leasehold arrangements, terminal management contracts and terminal concessions to facilitate private sector intervention in port operation and management. In 1997 the Terminal Operating Company (TOC) scheme was introduced in nine seaports out of 28 trade ports. The local representative of the MOMAF leases general piers to private stevedoring companies, which independently operate the piers on a one-year provisional contract, as part of a three-year contract. Based upon the evaluation of the performance during the first year, the companies are granted permission for continuous operation for the remaining two years.

In 1999, Jasungdae container terminal, previously operated by the state-owned Busan Container Terminal Operating Company (BCTOC), was leased to Hyundai Busan Container Terminal. Currently, other container terminals at Busan port such as Shinseondae, Uam and Gamman terminals are operated under leasehold arrangements. As the lessor, BPA leases terminal facilities and handling equipment to terminal operators that are responsible for daily terminal operations, including cargo handling, berth allotment and labour supply (Moon, 2001).

The central government enacted a new law to induce private capital directly into the development of port facilities through the New Port Development Facilitation Act in 1996. The objective of this legislation was to improve efficiency in port operation and to diversify sources of capital inflows. The private sector is able to participate in the port development project under a Build-Transfer-Operate (BTO) concept. Under this scheme, the port authority constructs nautical facilities such as breakwaters and dredges the channel, while the private sector provides other facilities including the construction of quay walls, land filling, warehouse and cargo handling equipment. The Busan New Port project is being carried out under this kind of scheme. Other seaports in

Korea such as Gwangyang, Pyongtack, Incheon, Mokpo, Ulsan, Pohang, Boryong and Saemankeum are also being developed through terminal concession arrangements.

3.3 Korean government policy on port development

3.3.1 Overview of port policy

Ambitious port development projects have been initiated to meet the growing demand for port services in Korea. As shown in Figure 3.6, it has been forecast that total container cargo throughput handled in Korean ports will increase to nearly 20 million TEUs by 2006 and 30 million TEUs by 2011, and 44 per cent of the container volume will be transhipment cargoes (MOMAF, 2001). The government is currently planning to add 59 new deep-sea berths spread over 11 phased port projects between 2002 and 2012. By 2011, Busan New Port (BNP) will be equipped with 30 berths and Gwangyang port will have an additional 33 berths. The government aims to develop Busan and Gwangyang as logistics hub ports in Northeast Asia by attracting global logistics firms targeting Northeast Asian hinterland markets and by establishing innovative integrated logistics service systems.

To achieve the status of logistics hub ports in Northeast Asia the government is implementing a number of strategies. For example, to generate port traffic and attract global logistics companies, it is planned to build large-scale logistics complexes in port hinterlands. The companies operating in the

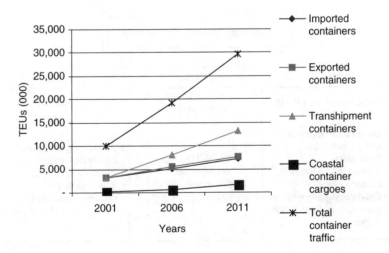

Figure 3.6: Forecast of container traffic in Korea
Source: MOMAF (2001).

complexes are allowed to conduct business activities such as reprocessing, assembling, packaging and labelling. Areas of 307 ha in the Busan New Port and 233 ha in the Gwangyang port respectively will be developed by 2013. The development of 82.6 ha in the BNP and 33 ha in Gwangyang is scheduled to be completed by 2006. Those complexes will also be designated as Free Trade Zones (FTZ) with the introduction of a new law for International Free Trade Zones, which provides corporations registered in the FTZ with favourable rates for leasing real estate and with tax benefits.

In addition, to ensure customer satisfaction and to increase terminal productivity the government is planning to introduce sophisticated IT in container terminal operation and management, especially in newly developed container terminals. At the BNP a semi-automated operational system will be introduced and an automated container terminal is being developed at Gwangyang port. To strengthen logistics competitiveness, flexible labour management will be adopted and around-the-clock operations systems powered by cutting-edge IT will be introduced (see Figure 3.7).

3.3.2   The development of Busan New Port

In order to develop the Port of Busan as a hub port for Northeast Asia, the government is concentrating its efforts on the rapid expansion of port infrastructure at Busan port. The present capacity alone is not sufficient to handle the rapidly increasing container cargo volumes. To meet increasing growth of container traffic the government launched a project for building Busan New Port in 1995.

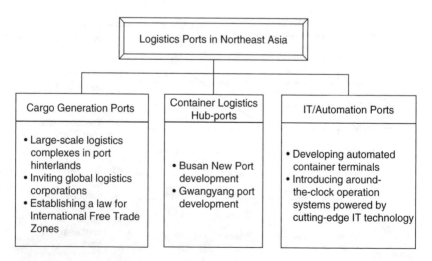

Figure 3.7:   A vision for port development policy in Korea
Source: MOMAF (2004).

Under the Busan New Port project, 30-berth container terminals will be developed by 2011. The first three berths were scheduled for completion by the end of 2005. An additional three berths will be built and in operation by January 2007. These six berths, which make up phase one of the entire development project, will have 2,000 metres of berth, an initial depth of 16 metres and a capacity of 3.4 million TEUs.

This project will involve the construction of 9.95 km of container berths, a breakwater of 1.49 km, dredging 72 million m^2 and bank protection of 20.7 km. The government will fund the construction of fundamental facilities, such as the breakwater, shore protection, transportation facilities and a multipurpose pier. Operational facilities, such as 29 container berths and the harbour site will be developed through private investment. Total project costs are estimated to be 9,154.2 billion won, consisting of 4,173.9 billion won from government and 4,980.3 billion won from the private sector (see Table 3.3).

The hinterland of the BNP will be designated as a free trade zone, in which various business activities such as manufacturing, processing, assembling and exhibition are allowed, with tenants being given budget and tax support. With the construction of the BNP it is anticipated that Busan would enhance national competitiveness through the smooth processing of export and import cargoes and increase cargo handling capacity by 8.04 million TEUs per year.

3.3.3 Designation of free trade zones

In the globalised economy, manufactured products are no longer produced in one country to be sent to another. Instead, manufacturers search the globe for the cheapest logistics system and produce their goods in those places offering the most advantageous conditions with respect to raw materials, workforce, transport systems, distribution channels and access to end markets.

Special customs-privileged places, so-called free trade zones, free ports and export processing zones provide facilities for firms to perform their business activities such as transit trade, storage, distribution and manufacture. Especially, multinational corporations prefer to conduct their commercial activities within the zones enjoying freedom from customs duties and taxes. Today, there are many free trade zones worldwide and a number of countries have spent millions of dollars to establish the zones with the aim of attracting foreign investment and strengthening their national or regional economy (Ryoo et al., 2001).

Particularly with the changes in logistics management systems and the emergence of hub/feeder networks, seaports in Northeast Asia are in fierce competition with each other to attract international traffic. As a result, they are expanding their port facilities and diversifying port functions in order to play a leading role in international logistics chains. In line with this development, the Korean government has recognised that the value added logistics function of a port is most important in gaining a competitive advantage over competing ports in Northeast Asia. This has led to the introduction of the Act on Designation and Management of Free Trade Zones for Building International

Table 3.3:   Project plan for Busan New Port[1]

Classification	Overall (1995–2011)	Stage 1 (1995–2008)	Stage 2 (2009–2011)
Total			
Project cost (100 million won)	91,542	55,519	36,023
Project scale (berth number)	30	14	16
Handling capacity (10,000 TEU)	804	352	452
Government			
Project cost (100 million won)	41,739	28,012	13,727
Project scale (berth number)	1.49 km of breakwater	1.49 km	–
	20.8 km of ground revetment	20.8 km	–
	62 million m² of dredging	40 million m²	22 million m²
	Connecting 0.3 km of pier	0.3 km	
	0.4 km of multi-purpose wharf (1 berth)	0.4 km (1 berth)	–
	1 fishery compensation	1	1
Private sector			
Project cost (100 million won)	49,803	27,507	22,296
Project scale (berth number)	9.55 km (29)	4.3 km of quay wall (13)	5.25 km (16)

[1] At the time of writing, the exchange rate was US$1 = 1,041 won.
Source: Busan Regional Maritime Affairs and Fisheries Office (2004).

Logistics Centres in 1999. In an attempt to attract global logistics firms and international traffic through utilising Busan's advantageous geographical location, the port was finally designated as a free trade zone in 2002. As shown in Table 3.4, Shinseondae container terminal, Hanjin container terminal and Cheil Jedang site at the Port of Busan were appointed as FTZs. Port hinterland and reclaimed sites were also designated as prearranged FTZs.

As with free trade zones operated in other countries, in Korea's FTZs commercial activities are allowed with minimum customs formalities – to the mutual benefit of the country in which the companies are located and the companies

Table 3.4: Designation of Busan port as a free trade zone

FTZ	Expected zone
Shinseondae container terminal	Hinterland adjacent to FTZ
Part of Kamchon western terminal	Yongdang site (near Shinsundae terminal)
Hanjin container terminal	Reclamation site for Korea Ship
Ex-Cheil Jedang (CJ) site	Repairing Industry Cooperatives and Dae Sun Shipbuilding and Engineering Co. Ltd. (Near Kamchon terminal)
Total: 1.277 million m²	Total: 890,000 m²

Source: Busan Regional Maritime Affairs and Fisheries Office (2004).

which operate from them. Within the zone, customs law is not applied and it is considered to be a foreign location in accordance with customs law. In FTZs, foreign registered firms are exempted or have a reduced direct tax, such as corporate tax, income tax, acquisition tax, registration tax, property tax and aggregate land tax. Moreover, diverse indirect tax exemptions are offered, such as the customs duties in the FTZ.

With its designation as a FTZ, Busan port is expected to operate beyond the traditional roles of cargo handling to encourage value added logistics activities including repacking, customising, assembly, repair and processing. Other businesses such as financing, insurance, exhibition and manufacturing are also permitted in the zone (Table 3.5).

The economic benefits of free trade zones to the host country vary with the type of free trade zone activities. Different types of free trade zones are, therefore, developed in response to a particular government's objectives and policies. In the case of Busan port, the anticipated benefits of designating the port as a free trade zone include:

- Employment creation effects as the result of attracting investment from both foreign and domestic companies;
- Creation of added value in port-related industries;
- Increased income from marine freight rates as the result of an increase in goods transference and transit cargoes;
- Activation of mediation/processing trade by trade agents both from Korea and overseas;
- Increase of income from port and related businesses;
- Reduction in transaction cost due to the simplification of processes in product trading within the zone;
- The development of the financial sector due to the required distribution of vast funds; and
- The attraction of foreign capital and technology.

Table 3.5:   Areas subject to designation and the status of areas due for designation

	Yongdang region in North Port			Seopyeon region in Gamcheon	
	Shinseondae terminal region	*LME warehouse region*	*Chunil CY region*	*Hanjin terminal region*	*Reclamation site of CJ*
Company name	Shinseondae Container Terminal Co. Ltd.	Global Enterprises Ltd.	Chunil Cargo Transportation Co. Ltd.	Hanjin Shipping Co. Ltd.	Korea Land Corp.
Lot address	123, Yongdang-dong, Nam-gu	128–12, Yongdang-dong, Nam-gu	128–14, Yongdang-dong, Nam-gu	468, Gupyeong-dong, Saha-gu	468, Gupyeong-dong, Saha-gu
Area size	1 million m^2	16,000 m^2	7,000 m^2	130,000 m^2	148,000 m^2
Proprietor	Ministry of Maritime Affairs and Fisheries	Ministry of Maritime Affairs and Fisheries	Ministry of Maritime Affairs and Fisheries	Hanjin Shipping Co. Ltd.	Korea Land Corp.

Source: Busan Regional Maritime Affairs and Fisheries Office (2004).

3.4   The financing of port development projects

3.4.1   Overview of financing port projects

Port infrastructure expansion projects in Korea are currently supported through a mix of government funding, funding from revenues of existing container terminals and private investment.

In the early 1990s the government realised that private investment in port development projects was necessary in order to accommodate growth of container traffic. Because of budget restrictions, the government could not maintain an acceptable pace of port construction. Therefore, in 1990, the establishment of the KCTA became part of the solution, as it is supported by government funding, revenues from the existing container terminals and private investment. Container terminals at Busan port operated by private terminal operating companies were built through the KCTA.

The government has estimated that timely expansion of port facilities to meet the demand for a rapid growth of container trades would need to be as high as 3.3 trillion won over the period 2002–11. However, the government was able to allocate only 1.8 trillion won per year to the port development budget. As a result, the government introduced numerous incentive measures to attract private investment into developing urgently needed facilities and to secure the nation's port competitiveness.

To ease the burden which private investment firms might face, the government provides financial aid for port construction, guarantees minimum revenue, protects against currency exchange rate risk and reduces tax credit for port investors. For example, the government maintains the rate of return at a high level by comparing the port-user charge utilised to calculate projected income with the prevailing market price. If annual operational income falls short of the minimum level set forth in the settled agreement, either the period of investment returns is expanded or adjustments to user fees are considered to make up for the loss. In addition, when the currency exchange rate fluctuates by more than 20 per cent and the investors are hit hard by losses in borrowed foreign capital used as construction finance, the government compensates for the loss with financial aid or by altering charges based on losses of more than 20 per cent of the exchange rate. For SOC facilities built using the BTO or BOT method value-added tax is exempted. As shown in Table 3.6, in the BOT case registration tax and acquisition tax on real estate are exempted (MOMAF, 2004).

3.4.2 Financing for the Busan New Port project

The Pusan New Port Corporation (PNC), a consortium of Korean construction and transportation companies, has been established to construct the Busan New Port and the consortium is now responsible for building Phase 1-1A, Phase 1-1B and Phase 1-2. The other phases of the BNP are being developed by the KCTA (Phases 2-1 and 2-2) and by the government (Phase 2-2).

In 1997, the consortium was awarded a 50-year concession by the Korean government to build and operate the Busan New Port. The proposed Busan New Port terminal is 3.2 km of berth connected to 192 hectares of on-dock storage which is to be built in three phases (1 km of berth for Phase 1-1A, 1 km for Phase 1-1B and 1.2 km for Phase 1-2).

Most shares of PNC are held by Samsung with 25 per cent and Dubai Ports World, also with 25 per cent. Dubai Ports World has the exclusive right to operate the new terminal for a minimum of 30 years (see Figure 3.8).

3.5 Competitiveness of the Port of Busan

In recent years the Port of Busan has been achieving considerable success in attracting transhipment container cargoes. The growth of transhipment cargoes has improved Busan's performance, because container lines are using the port to serve destinations in China, Japan, the Russian Pacific coast, and even countries in Southeast Asia. In 2003, Busan handled transhipment cargoes of 4.25 million TEUs, accounting for 41 per cent of total container throughput in Korea. This is mainly attributable to an advantageous geographical location and cheaper port charges compared with neighbouring ports in China and Japan.

In this section the competitiveness of Busan port is discussed by employing a SWOT analysis, a tool for auditing an organisation and its environment.

Table 3.6: Investment conditions for port development projects

Classification	Total investment cost	Investment return rate	Equity capital	Borrowed capital	Government construction aid	Guarantee of minimum level of operation income
Busan New Port (1st Phase)	2,388.6 bn won 100%	14.97% (9.5%)	477.7 bn won 20.0%	13,022.2 bn won 54.5%	608.7 bn won 25.5%	90% for 20 years (withdrawn, May 2003)
Mokpo new outport (1-1 Phase)	101.3 bn won 100%	15.19% (9.62%)	23.8 bn won 23.5%	34.5 bn won 34.0%	43.1 bn won 42.5%	90% for 20 years
Mokpo new outport (1-2 Phase)	26.6 bn won 100%	14.0% (8.57%)	6 bn won 22.6%	9 bn won 33.8%	11.6 bn won 43.6%	80% for 20 years
Incheon north port (INI Steel)	110.3 bn won 100%	14.45% (9.0%)	27.6 bn won 25.0%	56.3 bn won 51.0%	26.4 bn won 24.0%	80% for 20 years*
Incheon north port (Dongguk Steel)	53.3 bn won 100%	14.35% (8.9%)	13.3 bn won 25.0%	24.2 bn won 45.4%	15.8 bn won 29.6%	80% for 20 years*
Incheon north port (2-1 Phase)	254.4 bn won 100%	14.3% (8.86%)	55 bn won 21.6%	128.3 bn won 50.4%	71 bn won 27.9%	80% for 15 years
Gunsan Biueng harbour	123.8 bn won 100%	13.8% (8.38%)	38.8 bn won 31.3%	25.5 bn won 20.6%	59.4 bn won 47.9%	No guarantee

Note: * Limited to general miscellaneous cargo.
Source: MOMAF (2004).

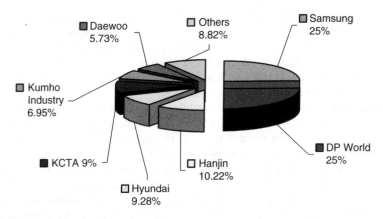

Figure 3.8: PNC consortium shareholders

Table 3.7: SWOT analysis of Busan port

Strengths	Weaknesses
Advantageous geographical location	Shortage of port facilities
Natural deep-water harbour	Limited port hinterland area
Low port costs	Insufficient port promotion activities
Value added logistics functions	
Opportunities	**Threats**
Growth of container traffic in Northeast Asia	Severe port competition in Northeast Asia
Construction of Busan New Port	Development of 'mega-port' in China and Japan
Designation of free trade zone	Active port marketing by competitors
Development of business complex in port hinterland at BNP	

Table 3.7 presents the strengths, weaknesses, opportunities and threats relevant to the Port of Busan.

3.5.1 Strengths

Busan port has competitive advantages over its competitors in Northeast Asia. Some of the strengths of Busan port are:

- Advantageous geographical location;
- Natural deep-water harbour;
- Low port costs; and
- Value added logistics functions.

According to the literature with regard to key success factors for transhipment hubs, strategic location has been identified as one of the main success factors. A port is strategically located, if it is situated on the main maritime routes or situated in or near production and/or consumption centres with natural deep-water harbours (Tongzon, 2001). As Busan is geographically located on the east–west main trunk route and close to China, one of the world's dynamic economies, it has a strong position in attracting transhipment cargoes to and from northern China and Japan.

According to a recent origin and destination (O/D) analysis of container cargoes at Busan, a total of 536,595 TEUs handled at Busan port were bound for China in 2000. Among them 170,369 TEUs were transhipment cargoes and 67 per cent of total cargo volumes was destined for four ports in northern China such as Shanghai, Qingdao, Tianjin and Dalian. For inbound container cargoes from China, Busan handled a total of 918,880 TEUs consisting of 304,489 TEUs of imported container cargoes and 614,391 TEUs of transhipment cargoes. This proves that large amounts of Chinese container cargoes are transhipped via Busan. In 2000 a total of 640,114 TEUs handled at the port were bound for Japan. Among them 45 per cent of cargoes were transhipment containers. It was found that the majority of cargoes were transported to Tokyo, Osaka, Hakata, Yokohama, Tomakomai and Nagoya. At the same time, Busan handled 398,621 TEUs originating in Japan. Transhipment cargoes accounted for almost 36 per cent of the total. Major trading partner ports in Japan included Yokohama, Kobe, Osaka, Nagoya, Tokyo and Hakata (KCTA, 2002).

Another strong position of the port is its natural deep-water harbour compared to its competitors. This enables the port to attract larger size container ships. For example, CMA/CGM's 8,200 TEU container ship *Hugo*, one of the largest container ships currently operated in the world, started visiting the port in 2004. Its lower handling costs have also contributed to an increase in transhipment cargoes over the last few years. Transhipment cargo handling costs at the Port of Busan are 47 per cent less than at Kobe, and 28 per cent less than at Kaohsiung.

Nowadays, the increasing number of distribution centres and free trade zones in ports worldwide explains the important role of ports in terms of their logistics function. Aiming to strengthen the logistics function of Busan port, MOMAF designated the port as a free trade zone as of 1 January 2002. Within the FTZ, free business activities are ensured since tariffs, dues and taxes are exempted on goods brought in while international logistics activities are available to generate high added value through repacking, customising, assembly, processing and quality control. As a result, the port is expected to operate beyond simple functions such as loading, unloading and storage of cargoes, and attract more port traffic. With the establishment of the FTZ at Busan port it is estimated that the volume of transhipment cargoes will increase to about 9.8 million TEUs in 2010 and 19 million TEUs in 2020 (KMI, 2000).

3.5.2   Weaknesses

One of the crucial problems the Port of Busan faces is a shortage of handling capacity. Containers at Busan port are currently handled far beyond its planned capacity. When considering the future growth of container traffic in Northeast Asia, the expansion of its port facilities is clearly desperately needed. In particular, due to its shortage of on-dock container yard spaces a large number of containers are currently handled at off-dock container yards (ODCYs) and Yangsan inland container depot (ICD). ODCYs are located in 26 different regions in Busan and operated by 13 companies. In 2003, the ODCY handled a total of 3 million TEUs of import and export containers, a 14 per cent increase over the previous year. This group accounts for 30 per cent of total container throughput in 2003 (KCTA, 2004). Eighty-five per cent of all imported and exported cargoes arrives or exits the port via local loads. As these containers need to be transported to and from container terminals for stuffing, devanning and storage in the ODCYs or Yangsan ICD, this has been a major cause of traffic congestion in Busan and social and environmental costs have been incurred which might be reduced by handling containers in the on-dock container yard (Hur et al., 2001) (see Table 3.8).

Figure 3.9 shows a quadrant analysis matrix for the marketing mix (4Ps: product, place, price and promotion) of Busan port. Port users believe price

Table 3.8:   Social costs incurred by using the ODCY and ICD

	Transport costs ($1,000)	Environmental pollution costs ($1,000)	Road maintenance costs ($1,000)	Road accident costs ($1,000)	Total ($1,000)
1999	13,563	428	140	12,820	26,951
2001	5,392	259	84	3,271	9,007
2003	8,517	587	191	11,326	20,621

Source: Hur et al. (2001).

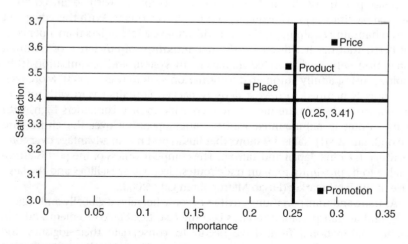

Figure 3.9:   Importance-performance analysis (IPA) of marketing mix
Source: Hur and Jeong (2002).

is an important factor for using a port and they provide a high rating on this attribute for the port. Port promotion is considered to be important to port users, but it is found that Busan scores low on this attribute (Hur and Jeong, 2002). The implication of this result is that the port needs a successful promotion strategy. In particular, container terminal operating companies at Busan port are currently promoting their terminals independently. There is a lack of promotional activities in co-operation with a port authority and government organisations. As the port is administered and managed by a number of organisations such as the Busan Regional Maritime Affairs and Fisheries Office, the KCTA, Busan City and Busan Customs a more co-operative and aggressive marketing strategy should be implemented to promote Busan port successfully (Hur and Jeong 2002).

3.5.3 Opportunities

China's entry into the World Trade Organisation (WTO) in 2001 will have profound effects not only on the global trading system but also on the maritime industry. According to the World Bank, China is expected to become the world's second-largest trading nation with its 10 per cent share of world exports. The most immediate effect on the container market will be a dramatic increase in the proportion of containerised cargoes in China and a growth of transhipment volumes in Northeast Asia. Container ports in Northern China currently have problems of capacity shortage and a lack of deep-water access channels. Busan port is in a strong position to attract more transhipment cargoes to and from northern China until it develops its own deep-water berths and transhipment capabilities.

The development of Busan New Port will enable Busan to achieve a competitive advantage in attracting more shipping lines as their port of call and increase port traffic. Busan New Port will be equipped with advanced operational facilities to provide quality services to customers. With this advanced cargo handling equipment, the port will achieve a rate of less than 1 per cent of berth waiting. It will realise the maximisation of efficiency of terminal operation with an integrated management system and optimisation technology, using a fully automated information system (Kim, 2003). Moreover, the port is planned to have a densely packed container yard with rows of container stacks that are nine containers wide by five containers high, with semi-automatic rail-mounted gantry cranes operating over the entire yard (Woodman, 2001). Table 3.9 shows that Busan port has an advantage over competitors in China, Japan and Taiwan. The competitiveness of the port is attributable to its proximity to main trade routes, deep-water facilities and the large size of the local market (Busan Metropolitan City, 2003).

As trade and transportation activities become liberalised globally and regionally, and as transportation services become fast, flexible, convenient and efficient, multinational firms have begun to consolidate their logistics and distribution activities into one or two centres. The centralised distribution

Table 3.9:   Competitiveness of Busan New Port in Northeast Asia

Index	Busan NP	Kobe	Shanghai	Dalian	Qingdao	Kaohsiung	⓪ → ① → ② → ③ → ④
Proximity to trade route	④	③	②	⓪	①	④	Distance 500 mile → 100 miles
Cost of labour	②	⓪	④	④	④	①	Expensive → Cheap
Deep-water	④	③	①	①	⓪	③	0–9, 10–11, 12–13, 14, 15 m+
Size of local market	④	②	④	④	③	④	Population <1 million → +3 million
Subsidies & incentive	④	③	②	②	②	③	No Programme → Duty free
Average score	④	②	③	②	②	③	

Source: Busan Metropolitan City (2003).

centres in Singapore and in the Netherlands are good examples. The liberal-ising economic environment in Northeast Asia will make it increasingly feas-ible for multinational firms to consolidate their logistics and distribution activities in the region to fewer distribution centres. To cater for this new business environment the Korean government is very keen to develop logis-tics centres in port hinterlands. The BNP will be accompanied by spacious sites which encourage logistics and distribution activities. A business com-plex will be developed in its hinterland and it will be designated as a free trade zone. The construction of a logistics centre and the designation of the hinterland as a free trade zone would generate more container cargoes and encourage more liner carriers to call directly at the port.

3.5.4   Threats

The increase in containerised traffic in the 1990s has led to a dramatic increase in the transhipment market. This has been a particularly welcome development for ports located in strategically advantageous geographical locations on major trade routes. Busan has taken advantage of its geographical location and the growth of container traffic in Northeast Asia for the last decade. However, the port is facing stiffer competition from neighbouring ports in Korea, China and Japan. The development of Gwangyang as part of the government's twin-hub port strategy would have a negative effect on container volumes at Busan port. The government has developed Gwangyang to serve the excess capacity of Busan port. Four berths became operational in 1998 and a total of

33 berths will be constructed by 2011. The port has recorded a cargo growth rate of 22.6 per cent and handled about 1.2 million TEUs in 2003.

Gwangyang is making a concerted effort to attract shipping lines and increase port traffic, with a range of measures such as tax benefits, reduced service fees, incentives on transhipment cargoes, the designation of the port as a free trade zone and the development of a logistics centre. The port introduced a 'Volume Incentive System' in December 2003, which offers up to 50 per cent discount on transhipment cargo handling fees to high-volume shipping companies. The new incentive system, along with other exceptional measures, is expected to boost trade at Gwangyang port (KCTA, 2003).

Shanghai, the main competitor to Busan port, has emerged as one of the largest container ports and commercial centres in the world over the past five years due to the fast growth of China's economy. Its annual growth rate of container traffic amounted to 28 per cent over the last five years. In 2003, the Port of Shanghai handled 11.2 million TEUs and was positioned as the third biggest container port in the world.

As container carriers have invested in new post-panamax vessels to serve main east–west trades, draught has increasingly become a problem for Shanghai port. As a result, import and export container cargoes at Shanghai port have been transhipped by feeders to neighbouring ports such as Busan and Kobe. However, to solve both draught and capacity problems Shanghai is driving hard forward with its 'Yangshan project' to build 52 berths by 2020 on the islands of Xiao Yang Shan and Da Yang Shan. The main advantages of the site include its relative proximity to the existing container terminals, its deep-water draught of 15 m and its fast currents that will prevent the main channel from silting up. In 2005, the first phase of the project was completed. It consists of five container berths with an annual handling capacity of 2.2 million TEUs. By 2010, the terminal's annual capacity will increase to 15 million TEUs (Dekker, 2002).

The Port of Yokohama in Japan is also investing heavily in developing its port facilities to become an international hub for East Asia. The port is increasing the water depth of the MC-1 and MC-2 container berths at Minami-Honmoku Pier, as well as the berth lengths and the terminal areas, in response to the growing size of container vessels. The Minami-Honmoku MC-1 and MC-2 container terminals boast Japan's first 16-metre berths. The largest container vessels navigating main routes connecting North America, Asia and Europe will be able to smoothly enter and exit the port via these terminals. The combined length of the MC-1 and MC-2 berths will be 750 metres and they will be equipped with five mega-gantry cranes capable of accommodating 22 rows of containers (City of Yokohama, 2004).

3.6   Business strategies for building a hub port in Northeast Asia

The Port of Busan has introduced a number of business strategies to maintain its status as one of the world's top container ports and to become a logistics hub port in Northeast Asia. This section discusses its business strategies in terms of modernising existing port facilities, improving port services, implementing port marketing activities and designating the port as a free trade zone.

3.6.1   Upgrading of port facilities

Busan is undertaking a number of activities to modernise general cargo piers and improve their port facilities. For example, old warehouses in the general cargo piers, which handle 30 per cent of container volumes, will be removed so that the site can be used as container yards. Also, stevedoring equipment such as transfer cranes and gantry cranes will be upgraded. In addition, these piers were equipped with a totally automatic gate system in 2003 and, since that time, have been offering real time information on cargo and terminal operations to port users.

The dedicated container terminals at the Port of Busan will be equipped with four gantry cranes per berth by 2004, instead of the current three, and this will increase to five cranes per berth by 2005 to improve stevedoring productivity. Also, to accommodate larger containerships Busan East Container Terminal (PECT) is planning to extend its 1,200 m quay length to 1,500 m and add new super post-panamax gantry cranes. With this 300 m berth extension, PECT will have additional back-up space of about 52,900 m^2.

The operating company of Shinsundae terminal revealed that it would dredge its third and fourth berths to make water depths of 15–16 metres by early 2005. The dredging started in 2003 at a cost of 7.2 billion won per metre per berth. The 14 metre-deep third berth will be dredged to 15 metres and the 15 metre-deep fourth berth to 16 metres. After dredging, the third berth will accommodate 6,000 TEU vessels and the fourth berth up to 8,000 TEU vessels.

The dredging aims to provide better service to shipping companies and shippers by accepting bigger container vessels. In the meantime, Shinsundae terminal also has plans to develop a fifth berth of 16 metres depth with a 146.9 billion won investment to accommodate 8,000 TEU vessels (Busan Regional Maritime Affairs and Fisheries Office, 2003a).

The government has purchased land in Gamcheon to secure a large port hinterland and also to attract high value-added logistics companies. Furthermore, it is drawing up a project to establish a new logistics complex behind Shinseondae container terminal after removing the old existing facilities. To facilitate the construction of the logistics complex, the government has enacted a law reducing the direct tax burden on the investors. The tenants will be authorised to open their business for the exporting of manufactured goods, processing and assembling.

3.6.2   Improvement of port services

One of the notable actions that has been taken for the improvement of port operation is the formation of the Labour Administration Committee in which management and labour jointly participate to manage and employ port labour and maintain 24-hour operations.

In order to meet customer requirements for better cost-effectiveness and higher standards of service, PECT has brought on-dock service into operation. This provides a comprehensive range of services, performed on the terminal premises, including loading, unloading, storage and customs clearance of containers. As a result, container movements are streamlined because there is no need for containers to go through off-dock container yards. In this way, PECT is promoting a win-win strategy based on an on-dock service that yields cost savings for shipping lines, whilst securing a volume base for the terminal (Busan Regional Maritime Affairs and Fisheries Office, 2003b).

At the same time, the MOMAF has recently lifted a cabotage ban imposed on foreign container vessels so as to loosen bottlenecks in inland transportation. It is deemed that the policy change will be a major step towards making cargo flow in a more economical and streamlined manner by matching commercial demand.

As more than two stevedoring companies are involved in cargo handling on conventional wharves that usually handle transhipment cargoes, there is a purported problem of inefficiency in port operation, in that terminal resources are not effectively utilised. Therefore, the government has recommended companies such as Kukje Express, Global Enterprises and Korea Express to temporarily integrate into a single operating company by June 2004 through the means of a consortium.

The operating companies have agreed to leave the details of the consortium constitution to the Busan Port Stevedores Association and to decide shares through external appraisals. In October 2003, the association launched research projects for asset and value appraisals of seven terminal operating companies of conventional wharves and to find ways to improve terminal operating efficiency. The association also plans to automate terminal gates like those of the specialised container terminals. The restructuring of terminal operation companies and the upgrading of terminal facilities on conventional wharves are, therefore, expected to improve the productivity of their port operations (Busan Regional Maritime Affairs and Fisheries Office, 2003c).

3.6.3   Implementation of port marketing

Busan has launched a number of marketing activities to attract customers and increase container traffic. For instance, sales delegates regularly visit existing and potential customers to promote Busan port and all kinds of incentive systems have been introduced to attract container traffic. Port sales delegates regularly visit Hong Kong, Singapore, China and Japan to promote Busan port in the face of strong competition from other ports in Northeast Asia. Recently, the port began to realise the need for a marketing activity jointly with public and private sectors. As a result, the port formed a port promotion delegation consisting of the Busan Regional Maritime Affairs and Fisheries Office, Busan city and terminal operators.

As a means of attracting transhipment containers, the government introduced a volume incentive programme in 2003. Shipping lines bringing transhipment cargoes to the port will be offered a cost reduction as an incentive if the growth in cargo volume exceeds that of the previous year. For example, if a shipping line calling at the port handles 250,000 TEUs this year, then it may be subject to a reduction in cargo handling charges on a growth of 50,000 TEUs next year. This incentive system was applied until November 2005 (Busan Regional Maritime Affairs and Fisheries Office, 2003d).

3.6.4 Designation of free trade zones

To attract foreign investment and increase port traffic the government has a plan to designate hinterlands at Busan New Port as free trade zones and build a distribution centre, sized between 132,000 m^2 and 330,000 m^2 in the zone. Foreign manufacturing and logistics companies investing in the FTZ will receive tax incentives and other benefits. A number of special incentives offered to foreign companies are as follows (Roh, 2003):

- Low corporate, income registration and property taxes;
- No corporation tax for tenants entering in 2004 for the first seven years and a 50 per cent discount for the next three years. Tenants entering in 2005 will get three years tax-free and a 50 per cent discount for the next two years;
- Exemption from acquisition, registration, property and land tax for the first five years and discounted 50 per cent for the following three years;
- Exemption from customs reports and duty payments for foreign imports;
- Exemption from customs duties and special consumption taxes on products brought into FTZs from Korea with favourable VAT rates applying to them;
- Exemption from alcoholic beverage tax and transportation tax;
- Low rent at the level of Masan FTZ;
- Maximum 50-year rent contract and permanent facilities construction within national or public land;
- Simplified customs report procedures for transfer of products between registered companies; and
- Simplified usage/consumption of foreign products and conducting value-added logistics activities.

3.7 Summary

The Port of Busan has established a strong position in the transhipment market in Northeast Asia by providing quality service, low handling charges and a strong local cargo base. Its proximity to the main trade routes and the growth of China's container trade has also contributed to the increase of transhipment cargoes at Busan over the last decade. However, the port is facing strong competition from ports in northern China, which is expected to increase its domination of the container market in Northeast Asia. It is expected that shipping companies will turn to direct callings at Chinese ports due to the rapidly growing Chinese economy, instead of keeping to the main trunk route through the ports in Taiwan, Korea and Japan. This indicates that transhipment containers at the Port of Busan will gradually decrease in the near future.

Busan needs to adjust to changing markets in order to ensure the competitiveness of the port and remain successful in the future. To offer and sustain transhipment business the port has launched numerous business strategies such as the introduction of volume incentive systems, the dredging of its approach channel, the designation of the port as an FTZ, the modernisation of conventional piers and the establishment of the Busan Port Authority. In addition, a variety of projects at Busan New Port are underway to meet the increasing growth in container traffic and the development of a logistics centre. A free trade zone is also planned in the hinterland of the New Port to generate more container cargoes.

To gain a competitive advantage it is important to implement these business strategies efficiently and effectively. The port's future success will hinge on its ability to meet the needs of port users and to offer a competitive transhipment service. Shipping lines have been trying to make as few port calls as possible to minimise round voyage times, and have tried to benefit from economies of scale. In selecting a hub port, shipping lines seek locations with certain key characteristics. The strategic requirements that shipping lines require from ports include minimised waiting and cargo handling times, flexible and reliable services, access to deep-water berths, lower port costs and minimal intervention in overall cargo flow. These elements are directly related to the overall performance of port operation, which is of interest to container lines. To enhance port performance, close co-operation between the BPA, KCTA, MOMAF, terminal operators and port labour unions has become more important than ever before. They should work closely together to satisfy the final customers and to prepare to become the future logistics hub of Northeast Asia.

References

Baird, A. J. (2001) 'Privatisation Trends at the World's Top-100 Container Ports', *Proceedings of the International Association of Maritime Economists Conference*, July, Hong Kong: 249–67.

Busan Metropolitan City (2003) *A Study on the Revitalization of Free Trade Zone in Busan Port*, Busan.

Busan Regional Maritime Affairs and Fisheries Office (2003a) 'News in Busan', *Dynamic Busan*, 2: 31–3.

Busan Regional Maritime Affairs and Fisheries Office (2003b) 'Why is PECT different?' *Dynamic Busan*, Summer: 28–9.

Busan Regional Maritime Affairs and Fisheries Office (2003c) 'Introducing the Single Operating System', *Dynamic Busan*, 2: 15.

Busan Regional Maritime Affairs and Fisheries Office (2003d) 'Volume Incentive', *Dynamic Busan*, 2: 14.

Busan Regional Maritime Affairs and Fisheries Office (2004) http://www.portbusan.or.kr/.

City of Yokohama (2004) http://www.city.yokohama.jp/.

Dekker, N. (2002) 'Shanghai in Deep Water?' *Containerisation International*, February: 78–9.

Hur, Y. S. and Jeong, T. W. (2002) 'A Study on Marketing Analysis and Role Sharing for Busan Port', *Journal of Korean Society of Transportation*, 20(6): 17–30.

Hur, Y. S., Nam, G. C., Moon, S. H. and Ryoo, D. K. (2001) 'A Case Study on the Improvement of Container Transportation Systems in Busan Port', *Journal of Korean Society of Transportation*, 19(2): 29–40.

Kim, Y. B. (2003) 'Strike while the Competition is Hot', *Dynamic Busan*, Summer: 12–13.

Korea Container Terminal Authority (2002) *An Analysis of Container Cargo Transport System in China and Japan and the Development of Marketing Strategy of Korea Seaports*, Busan.

Korea Container Terminal Authority (2003) 'Gwangyang Port, Launching Volume Incentive System', *Port News*, August: 2.

Korea Container Terminal Authority (2004) http://www.kca.or.kr/.

Korea Maritime Institute (2000) *The Establishment of Free Trade Zones in Port Areas in Korea*, Seoul.

Ministry of Commerce, Industry and Energy (2002) *Progress Report 2002*, Seoul.

Ministry of Commerce, Industry and Energy (2004) http://www.mocie.go.kr/.

Ministry of Maritime Affairs and Fisheries (2001) *Adjusted Port Development Plan*, January.

Ministry of Maritime Affairs and Fisheries (2004) http://www.momaf.go.kr/.

Moon, S. H. (2001) 'The Privatisation of Korean Seaports', *Proceedings of the International Association of Maritime Economists Conference*, July, Hong Kong: 268–81.

Moon, S. H., Kwak, K. S., Nam, K. C. and Song, Y. S. (2003) 'An Analysis on the Distribution of Transhipment Container Cargoes in Northeast Asia: with Particular Reference to Korea and China', *Proceedings of the International Association of Maritime Economists Conference*, 3–5 September, Busan, Korea: 332–42.

Roh, M. H. (2003) 'Busan Lures Foreign Investment', *Dynamic Busan*, 2: 28–9.

Ryoo, D. K., Moon, S. H., Lee, T. W. and Kil, K. S. (2001) 'Charting a New Course of Korean Seaports with the Establishment of Customs-Free Zones', *Proceedings of the International Association of Maritime Economists Conference*, 18–20 July, Hong Kong: 237–47.

Ryu, J. Y. (2003) 'Port of Busan Breaks 10 Million Containers Record', *Dynamic Busan*, 2: 12–13.

Song, D. W. and Cullinane, K. P. B. (1999) 'Port Privatisation: Principle and Evidence', *Proceedings of the International Association of Maritime Economists Conference*, 13–14 September, Halifax, Canada.

Tongzon, J. (2001) 'Key Success Factors for Transhipment Hubs: the Case of the Port of Singapore', *Proceedings of the International Association of Maritime Economists Conference*, 18–20 July, Hong Kong: 85–101.

Woodman, R. A. (2001) 'Facing Up to the Future', *Port Development International*, October: 15–17.

4
Kobe: One of the Most Developed Ports in Japan[1]

Hajime Inamura, Ryuichi Shibasaki and Kazuhiko Ishiguro

4.1 Introduction

The Port of Kobe grew as the main Asian hub port throughout the 1970s and 1980s. However, growth slowed in the 1990s. In particular, the Port of Kobe suffered extensive damage as a result of the Great Hanshin-Awaji earthquake in 1995. Since all of the container berths equipped with gantry cranes were not available for more than two months, many shippers and carriers moved away to other ports. The proportion of international transhipment container cargoes to total container volume handled at the Port of Kobe has fallen to less than 10 per cent. In reaction to this situation, the Port of Kobe has begun to implement measures to reduce costs, shorten processing time and improve service levels. If all of these measures work out well, the Port of Kobe will recover. This chapter summarises the current situation at the Port of Kobe and discusses its future prospects. Geographical features of the port and the current liner services are summarised in section 4.2, and the status of facilities is presented in section 4.3. Features of each area of the port are introduced in section 4.4 and the role of Kobe Port Terminal Corporation (KPTC), as an agent that develops and manages container terminals, is explained in section 4.5. In sections 4.6 and 4.7, long-term development plans and currently implemented measures are discussed.

4.2 Outline of the Port of Kobe

4.2.1 Geographical features

Located at the centre of the Japanese archipelago and on the world's main marine transportation route, the Port of Kobe plays an essential role as an Asian hub port (See Table 4.1). Its natural features are as follows:

1. The Rokko Mountains extend parallel to the port and block the seasonal winds.
2. Since no rivers flow into the port, dredging is unnecessary.

Table 4.1:   Statistics of the Port of Kobe (as of 2003)

Area	Port water area	9,342 ha
	Waterfront area	1,885.6 ha
	Commercial zone	1,135.5 ha
	Industrial zone	677.4 ha
	Scenic and recreation zone	47.6 ha
	Marina zone	2.4 ha
	Non-designated zone	22.7 ha
Facilities	Total: 226 berths	
	Public & Kobe Port Terminal Corporation Berths: 174 (including 23 container berths) Private berths: 52	
Port activities	Number of incoming ships: 40,868 (including 7,887 international ships) Volume of cargo loaded and unloaded: 78.76 million tonnes Number of containers loaded and unloaded: 2,045,714 TEU Value of trade: 6,388.0 billion yen	

Source: Kobe City.

3. The port stretches from east to west and can be accessed from various directions.
4. The port is ideal for mooring, since it has little tidal variation.
5. Having the Rokko Mountains at its rear and the City of Kobe nearby, the Port of Kobe has outstanding scenic beauty.

The Port of Kobe has the whole of western Japan and the Chubu and Hokuriku regions as its hinterland. The port and its hinterland are directly linked via expressways, domestic feeders and ferryboat networks. In addition, progress is well underway on improving and expanding the Kobe Air Cargo City Terminal (K-ACT), which connects the port to the airport, ensuring punctual delivery.

4.2.2   Regular liner services

The port has many regular liner services that call, including: connections to North America (West Coast), Europe, Southeast Asia and China (see Table 4.2). The port is linked via these lines to 500 ports in 135 countries. Major shipping companies supply their main service routes on fixed weekly schedules and ships from the main sea routes call at the Port of Kobe nearly every day.

4.2.3   Access to the port

The port's hinterland covers the whole of western Japan. Transportation efficiency is secured by expressway networks, domestic feeder services and ferry services. Within the port area, the Harbour Highway, linking Port Island and Rokko Island, ensures smooth traffic flow between port facilities. As a result of

Table 4.2:   Number of container liner services (as of July 2004)

Service routes	Number	Frequency of service per month
North America West Coast	9	48
North America East Coast	2	8
North America/Europe	3	20
Europe/Mediterranean	4	16
Africa	1	4
Central and South America	2	6
Oceania	6	12
South East Asia	24	96
China	31	134
Korea	10	44
Nakhodka	1	3
Total	93	391

Note: Double-calling of westbound and eastbound services is counted as two in the frequency column.

the opening of the Sumiyoshihamawatari Line in December 1997, the Harbour Highway is directly connected to the Hanshin Expressway Bay Route. The Minatojima tunnel, which connects Shinko-Higashi Wharf to Port Island, was opened at the end of July 1999, and further improved access to the port. The construction plan for the Hanshin Expressway Bay Route has not yet been finished. When the remaining stretch has been constructed, accessibility to and from the west will be improved. The Japan Railway Freight Company (JRF) is the only nationwide railway company to operate a container freight station on Rokko Island. International container cargo can be reloaded there onto JRF's uniquely standardised containers. Reloaded container cargo is transported by the JRF through the Kobe Freight Terminal Station approximately 15 km from the container freight station.

4.2.4   Improving port services

The port is improving various services in terms of user convenience and friendliness.

1. On 1 July 1998, the compulsory pilot system was deregulated in the Port of Kobe. As a result, the tonnage level at which ships are required to use pilots was raised from 300 G/T to 10,000 G/T.
2. Port dues and wharfage for first-call ocean-going vessels were exempted from 1 July 1998.
3. An EDI (electronic data interchange) system for submitting various forms of documentation was inaugurated on 1 October 1999.

Future plans for the Airport Project include the creation of a meeting-place for people, merchandise and information. The Port of Kobe intends to develop such projects further.

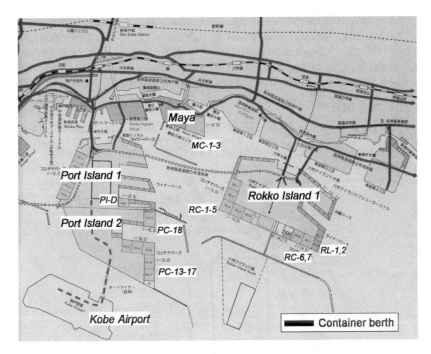

Figure 4.1: Map of the Port of Kobe
Source: Kobe City.

4.3 Container terminal facilities

The Port of Kobe has 19 container terminals equipped with the latest loading and unloading facilities, including super post-panamax gantry cranes, for safe and effective cargo-handling work. There are six high-standard 15 m deep working container berths on Rokko Island (see Figure 4.1). The current port consolidation plan is now complete in terms of new berth construction. Old and smaller berths have been diverted to other purposes with the development of these new berths. Currently, the most highly promoted project is the berth deepening on Rokko Island.

Financiers of berths are classified into the following three types: public, corporation and joint. Public berths are financed and constructed by the Kobe City government and commonly used by various shipping companies. Corporation berths are financed and constructed by the Kobe Port Terminal Corporation (KPTC) and each berth is dedicated to the exclusive use of one or only a few shipping companies. Joint berths are financed by the national government, the Kobe City government, and the KPTC. These three players take respective responsibility for developing quays, marshalling yards and for equipment. The concept of joint berths has been recently introduced in order to remove the negative aspects of the other two types of berths. Public berths are not particularly convenient for large-scale ocean carriers because they are never available for exclusive use. Corporation berths entail huge fixed rents with resultant high operating costs. In principle, joint berths are common user facilities. However, two joint berths are leased to particular shipping companies.

4.3.1 Port Island

Port Island is a man-made island (436 ha) completed in 1981 after 15 years of construction (see Figure 4.2). Port Island provides berths around the island.

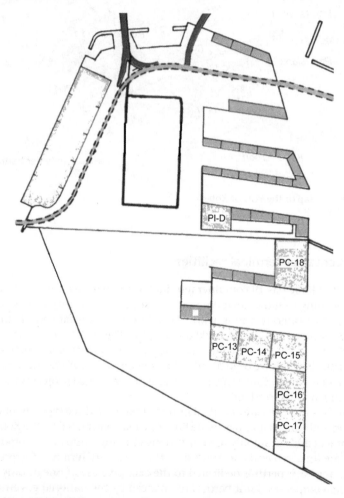

Figure 4.2: Layout of the container terminal on Port Island
Source: Kobe City.

Behind these are port facilities such as transit sheds, warehouses and marshalling yards. In the central area are housing, schools, hospitals, conference facilities and a variety of commercial facilities providing general urban functions for living, working, recreation and study.

Port Island (2nd Stage), to the south of Port Island, was mostly completed in 2002. The area is 390 ha. Six 15 m deep container berths, Kobe Harbour Polytechnic College, and various other facilities have opened (see Table 4.3). The City of Kobe enacted the Kobe Enterprise Zone Ordinance in 1997, which stipulates various incentives to attract enterprises in a number of promising industries to this district. In addition, the Special Port Function Zone was set up in 1999 to attract various industries.

4.3.2   Rokko Island

Rokko Island, the second man-made island, was completed in September 1992 after 20 years of reclamation work.

The total area of this island is 580 ha and a variety of harbour facilities were constructed to accommodate larger ships and a diversified distribution system (see Figure 4.3 and Table 4.4). K-ACT, as an access point for air cargo to Kansai International Airport, and a cold-storage complex, are also located here. These facilities make the island a comprehensive distribution terminal for marine, air, and land transport.

In the central urban function zone, a multifunction town with a population of 30,000 is planned, in response to the needs of internationalisation, and an information-based ageing society.

Table 4.3:   Container terminals in Port Island

Berth	Length (m)	Depth (m)	Terminal area (ha)	Gantry crane	Managing body	Contractor (Corporation Pier) Main user (Public Pier)
PI-D	300	12	7.9	2	Public	
PC-13	350	15	12.3	2	Corporation	APL
PC-14	350	15	12.3	3	Corporation	MOL
PC-15	350	15	12.9	2	Corporation	MOL and three terminal operators (Nickel & Lyons, Sankyu and Sumitomo Warehouse)
PC-16	350	15	12.9	3	Corporation	Two terminal operators
PC-17	350	15	12.3	2	Corporation	(Shibusawa Warehouse and Mitsui Soko), many carriers use it.
PC-18	350	15	13.4	3	Corporation	One terminal operator (Kamigumi), many carriers use it.

Note: Corporation berths are for the dedicated use of contracted customers and public berths are common user.

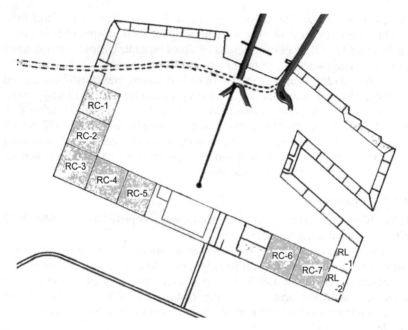

Figure 4.3:   Layout of the container terminal on Rokko Island
Source: Kobe City.

Table 4.4:   Container terminals on Rokko Island

Berth	Length (m)	Depth (m)	Terminal area (ha)	Gantry crane	Managing body	Contractor (Corporation Pier) Main user (Public Pier)
RC-1	350	13	12.3	2	Corporation	
RC-2	350	13	12.3	3	Corporation	
RC-3	350	14	12.3	2	Corporation	K-line and Maersk Sealand
RC-4	350	14	12.3	3	Corporation	
RC-5	350	14	12.3	2	Corporation	
RC-6	350	14	12.3	3	Corporation	NYK
RC-7	350	14	12.3	2	Corporation	
RL-1,2	600	13	12.0	2	Public	Hanjin, etc.

Note: Corporation berths are for the dedicated use of contracted customers and public berths are common user.

4.3.3   Maya Wharf

The construction of the Maya Piers was started in 1959 and completed in 1967. The Piers consisted of four piers in a comb shape. Maya Pier No. 4 was the first container terminal in Japan. In order to achieve greater container handling efficiency, redevelopment commenced in 1987 on Pier No. 4, and, by reclaiming a 9.5 ha area between Piers 3 and 4, a full-scale container terminal

Table 4.5: Container terminals on Maya Wharf

Berth	Length (m)	Depth (m)	Managing body	Main user
MC-1-3	900	12	Public	MISC, OOCL, Heung-A, etc.

was completed in 1991 for public use (see Table 4.5). Further redevelopment projects are also proceeding on the reclamation area (about 18.5 ha) between the other three piers, using rubble from the earthquake.

At the rear of the wharf is a distribution centre for foodstuffs and general merchandise. Accordingly, the wharf is now developing as a waterfront distribution base with an excellent level of accessibility.

4.3.4   Other wharves

There used to be three piers at Hyogo Wharf, which handled daily commodities. In order to expand the functions of these special piers for the handling of vegetables and fruit and to add to the overall redevelopment of Hyogo Piers, an additional reclamation of approximately 39 ha was completed between the piers in October 1997. The wharf will be renovated into a modern facility through the reinforcement of its functions and its linkages with the Central Wholesale Market. Distribution enterprises have relocated to the wharf in order to take advantage of its location. The opening of the Kaigan Line of the Municipal Subway in 2001 has enhanced the convenience for commuters.

The first phase of the Shinko Piers (1 to 4) at Shinko-Higashi Wharf was completed in 1922. Piers No. 5 and No. 6, constructed in the second phase and completed in 1939, made the Port of Kobe Japan's leading trade port. Piers No. 7 and No. 8 were built in the 1950s and 1960s. Pier No. 4, which includes the port terminal, is used for ocean-going passenger ships and international ferry services. The water between Piers No. 5 and No. 8 (approximately 34.5 ha) has been reclaimed, in line with a redevelopment plan that aims to construct more modern port facilities. This 96 ha area is now called the Shinko-Higashi Wharf. The opening of the Minatojima tunnel in July 1999, together with the completion in the near future of a new access road linking the wharf to Routes 2 and 43, will further improve the accessibility of Shinko-Higashi Wharf.

4.4   Kobe Port Terminal Corporation

4.4.1   History

The dissolution of the Hanshin (Osaka & Kobe) Port Development Authority, which had been constructing container and conventional liner terminals in Osaka and Kobe ports since 1967, was formalised by the Law Related to the Dissolution of Foreign Trade Port Development Authorities promulgated on 25 August 1981. In order to take over the business from the Hanshin Port Development Authority, the Kobe Port Administrator decided to reorganise the existing

Kobe Municipal Ferry Terminal Corporation and established the Kobe Port Terminal Corporation on 25 December 1981. Thereafter the KPTC took over the business at Kobe port from the Hanshin Port Development Authority on 31 March 1982. Currently, the KPTC is a subsidiary wholly owned by the Kobe City government with an amount invested of 8,706 million yen.

4.4.2   Role

In compliance with the port and harbour master plan authorised by the port administrator (Kobe City government), the KPTC's role is to build, lease and maintain container, liner and ferry terminals in Kobe port which are rented by vessel operating and harbour transportation companies. KPTC's role will proceed systematically and efficiently and will contribute to the strengthening of the port's function, that is, to increase foreign trade volumes and to develop the local economy. Apart from the KPTC terminals, the Kobe port administrator manages those port and harbour facilities that are shared.

4.4.3   Business

The main businesses of the KPTC are as follows:

1. Construction of foreign trade and ferry terminals.
2. Leasing of the terminals (the lease period of both foreign trade terminals and ferry terminals is 10 years, and can be extended).
3. Maintenance and improvement of the terminals.
4. Construction, maintenance and control of facilities related to the foreign trade terminals and ferry terminals.

4.4.4   Funds

The funds required for the construction and improvement of terminals are raised by interest-free loans from the central government and the port authority (City of Kobe), by interest-bearing loans from the port authority and lessee, or the issuing of bonds. Repayments are made from the lease income of terminals.

4.4.5   Statistical data

Recent trends in foreign trade container cargo and container vessel calls are shown in Tables 4.6 and 4.7, respectively. Volume handled and the number of vessels calling decreased drastically in 1995 due to the damage caused by the great Hanshin-Awaji earthquake. These statistics show vividly that the Port of Kobe has not returned to the levels pre-dating the disaster.

4.5   Perspectives on the long-term development plan

4.5.1   Outline

Kobe's port facilities will be improved in accordance with the Kobe Port Development Plan, which will be completed in 2005. This plan was developed

Table 4.6:   Foreign trade container cargo handled in the Port of Kobe and KPTC terminals (million tonnes)

Year	1993	1994	1995	1996	1997	1998	1999	2000	2001	2002
Total volume	39.8	42.2	21.1	32.0	30.3	28.7	29.4	32.2	28.7	27.6
Handled at KPTC	29.6	32.4	15.1	24.4	24.5	25.1	25.4	26.4	24.6	23.6
Percentage (%)	74.3	76.9	71.6	76.3	80.8	87.6	86.4	82.2	85.7	85.6

Table 4.7:   Container vessels calling at KPTC terminals

Year	1993	1994	1995	1996	1997	1998	1999	2000	2001	2002
No. of vessels	4,035	4,312	2,196	3,602	3,535	3,812	3,676	3,756	3,831	3,636
Million tonnes	98.1	98.6	52.4	90.5	94.6	98.6	98.8	100.3	100.8	100.4

in February 1995, based on the Kobe Port Long-term Development Plan prepared in March 1993, with a long-term view encompassing the twenty-first century. The Kobe Port Development Plan outlines Rokko Island South, Kobe Airport and other redevelopments such as the Eastern Waterfront Development Plan, and aims to be the basis for the following:

1. The development of state-of-the-art port facilities through the expansion of foreign trade functions and the redevelopment of existing wharves.
2. The improvement of the area's environment through the promotion of modal shifts and the enhancement of ocean-based transportation facilities.
3. The development of a port environment that is welcoming to citizens, providing marine recreation and ensuring user-friendly waterfront spaces.

4.5.2   Recent implementation

In order to augment the port's international competitiveness, it is of vital importance that its level of user friendliness, as well as the port facilities, be improved. The Port of Kobe has therefore actively promoted cost reduction measures for port users. For instance, the port has revised port facility charging systems, including a drastic reduction of land rentals to the rear of the berths. In March 1998, in order to reduce drayage cost, the port allowed domestic container feeders to use overseas berths. Deregulation of the compulsory pilot system in July 1998 raised the tonnage levels at which ships are required to use pilots from 300 G/T to 10,000 G/T, with the proviso that vessels below 10,000 G/T must be steered by experienced captains. Port dues and wharfage are exempted for ocean-going ships that enter the Port of Kobe for the first time.

Enterprise zones have been established in the newly reclaimed districts on Port Island Second Stage. Various incentives, including tax exemption/reduction, are offered to enterprises located within these zones. These incentives are expected to attract more and more enterprises to these newly developed districts.

4.6   Super-hub port policy and airport construction

4.6.1   Super-hub port policy

4.6.1.1   *Collaboration with the Port of Osaka*

The Kobe City government drew up the Super-hub Port Project in collaboration with the Osaka City government, the administrator of the Port of Osaka. The Port of Osaka is one of the major hub ports in Japan and is the neighbouring port to the Port of Kobe. The Yumeshima container terminal at the Port of Osaka is about five nautical miles from Rokko Island container terminal at the Port of Kobe. Both ports are connected by a number of expressways and arterial highways.

According to the Port Regulation and Customs Laws, the Ports of Kobe and Osaka are both individual and separate ports. Therefore, a vessel which calls into both ports successively is required to pay tonnage tax and special tonnage tax to the national government at each port. Both city governments are urging the national government to make some legal changes, in view of the fact that the Port of Tokyo and the Port of Yokohama are integrated from an institutional perspective.

4.6.1.2   *Integration of information platforms*

Currently, individual port authority EDI systems operate at each port. Administrative procedures at each port will be standardised and centralised but handwritten forms are still used. At the Port of Kobe 85 per cent of documentary procedures are dealt with using the EDI system.

An integrated EDI system will be introduced between the container terminal, harbour transportation and land transportation companies to encourage efficient container handling and transactions.

4.6.1.3   *Cost reductions*

What had previously been the temporary adoption of new policies giving a 50 per cent discount in gantry crane charges on the loading or unloading of coastal feeder ships will be continued. Permission for domestic feeder ships to berth at an international berth will also be continued. An incentive payment structure will be adopted for port dues and towage. The establishment of a joint terminal company is being promoted to enlarge the operating scale of container terminals. Efficient operation by the company, leading to a 30 per cent reduction in handling costs, is widely expected. Unit handling cost will be reduced by nearly 40 per cent.

4.6.1.4   *Target volume of containers handled at the Port of Kobe*

The target volumes of containers to be handled in 2008 compared to performance in 2004 are shown in Table 4.8. The qualifications needed to locate enterprises within the transaction area near the container terminal have been relaxed.

Table 4.8:   Target volume of containers handled in
2008 (unit: thousand TEUs)

Year	2008	2004
Local cargo	1,680	1,390
Transhipped domestic cargo	300	250
Transhipped foreign cargo	220	110
Total	2,200	1,750

In the past they have been required to have at least one business licence for a warehouse, harbour transportation, or water transportation. Currently, in the case of a company ship receiving half of the total cargo handled through the port in terms of amount or volume, the company qualifies for the right to be located there. This relaxation of qualifications has led to several dozen companies taking out leases. There are 12 ha of vacant lot with the potential to generate 290,000 TEU of containerised cargoes. The volume of transhipped domestic cargo is expected to increase in accordance with past trends. The volume of transhipped foreign cargo is expected to account for 10 per cent of total volume.

4.6.1.5   *Establishment of a joint enterprise*

Five harbour transportation companies (Kamigumi, Mitsui Soko, Nickel & Lyons, Sankyu and Sumitomo Warehouse) established a joint enterprise, the Kobe Mega Container Terminal Co. Ltd. on 30 June 2004. The terminal will operate three container berths, PC-16, 17 and 18, as an integral unit.

4.6.1.6   *Facility improvement*

In 2005 and 2006, container berths at Port Island and Rokko Island will be improved and the width of the terminal will be expanded from 350 m to 500 m. Container berths at Rokko Island will be 15 m deep. The terminal gate of the terminals will be centralised and, in 2008, the operating system will be integrated for each island.

4.6.2   Kobe Airport

In response to the increased demand for air transportation resulting from socio-economic development, the City of Kobe believes that an airport is as indispensable as a seaport to a rich community life and the creation of an attractive urban future. Today, an airport serves as an exchange centre not only for people and goods, but for information and cultures as well. Attributes unique to an airport can be utilised to bring about new industrial development, a shift in focus to more knowledge-intensive industries, the promotion of fashion, conventions, tourism and information industries, and so on. Moreover, the presence of an airport in a community can have a major positive effect on various aspects of its residents' lives. In other words, an airport can be viewed as an urban facility indispensable in terms of enhancing the attractiveness and vitality of a city.

Kobe Airport will be developed as a pollution-free, safe, convenient airport, located near the city centre, serving the people in the Greater Kobe area, and functioning as the hub of a Hyogo Prefectural local air transportation system that is responsive to new air transportation needs, including the main domestic, local, and commuter routes.

In conjunction with the existing Osaka and Kansai International Airports, Kobe Airport will also operate as a key local airport that contributes to the development, not only of Kobe, but also the entire Kansai district.

After all the preliminary procedures were completed, the airport island reclamation project started in September 1999. Construction is proceeding steadily towards the opening of the airport, scheduled for 2006.

4.7 Conclusion

This chapter has presented the current situation and future plans for the Port of Kobe. A number of container terminals within the port have already been developed, although deeper berths are required to accept greater numbers of post-panamax container ships. A new terminal operator has been jointly established by several companies which, as from 2004, is currently operating at the Port of Kobe. It is expected that terminal handling costs and handling time will be reduced. The volume of local cargo will increase through the continual efforts of the operator. Related organisations are considering the possibilities of increasing the volume of transhipment cargo. One other important issue is how the port can improve its attractiveness and quality in order to attract greater volumes of both gateway and transhipment container traffic.

Note

1. The authors would like to acknowledge the Port and Urban Projects Bureau of the Kobe City government and the Kobe Port Terminal Corporation for providing the relevant data and information and for giving valuable comments.

References

Container Age, January (2005).
Port and Urban Projects Bureau (2003) Kobe City government, *Port of Kobe*.
Kobe Port Terminal Corporation (2003) *Kobe Port Terminal Corporation*.
Kobe City government and Osaka City government (2004) *Hanshin Port Development Programs*.

5
Yokohama: Japan's Next Superport?

Hajime Inamura, Ryuichi Shibasaki and Kazuhiko Ishiguro

5.1   Introduction

The Port of Yokohama was opened in 1859 as Japan's gateway to the world. For more than 140 years, it has played an important role as Japan's leading international trade port, supporting the development of all social activities in Japan, as well as having an impact on its economy. Even now, the Port of Yokohama is one of the most important ports in Japan, handling more than 100 million tonnes and 2,000,000 TEU in 2003, making it the third and second largest in terms of tonnage and TEUs handled respectively, of all Japanese ports.

Although true for almost all major Japanese ports, the amount of cargo handled is stagnating, reflecting the prolonged Japanese economic downturn. On the other hand, the amount handled in ports in neighbouring countries, such as China, has increased rapidly due to the fast pace of their economic growth. It can be stated, therefore, that in relative terms the position of Japanese ports is decreasing. The Japanese government, in the form of the Port and Harbour Bureau within the Ministry of Land, Infrastructure and Transport, has begun to undertake a policy, known as the Super-Hub Port Project, in order to revive the major ports in Japan. This project will also enable Japan to keep pace with ports in other Asian countries, in order to avoid, in particular, increased transport costs resulting from their becoming feeder ports.

The Port of Yokohama has another problem. The Port of Tokyo, which is very close to that of Yokohama, is the largest port in Japan, in terms of container handling. The Port of Tokyo has a very large hinterland, covering the entire Tokyo metropolitan area. The Port of Yokohama also has good access to the metropolitan area, however, especially in terms of imported cargo where direct access to the market is preferable. As a result, while the Port of Tokyo is extremely congested, the Port of Yokohama has spare capacity.

In this chapter, we will focus on the past, present and future of the Port of Yokohama, especially in terms of international maritime container cargo. We will look at what has been done, as well as what will be done, to achieve more convenient transport, as well as what concrete actions are currently being undertaken, such as the super-hub port policy in the Port of Yokohama, and how effective this will be. This chapter consists of the following. The next section contains a brief analysis of the Port of Yokohama's past and summarises the historical changes that have followed World War Two, especially in terms of volume handled. Secondly, a brief description of the present situation at the Port of Yokohama focuses particularly on the several container terminals within the port. Then, the future of the Port of Yokohama is discussed. In particular, the focus rests with the unique policies that have been implemented by the port itself, before the implementation of the super-hub port policy, and how these policies could be connected. Finally, other appropriate topics concerning the Port of Yokohama are referred to, namely land development of the port area and land connection. This section is followed by the conclusion.

5.2   Historical development

The Port of Yokohama was opened at the end of the Edo era, as one of the first ports to open for foreign countries after the Tokugawa shogunate stopped Japan's isolationist policy. When the urban infrastructure and port facilities were developed, the Port of Yokohama came to play an important role as a distribution base, not only for the cities in the Kanto area, but for the entire country. Although it was just one small village when the port opened, following the renovation of port facilities after the severe damage caused by the great Kanto earthquake in 1923, Yokohama developed as a large industrial and trading city. By the beginning of World War Two, it had grown into part of the Keihin (Tokyo and Yokohama) industrial zone, which was constructed on reclaimed coastal land in the western part of Tokyo Bay.

All of the port facilities were requisitioned after being completely destroyed by air raids during World War Two. But, as the restoration of domestic industry proceeded, Yamanouchi Pier and Osanbashi Pier were derequisitioned. Since the construction of Yamashita Pier in 1953, the port has continued with the construction of Honmoku Pier in 1963, Daikoku Pier in 1971, and Minami Honmoku Pier in 1990, in order to meet the needs of port logistics, especially container cargo. Minami Honmoku Pier, one of the largest container terminals in Japan, opened in April 2001.

Figure 5.1 shows the historical changes in total cargo volume handled by the Port of Yokohama and its share of all cargoes handled by all Japanese ports. This period, from the 1960s, was a high economic growth period in Japan. The economy steadily increased until about ten years ago. In recent years, however, it has hovered around the same level due to a stagnant Japanese economy. Yokohama's share of all Japanese cargo has decreased, as a result of the development and growth of other ports, such as the Port of Tokyo and other local ports across Japan. The share of landed cargo has tended to increase, although it is still lower (around 55 per cent) than that at the Port of Tokyo (more than 60 per cent), which is much closer to the very large market of the metropolitan area.

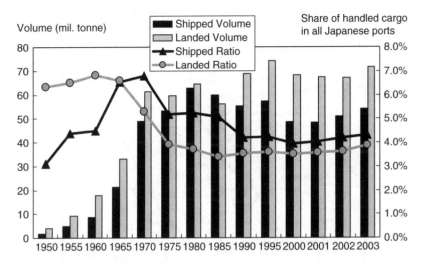

Figure 5.1: Change in total volume of cargo handled in the Port of Yokohama and its share of all cargoes handled in all Japanese ports
Source: Annual port and harbour statistics in Japan, annual statistics of the Port of Yokohama, and the history of the Port of Yokohama.

In 2003, exports worth 6.09 trillion Japanese yen and imports worth 2.87 trillion yen moved out and into the Port of Yokohama. Its share of trade volume in comparison to all Japanese trade amounted to 11.2 per cent and 6.5 per cent respectively.

5.3 The present: an outline of the Port of Yokohama

5.3.1 Overall description

The Port of Yokohama is located on the western side of Tokyo Bay. It is a port naturally blessed with the best wind, current and water depth conditions. It is approximately 30 km from the heart of Tokyo, which is the political and economic centre of the country, as well as a vast centre of consumption (see Figure 5.2).

This location enables the Port of Yokohama to be a comprehensive port, providing services as both Japan's leading commercial port with an enormous hinterland, as well as an industrial port supporting the Keihin and Negishi Bay industrial zone. The Port of Yokohama, with over 140 years of tradition and experience, is connected to ports all over the world and is visited by approximately 11,000 ocean-going and approximately 37,000 coastal vessels a year (see Table 5.1).

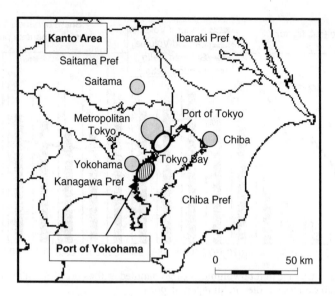

Figure 5.2:   Location of Port of Yokohama

Table 5.1:   Statistics of Port of Yokohama (as of June 2004)

Area	Port water area	7,315.9 ha
	Water front area	2,828.4 ha
	Commercial zone	972.9 ha
	Industrial zone	1,697.7 ha
	Scenic/recreation zone	95.7 ha
	Marina zone	5.7 ha
	Non-designated zone	56.4 ha
Facilities	Total: 221 berths	
	Public & Yokohama Port Development	
	Public Corporation berths: 85 (including 23 container berths)	
	Private berths: 136	
Port activities (as of 2003)		
	Number of incoming ships: 43,996 (including 10,982 international ships)	
	Volume of cargo loaded and unloaded: 125.97 million tonnes	
	Number of containers loaded and unloaded: 2,414,000 TEU	
	Value of trade: 8,958.2 billion yen	

Source: Port of Yokohama website.

Table 5.2: Number of container liner services (January 2004)

Service routes	Number	Frequency of service per month
North America West Coast	12	56
North America East Coast	6	22
Europe/Mediterranean	2	8
Central and South America	7	30
Oceania	4	16
Southeast Asia	24	96
China	40	170
Korea	8	42
Others	2	5
Total	105	445

Source: Port of Yokohama website.

5.3.2 Container terminal facilities

The amount of containers handled at the Port of Yokohama totalled some 2.4 million TEUs in 2003, putting the Port of Yokohama in second position among Japanese container ports in terms of volume handled. The number and frequency of container liner services are shown in Table 5.2. Port-related industries in the Port of Yokohama have a great impact on the economy. The economic effect and employment generated from port activities directly facilitates the development of the local economy and will ultimately improve the living standards of the citizens. However, the growth of neighbouring Asian ports is raising concerns such as the decline of the international status and competitiveness of the major Japanese ports, as well as the hollowing-out of industries in Japan. The container terminals in the Port of Yokohama have a total of 23 berths situated at the Honmoku, Daikoku and Minami-Honmoku (South Honmoku) piers. All terminals have world-class facilities that are able to accommodate the largest container vessels in the world. Details of each berth are shown in Tables 5.3–5.5. In order to further strengthen the port function as a logistics base, the continuous development of Minami-Honmoku Pier (MC-3 and 4 terminals) and the redevelopment of Honmoku Pier (jetties B and C), are underway.

5.3.2.1 *Minami-Honmoku Pier*

The first stage of Minami-Honmoku Pier, equipped with the deepest container berth in Japan, was opened in April 2001. It has been under construction since 1990 to serve as a new logistics hub for the Port of Yokohama. After construction is complete, it should be able to cope with the increasing container cargo volume and increasingly large container vessels. To date, 40 per cent of the construction of the total area has been completed. Two of the high standard largest-scale container terminals in Japan, the MC-1 and 2 berths, which have a quay length of 700 m and a container yard with a storage capacity of approximately 17,000 TEU containers along with a distribution zone, have been in operation since April 2001 (see Table 5.3). With their deepest water depth of 16 m, these two berths can be used together as one berth and are equipped with five mega-gantry cranes. Maersk Sealand uses these berths to handle its import/export cargo for eastern Japan and as an Asian hub. Future plans include the further improvement of facilities to meet the demands of port logistics, as well as reclamation work and the construction of facilities for the MC-3 and 4 container terminals. When these berths are completed, this pier will have four container terminals with a total area of 175,000 m². Along with its distribution facilities, Minami-Honmoku Pier will be a new logistics base meeting the future demands of diverse and complex port logistics.

5.3.2.2   Honmoku Pier

Honmoku Pier, a finger-type pier consisting of Jetties A-D, is the main pier of the Port of Yokohama (see Table 5.4 and Figure 5.3). The reclamation work for this pier was completed in 1970. It has played a major role for the Port of Yokohama over many years, handling various types of cargo carried by many types of ship including: full container, conventional, RO/RO, semi-container, and other vessels. The reclamation of the body of water between Jetties B and C was completed in 2004. This work reflects the increasing volume of container cargo and the growing size of container vessels in recent years, and was carried out in order to raise the efficiency of the container cargo operation. The existing facilities were also reorganised and remodelled. The water alongside the reclaimed land has now been formed into a 15–16 m earthquake-resistant deep-water container berth. This will be one of the first deep-water terminals developed following the implementation of the super-hub port plan by the Japanese government.

5.3.2.3   Daikoku Pier

Daikoku Pier is the largest island-type pier in the Port of Yokohama. The reclamation work for this pier started in 1971 and was completed in 1990. It is

Table 5.3:   Container terminals on Minami-Honmoku Pier

Berth	Berth length	Depth	Mooring capacity	Crane	Managing body	Main user
MC-1	350	16	105,000		YPDC* Public	CNC, MAERSK SEALAND POWICK SHIPPING, TSL
				5 (Mega G/C)		
MC-2	350	16	105,000		YPDC	

Source: Port of Yokohama Promotion Association.
* YPDC: Yokohama Port Development Public Corporation.

equipped with container berths C-1 to 4, multipurpose berths T-1, 2, 9, and modern distribution facilities, such as large-scale transit sheds, a cargo handling area, private warehouses, etc. (see Table 5.5 and Figure 5.4). Terminals C-3 and 4 are among the largest and most advanced container terminals in Japan. In addition, the Yokohama Port Cargo Centre has, since August 1996, been operating at Daikoku Pier, as a joint-stock company, providing a logistics hub designed to meet the needs of the ever-increasing volume of cargo and containerisation.

Table 5.4: Container terminals on Honmoku Pier

Berth	Berth length	Depth	Mooring capacity	Crane	Managing body	Main user
A5	300	13	35,000	2		APL, CCNI, CKL,
A6	300	13	35,000	2	YPDC	COLUMBUS, COSCO, DNA,
A7	250	13	25,000	2		DONG JIN, DONG YOUNG,
A8	250	13	25,000	2		EMC, FUJIAN, H-A, HASCO,
C5-9	200 × 5	13	15,000 × 5	7 (4 Super G/C)		HJS, HMM, IAL, KL, KMTC, LYKES, MARUBA, MISC,
D1-2	200 × 2	11	15,000 × 2	4	Public	MOL, NINGBO OCEAN, NSS,
D3	220	11	15,000			OOCL,
D4	300	14	40,000	3 (Super G/C)		PAN CONTINENTAL, PAN OCEAN, P&ONL, SDSG,
D5	300	15	60,000	3 (Super G/C)	YPDC	SINOKOR, SINOTRANS, SITC, SYMS, TMM, TMSC, UASC,WHL, YMM, ZIM

Source: Port of Yokohama Promotion Association.

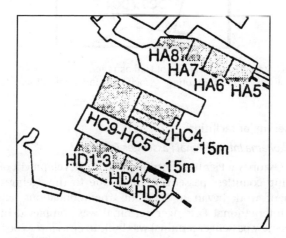

Figure 5.3: Container yard locations of Honmoku Pier
Source: Port of Yokohama Promotion Association and International Transportation Handbook.

Table 5.5:   Container terminals on Daikoku Pier

Berth	Berth length	Depth	Mooring capacity	Cranes	Managing body	Main user
C-1	300	12	35,000	0		
C-2	300	13	35,000	1 (Super G/C)		ANL, CSCL, CSAV, H-L,
C-3	350	15.5 (Tentative Depth 14 m)	54,500	3 (Super G/C)	YPDC	KHL, LU FENG, MISC, MSC, NYK, OOCL, P&O NL, SJSCO, SPIC,
C-4	350	15.5 (Tentative Depth 14 m)	57,500	3 (Super G/C)		TOYOFUJI, TSK, WWL
T1-2	240 × 2	12	30,000 × 2	2	Public	
T9	240	12	30,000	2		

Source: Port of Yokohama Promotion Association.

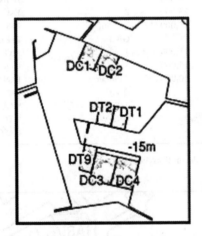

Figure 5.4:   Container yard locations of Daikoku Pier
Source: Port of Yokohama Promotion Association and International Transportation Handbook.

5.3.3   Other major facilities

5.3.3.1   *Yokohama International Passenger Terminal*

Since 1984, Osanbashi Pier has contributed to the development of Yokohama by welcoming countless passenger ships. Due to the ageing of the pier, redevelopment work began in 1989 on the foundations, and the new Yokohama International Passenger Terminal was completed in 2002. The height of the new passenger terminal was built to be as low as possible so that ships could stand out against this low building. The rooftop has unique, gently curved surfaces, portraying ocean waves. The interior of the terminal has been designed without columns or beams, creating a spacious environment for visitors. The design of this terminal was based on the work of two architects from the United Kingdom, who won the grand prize in the international design competition held from 1994 to 1995.

The terminal is capable of accommodating four 30,000 dwt or two 70,000 dwt vessels at the same time. The first floor is a parking lot for up to 400 standard-size vehicles. The second floor houses the lobby, CIQ (customs, immigration and quarantine), a shopping plaza and a multipurpose hall at the far end. Moreover, the rooftop plaza is open 24 hours a day, allowing visitors to view the cruise ships up close.

5.3.3.2   *The Minato-Mirai 21 area*

The Minato-Mirai 21 area (meaning Future Port for the 21st Century in Japanese) was named with the intention of being a harbour city of the twenty-first century; a city of the future covering 186 ha with a daytime workforce population of 190,000 and a residential population of 10,000. It is being developed in the inner area of the Port of Yokohama.

Construction started in 1983. The main construction body was the City of Yokohama. The land readjustment project was conducted by the Urban Development Public Corporation. By the end of 2003, it had attracted a workforce population of 50,000, as well as many tourists from all over Japan. The Minato-Mirai 21 area has many highlights, such as the Landmark Tower, several large shopping centres, historical warehouses, several large parks, etc. It has become one of the most famous sightseeing areas of not only the City of Yokohama, but also the Tokyo Metropolitan Area. Approximately 280,000 people per day visited the site in 2003. However, the development is only half complete, with the residential plan in particular well behind target. Before the completion of three 30-floor apartment blocks in 2003, the number of residents in this area was less than 1,000. The speed of development and construction has also slowed due to the prolonged recession affecting the Japanese economy. However, after the Minato Mirai Line (a railway going through the area and connecting directly to the Tokyo Metropolitan Area) was opened in February 2004, it seems to have changed. It was major news in June 2004 that Nissan Motor Co., which is the second largest auto manufacturer in Japan, announced that its headquarters would be transferred to this area. Now many apartments have been constructed and the Minato-Mirai 21 area, which has already succeeded as a commercial and sightseeing area, is entering a new stage of development.

5.3.4   Land connections with the port

In Japan, more than 95 per cent of international maritime containers are moved by vehicles such as semi-trailers for domestic transportation (cf. Yamaka et al., 2004). Although this also holds true for the Port of Yokohama, it is one of the very few ports in Japan that has railway connections capable of handling international maritime container transportation.

5.3.4.1   *Road transportation network*

The hinterland of the Port of Yokohama covers the whole Tokyo Metropolitan Area. The Metropolitan Expressway (Bay Shore Line) and Route 357 (a high-grade national road) have been fully opened to traffic. Thus, a complete road network, including expressways, connects Yokohama to all locations within its hinterland. However, there are some road connection problems. For example, there is only a bridge with a toll road on the Metropolitan Expressway that connects the two main piers, Honmoku and Daikoku, in the Port of Yokohama. Truck drivers have to pay more than 1,000 Japanese yen to cross this bridge, or take a 30-minute or more detour through central Yokohama city.

In order to remove this problem and mitigate traffic congestion along the detour route, a toll-free National Road 357 was constructed and opened in April 2004. By constructing a new road, the three main piers in the Port of Yokohama – Honmoku, Daikoku and Minami-Honmoku – can now promote the efficient and smooth distribution of cargoes to and from the port. The opening of the new road also drastically reduced the detouring of semi-trailers through the commercial and residential areas around the central district of the City of Yokohama, with a subsequent reduction of traffic jams and accidents. After starting operation, the flow of trucks around these areas has also drastically changed.

5.3.4.2   *Railway connections*

Yokohama-Honmoku Station, a freight-only station, is operated by the Kanagawa Coastal Railway Co., a group company of JR-Freight Co. It is one of a very few stations from which regular railway transportation of international maritime containers operates. The most important international maritime container transport railway line in Japan is the line between Yokohama-Honmoku Station and Sendai Station, Miyagi Prefecture. The distance between these two stations is approximately 400 km. One train with the capacity of 40 TEU operates every day and takes ten hours. In 2002 approximately 9,000 TEU of transported containers were moved both ways. Railway transportation is considered to have an advantage in terms of long-distance land transportation in countries such as the United States. Japan is a long and narrow country, consequently the potential demand for railway transportation is expected to be less (cf. Yamaka et al., 2004). However, if, for example, the connection between container terminal and railway station is improved through direct connections, direct cargo handling, and simplified procedures, the amount of rail transportation might increase. In December 2003, the Port of Yokohama, the Kanagawa Coastal Railway Co., and other related organisations established the Investigative Commission for the Promotion of Railway Transportation for International Freight in the Port of Yokohama in order to discuss this topic and improve railway transportation conditions.

5.4 The super-hub port policy and partnership in Tokyo Bay

5.4.1 Port development strategy before the super-hub port policy

5.4.1.1 *Creation of a user-friendly port*

In June 1997, the Port of Yokohama set up a Council for the Promotion of the Creation of a User-friendly Port, which comprised 26 organisations representing port-related governmental organisations and private bodies with the aim of strengthening the port's international competitiveness. The council worked out a plan called *Immediate and Future Measures to Create a User-friendly Port,* and made an effort to implement the measures so as to offer higher quality services and reduce total cost (see Figure 5.5). Measures that have been implemented include: (i) the Port and Harbour Bureau's operation of the EDI system; (ii) offering incentives on port charges, such as discounts given on port dues according to the number of containers handled; (iii) introduction of a reservations system for carrying container cargo in and out of the gate; (iv) cargo-handling at night on Sundays and holidays; (v) the simplification of advance application procedures for Sunday cargo-handling; (vi) the extension of opening hours for the container terminal gate; and (vii) partial cargo-handling at the year-end and the beginning of the year.

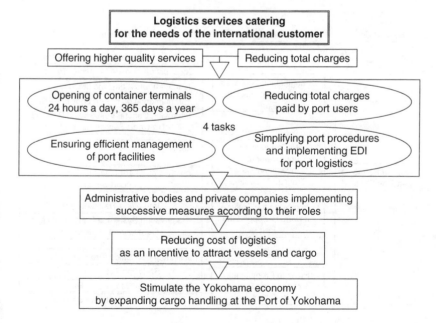

Figure 5.5:   Flow-chart of the creation of a user-friendly port
Source: Port of Yokohama Promotion Association.

5.4.1.2   *Strategy and measures for further development*

In order to further expand the role of the Port of Yokohama, the Council is promoting the creation of an energetic harbour, foreseeing the changes in the global economy and trade. Another aim is the development of a comprehensive harbour, which will contribute to the local economy by creating spaces close to local residents and international exchange zones by actively utilising the port's existing resources. In order to achieve these goals, the Port of Yokohama is striving to develop a vibrant and advanced port, which holds to the basic concepts of: 'a vibrant port leading the world', 'a charming port for local residents', and 'a port with an international character'.

Aiming to become 'a leading port of the world', it will implement concrete measures designed to promote: (i) strengthening of its functions as an international hub port; (ii) realignment and improvement of facilities for conventional cargo transportation; (iii) expansion of the supporting traffic network; and (iv) promotion plans to encourage its use. Details of this strategy are shown in Figure 5.6.

5.4.1.3   *Long-term vision of the Port of Yokohama*

The City of Yokohama, which is the managing body of the Port of Yokohama, established the *Long-term Vision of the Port of Yokohama* in May 2003. This vision describes future images of its role, covering the next 20 to 30 years from now. In

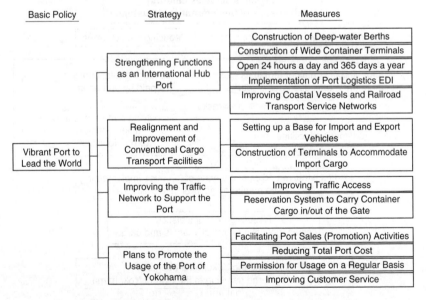

Figure 5.6:   Basic policy, strategy and measures for the Port of Yokohama
Source: Port of Yokohama Promotion Association.

addition to the year-long discussion, via the Exploratory Committee, participated in by academic experts, related organisations and citizens, an open forum was held, and public comments were collected. Basic philosophies of the vision include the following: (i) citizens as the leading players; (ii) interaction with the world; and (iii) respect and representation of history. Future images are determined as a result of discussion, as shown in Table 5.6.

The results of the vision are planned to be reflected in the revision of the Port of Yokohama Master Plan, scheduled for 2005, where a total of eleven challenges have been set by the municipal government, also shown in Table 5.6, based on the above six images of the future.

5.4.2 Super-hub port policy for the Port of Yokohama

5.4.2.1 Hub-port programme of Yokohama

In line with the super-hub port concept proposed by the Japanese government, the City of Yokohama government has also stood as a candidate; this has resulted in Yokohama being designated as one of the three super-hub port groups, on condition that it collaborates with the Port of Tokyo. The Port of Yokohama had already established the hub-port programme of Yokohama in November 2003 through the Council for the Promotion of the Creation of a User-friendly Port. This was before the Council for the Selection of a Super-hub

Table 5.6: Six images of the future and eleven challenges

Six Images of the Future
 1. Super-hub port in Eastern Asia
 2. Manufacturing port specialising in knowledge creation
 3. Intersection port of world cultures
 4. A port that can be enjoyed through the senses
 5. Resource and energy recycling port
 6. Ecosystem conservation and re-creating at the port

Eleven Challenges
 1. Strengthen functionality as an international trade gateway in eastern Japan
 2. Improve level of service as a user-friendly port
 3. Ensure safe and effective water area in the harbour
 4. Develop close partnership between three ports in the Keihin area (Yokohama, Tokyo, Kawasaki)
 5. Revitalise as an industrial port
 6. Promote the calling of passenger vessels and install waterfront area
 7. Redevelop harbourside area
 8. Revitalise the public use of coastal and water areas
 9. Address global environmental issues
10. Utilise extensive hubs in terms of disaster mitigation
11. Assist the disposal of waste material and construction-generated soil

---

Sources: Port and Harbour Bureau, City of Yokohama, 2003, 2004.

Port was set up by the national government. This programme consists of four main objectives and twelve action points, as shown in Table 5.7.

5.4.2.2   *Programme for fostering the super-hub port*

The national government's objective of designating certain ports as super-hubs is to selectively strengthen international competitiveness for that container port by offering port services at lower costs than the competing large-hub Asian ports. The basic concepts of the Port of Yokohama action plan for the super-hub port have already been described in the hub-port programme for Yokohama. However, in order to have been designated as a super-hub port by the national government, it was necessary to include two additional points to the established programme: one was the Development of High-standard Next-generation Container Terminals, the other a Development of the Managerial Environment for Terminal Operators (Ports and Harbours Bureau, Ministry of Land, Infrastructure and Transport, 2002). Another request by the national government before designation lies with a comprehensive coalition with the Port of Tokyo, since both ports are located in Tokyo Bay, in addition to the coalition of the Port of Kobe and Osaka in Osaka Bay and the Port of Nagoya and Yokkaichi in Ise Bay. In order to meet these requests made by the national government, the Port of Yokohama and Tokyo together proposed the Programme for Fostering the Super-hub Port (Tokyo Metropolitan Government and City of Yokohama, 2004).

In the proposed programme, the Port of Yokohama declared that its goal is to handle approximately 3.5 million TEUs per year over a five-year period, through the reduction of associated costs, the shortening of lead time before loading onto the container ships, and so on. A detailed action plan that has

Table 5.7:   The hub-port programme of Yokohama

I. **Strengthening the Function as a Transhipment Hub**
a. Construction and management of successive high-standard terminals
b. Upgrading hinterland transportation
c. Improvement of road access
II. **High Efficiency Operation**
a. Improvement of shipping operation efficiency
b. Improvement of terminal operation efficiency
c. Settlement of opening 24 hours a day, 365 days a year
d. Simplifying port procedures and implementing information technology
III. **Strengthening Functions as a Logistics Hub**
a. Treatment for upgrading port logistics
b. Enhancing aggregation of the logistics industry
c. Strengthening marketing
IV. **Reducing Total Charges**
a. Reduction of utilising port facilities
b. Reduction of service fees

Source: Council for the Promotion of the Creation of a User-friendly Port (2002).

recently been added to the hub-port programme of Yokohama is summarised in Table 5.8. In particular, although it also holds true for almost all Japanese ports, not much consideration had been given to the development of managerial environments for the terminal operators or the involvement of mega-operators. The programme would be a good opportunity to discuss how to improve services and lower costs based on the economies of scale related to the amount of containers handled.

5.4.2.3 Collaboration within Tokyo Bay

The concept of the super-hub port, proposed by the national government, is to strengthen the competitiveness of Japanese ports against other major world ports, by mainly reducing port charges through economies of scale. Collaboration between neighbouring ports is essential and the most important factor in assuring the competitiveness of Japanese ports on the world stage. In the Keihin Area, the Ports of Tokyo and Yokohama have been identified as competing with Keihin port. A Council for Wide-ranging Cooperation between the Three Keihin Ports (the Port of Kawasaki, which is in the middle range of ports, is located between the two large Ports of Yokohama and Tokyo, is also included) was organised last year. The main agendas of the co-operative framework are shown in Table 5.9. Although these three ports are located within 20–30 km of each other, in the same bay, there is almost no collaboration between them, especially in terms of infrastructure investment and management policy. This is mainly because the management bodies, which are usually the municipal governments in Japan, differ. Although having only one place for regular meetings would be a large advantage, work on identifying and establishing common concrete policies is just beginning.

5.4.2.4 Issues for future development as the super-hub port

Since the super-hub port policy was proposed by the national government a few years ago, it has been identified by the Japanese government as one of the most important port policies. As a result, all of the major Japanese ports have participated in the programme. However, until now, concrete measures taken by the national government and that are needed to achieve this policy have been very limited; namely, only direct investment in a deep container berth and preferential tax treatment for terminal operators. This situation is partly because the Japanese government has placed curbs on the amount of public works undertaken due to fiscal restraint. Therefore, the implementation of the super-hub port policy is actually dependent upon local management bodies. As already mentioned, the Port of Yokohama is now at the stage of revising its Port Master Plan for this year, 2006. In their new plan, they should be incorporating the effect of implementing the super-hub port policy, and considering the benefits of the policy compared to the cost involved. A provisional calculation of the effect is shown in the next section.

Table 5.8: Action plan list for a super-hub port

I. Action Plan for Effective Management for Terminal Operators

a. Establishment of the hub-port programme of Yokohama by the Council for Promotion of the Creation of a User-friendly Port, a co-operative organisation of the public and private sectors
b. Strengthening information technology infrastructure, such as opening a website, or portal site for the Port of Yokohama, and the Port of Yokohama System for Container Freight Information, or Y-CON 24
c. Ensuring smooth access from the hinterland transportation network including the social experiment of night time discounting of the Metropolitan Expressway toll
d. Making the Logistics Park in the terminal include a public warehouse demonstration experiment and the Yokohama Port Cargo Centre, as well as the utilisation of designated structural reform district institutions

II. Reduction of Port Charges and Improvement in the Level of Service

Reduction in port charges:
a. Introduction of broader, more targeted volume incentive systems
b. Research into a new port charging system
c. Reduction of shipping operational costs, such as pilot charges

Shortening lead times:
a. Construction of 24-hour, all-weather quarantine facilities and operations
b. Computerisation of all application procedures for port use
c. Introduction of a port logistics information platform for all terminals, such as a 24-hour reservation system for information on carrying-in and -out, as well as information on container status

III. Development of Next-generation High-standard Container Terminals

Development at three major piers at the port:
a. Minami-Honmoku Piers MC-1 and 2
   – Length: 750 m, Depth: −16 m, Width: 500 m (an expansion of the existing terminal)
b. Honmoku Pier between Jetties B and C
   – Length: 1,390 m, Depth: −13 to −15 m, Width: 500 m (under construction)
c. Daikoku Piers DC-3, 4, and T-9
   – Length: 940 m, Depth: −12 to −15 m, Width: 350 to 500 m (expansion of width and promotion of co-operative operation)

Invitation of mega terminal operators
a. Co-operative management of public and private berths
b. Improvement of the terminal charge system

Source: Summarised by the authors on the basis of a paper published by the Tokyo Metropolitan Government and the City of Yokohama (2004).

Table 5.9:   Port collaboration agenda in Tokyo Bay

I. **Strengthening the Logistical Network**
   a. Effective transportation, using various modes, between the three ports
   b. Common policy for the promotion of domestic container feeder transport

II. **Reduction of Port Charges**
   a. Introduction of common volume incentives and reduction of terminal lease payments

III. **Sharing of Application Procedure Systems and Promotion of Computerisation**

IV. **Development of a Common Risk Management System**
   a. Mutual use of quake-resistant berths when hit by earthquake
   b. Development and strengthening of common port security systems

V. **Joint request for national government policy**
   a. Financial assistance, construction of infrastructure, etc.

Source: Summarised by the authors and based on the paper published by the Tokyo Metropolitan Government and the City of Yokohama (2004).

5.4.3   An experimental estimate of the effects of the super-hub port policy

In this section, the effect of the super-hub port policy in Japan is simulated by using the 'International Maritime Container Cargo Flow Model' developed by Shibasaki et al. (2005). With the amount of origin-destination container cargoes as a given input, the model can produce maritime container cargo flows, including transhipments, through modelling carrier and shipper behaviour in selecting loading and unloading ports in Japan. The methodology applied in the model is a network assignment methodology, which is normally used for vehicle traffic simulation. A rough structure of the model is shown in Figure 5.7. Details of the model are given in several published papers such as Shibasaki et al. (2005). The model contains more than 100 ports, covering almost all container ports in Japan and the major hub ports in the Asian region, as well as representative ports in other regions. The major measures of the policy that are adopted in the simulation of the model are listed in Table 5.10.

Figure 5.8 shows the calculated results of the changes in Japanese ports and major Asian ports in terms of both the total amount of containers and transhipment containers handled. The findings from the figure are that the amount of both total and transhipped containers in all the Japanese super-hub ports except Yokkaichi will increase. For example, the total volume increases by around 20 per cent and the transhipment volume increases two to three times. In the Port of Yokkaichi, which is a relatively small port compared to the other super-hub ports, although the transhipped containers will increase to the same level as other super-hub ports, the total volume will decrease. Interestingly, in the other Japanese ports, the total and transhipped volumes

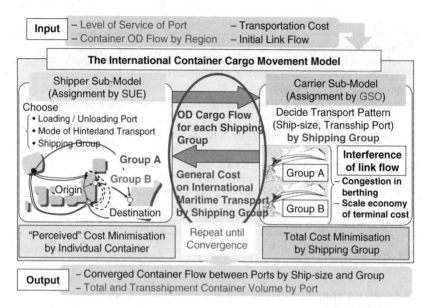

Figure 5.7:   Rough framework of the International Maritime Container Cargo Flow Model

Table 5.10:   Target ports of the super-hub port policy and the measures dealt with in the model

Target Ports ... *Tokyo, Yokohama, Nagoya, Yokkaichi, Osaka, and Kobe*

Concrete Measures
30% reduction of port entering charge by ship-size per vessel
30% reduction of port handling charge per TEU
30% reduction of port terminal charge per berth
Shorten to 24 hours for international loading and unloading time
Full opening of terminal 24 hours and 365 days
Direct handling at the same terminal of both international and domestic cargo

of containers, while they increase in Northern Kyusyu, they decrease in the other local ports. These results imply that the super-hub port policy encourages the 'selection and concentration' of the port for both carriers and shippers with a synergistic effect for larger ports and reduced usage for smaller ports. In terms of other countries' hub ports, such as Busan, which is a direct competitor to Japanese super-hub ports, the total and transhipped amount will decrease, while increasing in some ports such as Hong Kong and Kaohsiung. In these ports, there may be multiple effects to stimulate hub and spoke transport systems throughout Asian countries.

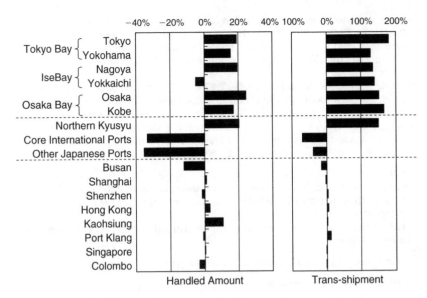

Figure 5.8: Changes in total and transhipment containers from the super-hub port policy

5.5 Conclusion

In this chapter, consideration has been given to the past, present and future of the Port of Yokohama, one of the largest ports in Japan. In particular, the focus has been on container transportation and the potential future problems associated with the super-hub port plan in the Asian region. For better or worse, the Port of Yokohama is very close to the Port of Tokyo and its large hinterland, the Tokyo Metropolitan Area. In order to survive and continue to develop in this era of international competition between Asia's large ports, the collaboration and coalition of these two ports (as well as the inclusion of the other ports in Tokyo Bay, such as the Ports of Kawasaki, Chiba, etc.) is essential. Because of its historical experience and the characteristics of its neighbouring city, as well as the fact that it is supported by port-related industries such as manufacturing, the Port of Yokohama might have the power to take the lead in this initiative.

References

Books, papers and other published documents
Japan Port and Harbour Association (1978) *History of Japanese Ports* (in Japanese).
Kobayashi, T. (1998) *Mega-city and Fishing Colony – Yokohama Waterfront*, Seizan-do Publishing Co. (in Japanese).
Port and Harbour Bureau, City of Yokohama (1989) *The History of the Port of Yokohama* (in Japanese).

Port of Yokohama Promotion Association (2002) *Port of Yokohama* (brochure).
Shibasaki, R., Kadono, T. and Ieda, H. (2005) 'Model Improvement of International Maritime Container Cargo Flow and Policy Evaluation for International Logistics in Eastern Asia', the First International Conference on Transportation Logistics, under review.
Shibasaki, R., Kadono, T. and Watanabe, T. (2005) 'An Analysis of Economic Loss Due to Bottlenecks in Domestic Land Transportation Network for International Maritime Container Cargo', *Transport Policy Studies Review*, 7(4): 15–26 (in Japanese).
Yamaka, T., Shibasaki, R., Kadono, T. and Watanabe, T. (2004) 'An Analysis of Japanese Inland Transportation of International Maritime Container Cargo by Rail and Ship', *Journal of Coastal Zone Studies*, 17(1): 39–50 (in Japanese).

Statistics
Ocean Commerce Ltd. (2004) International Transportation Handbook, 2004.
Port and Harbour Bureau, City of Yokohama. Annual Statistics of the Port of Yokohama (in Japanese).
Port and Harbour Bureau, Ministry of Transport. Annual Port and Harbour Statistics in Japan (in Japanese).

Other documents and statistics available through websites

1   About the Port of Yokohama:

Council for the Promotion of the Creation of a User-friendly Port (2002) Hub-port program of Yokohama.
Port and Harbour Bureau, City of Yokohama. Statistics on the Port of Yokohama.
Port and Harbour Bureau, City of Yokohama (2003) Report on the long-term vision for the Port of Yokohama.
Port and Harbour Bureau, City of Yokohama (2004) Discussion paper on the revision of the port master plan for Yokohama.
Tokyo Metropolitan Government and City of Yokohama (2004) Programme of developing a super-hub port.

(All of the above documents are available from the Port and Harbour Bureau, City of Yokohama website, http://www.city.yokohama.jp/me/port/. However, all of them, apart from the statistics, are only available in Japanese.)

2   Others:

Port and Harbour Bureau, Tokyo Metropolitan Government. Statistics on the Port of Tokyo. http://www.kouwan.metro.tokyo.jp/data/toukei/index.html (in Japanese).
Port and Harbour Bureau, Ministry of Land, Infrastructure, and Transport (2002) For port management bodies hopeful of being designated as super-hub ports. http://www.mlit.go.jp/kowan/super/super_bosyuu.html (in Japanese).

Part III

Ports in Central Asia

6

Kaohsiung: Pending Direction

Tao Chen

6.1   Introduction

In the 1980s, Hong Kong, Singapore and Kaohsiung were the world's top three container ports. Although the terminal operators in those places adopted different strategies, all of these ports attracted a great volume of transhipped containers and served as shipping hubs in Asia.

In the 1990s, China became a centre of manufacturing for the world, resulting in millions of TEUs of containers flowing through major Chinese ports and Asian hubs. The political impasse between Taiwan and China since 1949, however, has restricted shipping links between Kaohsiung and neighbouring Chinese ports. Thus, Kaohsiung has not been able to take much advantage of the activity on the other side of the Taiwan Strait, causing Kaohsiung's share of container volume handled to drop in comparison with neighbouring competitors.

This political dispute is unlikely to disappear in the near future. Meanwhile, competition between shipping hubs has been increasing, with many planning multi-billion-dollar expansion projects. Therefore, Kaohsiung port needs to re-evaluate its role in Asia. Should the port gamble hundreds of millions of dollars in investment to attempt to maintain its position as an Asian hub or should it settle for being the regional gateway of Taiwan? This chapter analyses the development of Kaohsiung port since 1980 from a global perspective. This chapter has three parts. The first examines the development of the strategies adopted by Kaohsiung port from both global and regional perspectives. The second introduces the development of container terminals, container berths and terminal operators in Kaohsiung port. The third part examines the constraints and challenges to be faced by Kaohsiung port from the viewpoint of port operators.

6.2   National policy and port development

Since the 1990s, China has become the engine of world economic growth. Political disputes between Taiwan and China, however, continue to prevent most cross-strait shipping links. The Kaohsiung Port Authority has thus had no choice but to seek business opportunities elsewhere. Meanwhile, the role Kaohsiung plays in Asia has to be examined again. Although external developments have limited the development of Kaohsiung, several strategies in recent years have been adopted to strengthen the competitiveness of Kaohsiung port.

6.2.1   The political dispute and its impact

Taiwan has enjoyed double-digit economic growth since the 1980s. The great volume of containerised export and import cargo has made Kaohsiung one of the largest container ports in the world. Hub and spoke shipping networks have further attracted transhipment business and expanded the hinterland of Kaohsiung port to cover most of the countries in Asia. The recent economic development of China has had a great impact on the development of Kaohsiung. In the early 1990s, the political enmity between Taiwan and China seemed to ease, opening the possibility that if Taiwan and China co-operated, Kaohsiung could become the gateway of central China and the main shipping hub in Asia. An offshore shipping centre was established in 1997; shipping lines were allowed to call at ports in both China and Taiwan. Kaohsiung had Taiwan's only offshore shipping centre, while the Chinese government opened only two minor ports, Fuchou and Xiamen.

In the late 1990s, however, the political disputes between Taiwan and China worsened. As a result, the shipping links could not be expanded to major ports in China. From 1997 to 2004, the transhipment container volume of Kaohsiung's offshore shipping centre was limited in comparison with neighbouring ports (Table 6.1). In 2004, China-based cargo accounted for only around 8 per cent of Kaohsiung port's total container volume. With the emergence of major ports in China, for example Shanghai and Shenzhen, Kaohsiung's competitive advantage seems to have disappeared.

Although Kaohsiung's geographic location is excellent for serving as a gateway for central China, the political disputes between Taiwan and China ultimately forced Kaohsiung port to lose its most valuable hinterland.

Table 6.1:   Comparison of the volume handled by Kaohsiung offshore shipping centre and total traffic (TEUs)

	1997	1998	1999	2000	2001	2002	2003	2004
China tranship	128,000	272,756	365,857	432,668	508,242	574,451	630,000	680,000
Total traffic	5,960,000	6,270,000	6,990,000	7,400,000	7,540,000	8,490,000	8,840,000	9,710,000

Source: Mainland Affairs Council, Taiwan.

Furthermore, because the traffic between Taiwan and China has to be transhipped by way of Hong Kong, that city has had its position as a shipping hub strengthened.

As a consequence, the foundation of Kaohsiung as a hub in Asia has been rocked by the cross-strait political dispute. In the early 1990s, international shipping lines evaluated that Kaohsiung had the potential to be the gateway for China and expected that a huge volume of transhipment business could be attracted from that country; the companies were thus happy to build long-term relationships with Kaohsiung. Rising political tensions, however, lowered or stopped their interest in bidding for the management of container berths at Kaohsiung. Since then, some container berths have had trouble securing tenants and the Kaohsiung Harbour Bureau has had to provide discounts to keep clients (shipping lines) once berth-leasing contracts expire. Kaohsiung, therefore, has had to examine the external environment carefully. Are there opportunities for Kaohsiung to maintain its position as a major shipping hub in Asia? Should hundreds of millions of dollars be invested to build container terminals and facilities in a risky bid to attract transhipment business? Or should Kaohsiung abandon the high-risk move and concentrate instead on providing cost-effective and efficient port service to its core customers and serve as the gateway for Taiwan?

Finally, in August 2004,[1] the central government conditionally approved a mega-container terminal project. The Kaohsiung Harbour Bureau was asked to develop a four-berth terminal. (For details, see section 6.3.6 below.) The other parts of the mega terminal will be built if there is a need.

6.2.2 Strategies of Kaohsiung port

Kaohsiung port has adopted three major approaches to strengthen its competitiveness over the last twenty years. The first is to provide value-added services, for example the export-processing zone established in the 1980s and the free-trade zone set up in 2004. The second is to attract transhipment business, for example through the dedicated terminal and offshore shipping centre (discussed earlier). The third is to restructure the organisation of the Kaohsiung Harbour Bureau, for example by liberalising and privatising port operations.

In the 1980s, Kaohsiung served as the gateway for Taiwan's export and import trade. To promote exports, the port area set up a free export-processing zone in which parts from neighbouring counties could be assembled into products and then re-exported. It has proved one of the world's most successful experiences in promoting export businesses. But the business of the export-processing zone dropped significantly when low-cost labour in neighbouring countries became more widely available.

For its container-terminal operations, Kaohsiung port has adopted a 'dedicated terminal' strategy, under which the shipping lines can lease container berths for container loading and unloading for a set period of time (e.g. five to ten years). The major objective of this strategy is to secure business between shipping lines and the port. In Kaohsiung, however, the vessels served by the dedicated terminals were at one time limited to only those of the shipping lines that leased the berths. This restriction to the vessels of the container berths has restricted the business opportunities of Kaohsiung port for more than two decades. This restriction was lifted in 1998 to allow the lessees of the container berths to handle containers of other shipping lines. The move, however, may have come too late because in the last twenty years most shipping lines had already transferred their focus to other Asian ports.

In the 1990s, to increase competitiveness with the Ports of Hong Kong and Singapore, Taiwan's central government decided to promote Kaohsiung as the shipping centre for the Asia-Pacific area. Several strategies have been implemented; the first one was to cancel the restriction to the users of the container terminals. This strategy has changed the container-handling service provided by container-terminal operators from 'private' to 'common-user', and the shipping lines that lease the berths have been upgraded from 'dedicated users' to 'terminal operators'.

The second strategy introduced was the 'liberalisation and privatisation' of port operations. Port labour is no longer employed by the Kaohsiung Harbour Bureau; instead, workers are employed by private stevedoring companies. Moreover, the number of stevedoring companies is no longer restricted; those that meet the conditions established by Kaohsiung Harbour Bureau can be freely set up to provide cargo-handling services, therefore providing both terminal operators and consignees with more choice in stevedoring service.

In the first decade of the twenty-first century, Taiwan's economy has shifted from an emphasis on high-volume, low-value goods to high-value, low-volume ones. Many factories have moved from Taiwan to China, resulting in a drop in Taiwan's trade volume. Meanwhile, China's trade volume has grown dramatically, with an accompanying huge increase in the volume of cargo going through major Chinese container ports, such as those of Shanghai and Shenzhen. The combined effect of Taiwan's economic restructuring and the emergence of Chinese container ports resulted in a drop in Kaohsiung port's world ranking in respect of container volume: from third in 2000 to sixth in 2004.

To boost the competitive advantage of Kaohsiung and attract business, the strategy of a free-trade zone was introduced in 2004, a move expected to upgrade the business of Kaohsiung port from an Asian 'transhipment' centre to a 'logistics and distribution' centre and a part of the global supply chain. In March 2004, container terminals 2, 3, 4 and 5 were approved as free-trade zones. As a consequence, the resources of the container terminals (such as warehouses and container yard) are expected to be better utilised and Kaohsiung port will be able to provide an integrated transport service to importers and exporters and attract new business opportunities.

6.3   Introduction of container terminals and operators

The Port of Kaohsiung opened in 1684. Although Kaohsiung has attracted international business since 1855, the systematic development of Kaohsiung port did not begin until 1908. Between 1855 and 1980, the development of Kaohsiung focused on the northern part of the city, near the city centre. The first entrance was built at this stage, and most of the berths were designed for handling conventional cargoes.

From the 1970s, due to the need for both deep-water container berths and modern container-handling facilities, the development of Kaohsiung has moved to the 'southern' area, where land is sufficient for large-scale expansion. The China Steel Company and China Shipbuilding Company were also located in the southern section of Kaohsiung port. As a consequence, a huge import volume of ore and coal, together with containerised cargo, has moved the business focus of Kaohsiung port from north to south. During these years, most modern facilities – including container terminals, bulk terminals, export-processing zones, and the second port entrance – were built stage by stage.

Kaohsiung port has five container terminals with a total of 26 container berths. One of the port's main competitive advantages in attracting the business of major shipping lines in the 1980s was that it was also one of the few major container ports in Asia at which shipping lines could manage their own container berths (the other ones were Japanese ports). Accordingly, shipping lines operate most of the container terminals.

6.3.1   Container Terminal 1 (CT1)

Container Terminal 1 (Table 6.2) has four container berths (berths 40–43), two of which are public (40 and 41). For those shipping lines that do not have dedicated container berths at Kaohsiung port, the 'public berths' are the only facility available for the loading and unloading of boxes to and from container ships. No stevedoring company has been assigned to berths 40 and 41; therefore, the shipping lines need to hire stevedoring companies to handle the loading and unloading of containers at these berths.

Handling costs at public berths are cheaper than at dedicated berths, mainly because of differences between the operations in the berths. In public berths,

Table 6.2:   Information on terminal operators in CT1

Operator	Berth no.	Quay length (m)	Terminal area (ha)	Storage capacity (TEUs)
Wan Hai	63, 64	520	22.0	7,000
OOCL	65, 66	684	22.6	12,000

Source: Kaohsiung Harbour Bureau.

most of the shipping lines use inland depots adjacent to the berths for both container storage and cargo consolidation. The import boxes are transferred to inland depots when they are unloaded; the export boxes are transferred from inland depots to quayside hours before they are expected to be loaded into the container ship. As a consequence, shipping lines need pay only the charge of quay gantry crane operation because there are no extra charges for container storage, terminal handling charges (THC), and so on.

Public berths, however, also have disadvantages. Their loading and unloading efficiency is lower. In comparison to dedicated terminals, the distance between quayside and inland depots is much longer, and sometimes the supply of trailers is insufficient for efficient transfer operations between inland depots and quayside.

The other two berths (berths 42, 42) are leased by Lien Hai, a terminal operator without a shipping-line background. In recent years, Lien Hai has handled around 200,000 TEUs in annual cargo volume, around 30,000 of which has been transhipped cargo (Table 6.3).

CT1 has only 10.5 hectares of land, or just 2.6 hectares per berth, which is not sufficient to meet the demands of modern container handling operations. In Asia, newly built container terminals have around 20 to 30 hectares per berth.

6.3.2 Container Terminal 2 (CT2)

Terminal 2 has four container berths (63–66). Berths 63 and 64 are leased to the Wan Hai Shipping Line, whose business focuses on intra-Asian container shipping. Berths 65 and 66 are leased by OOCL (Table 6.4), which ranked 14th in global container shipping in 2003. Although CT2 has much less space for

Table 6.3: Container volume handled by Lien Hai in recent years (TEUs)

	1999	*2000*	*2001*	*2002*
Lien Hai	48,148	165,262	200,215	203,262
Tranship	601	14,042	22,615	31,559

Source: Kaohsiung Harbour Bureau.

Table 6.4: Information about terminal operators in CT2

Operator	*Berth no.*	*Quay length (m)*	*Terminal area (ha)*	*Storage capacity (TEUs)*
Wan Hai	63, 64	520	22.0	7,000
OOCL	65, 66	684	22.6	12,000

Source: Kaohsiung Harbour Bureau.

container-handling operations than CT3, CT4, and CT5, the throughput achieved in recent years by terminal operators there is amazing (Table 6.5).

Berths 63 and 64 are operated by Wan Hai. Although the land assigned is limited, the number of containers handled has increased significantly in recent years. In 2002, for example, the throughput was around 800,000 TEUs, which is 400,000 TEUs per berth; and around 40 per cent of the containers handled were transhipped. The yard operating system adopted by Wan Hai uses a combination of straddle carriers and RTGs.

In contrast with Wan Hai, rail-mounted gantries were operated by OOCL. The throughput of the OOCL terminal dropped from 700,000 TEUs in 2000 to 500,000 TEUs in 2002. Like Wan Hai, around 40 per cent of the cargoes handled by OOCL were transhipped.

6.3.3   Container Terminal 3 (CT3)

CT3 has three container berths (berths 68–70). Berths 68 and 69 are leased to APL, while berth 70 is leased to Yang Ming (Table 6.6). The yard-operating system used by APL is a combination of rubber-tyred gantries (RTG) and chassis. Yang Ming, however, transferred from a combination of straddle carriers and RTGs to rail-mounted gantries (RMGs) in 2000.

With respect to the land area, CT3 has 50 per cent more assigned to terminal operations than CT2, allowing terminal operators to provide better services to customers. For example, Yang Ming established an international logistics centre there in 2000 (Yes Logistics) to provide value-added service and to gain competitive advantage.

Table 6.5: The container volume handled by terminal operators in CT2 in recent years (TEUs)

	1998	1999	2000	2001	2002
Wan Hai	336,373	456,160	516,760	660,650	809,102
Tranship	84,219	137,839	165,026	252,317	338,313
OOCL	672,881	710,290	723,700	557,035	513,168
Tranship	281,145	311,908	337,866	231,972	185,443

Source: Kaohsiung Harbour Bureau.

Table 6.6: Information about terminal operators in CT3

Operator	Berth no.	Quay length (m)	Terminal area (ha)	Storage capacity (TEUs)
APL	68, 69	752	33.3	9,243
Yang Ming	70	320	18.4	10,799

Source: Kaohsiung Harbour Bureau.

Table 6.7:   Container volume handled by terminal operators in CT3 in recent years (TEUs)

	1998	1999	2000	2001	2002
APL	1,141,277	1,224,461	1,277,168	1,376,066	1,297,127
Tranship	791,060	872,880	971,912	1,081,016	1,010,863
Yang Ming	335,555	318,996	377,378	476,062	502,865
Tranship	162,648	158,094	179,242	175,526	207,603

Source: Kaohsiung Harbour Bureau.

Table 6.8:   Information about terminal operators in CT4

Operator	Berth no.	Quay length (m)	Terminal area (ha)	Storage capacity (TEUs)
Evergreen	115–117	916	36.5	12,000
Maersk Sealand	118, 119	640	27.8	9,792
Yang Ming	120	320	12.9	5,000
NYK	121	320	13.4	5,000

Source: Kaohsiung Harbour Bureau.

The two container berths of APL have enjoyed the reputation of having astonishingly high productivity. The throughput of these two berths has topped 1 million TEUs in recent years; and around 70 per cent of the cargoes were transhipped. The performance of the Yang Ming terminal has also been outstanding. Throughput there in 2002 was over 500,000 TEUs; and around 40 per cent of the cargoes handled were transhipped (Table 6.7).

6.3.4   Container Terminal 4 (CT4)

Container Terminal 4 has eight berths (115–122). Evergreen leases berths 115–117, while Maersk Sealand leases berths 118 and 119, Yang Ming leases berth 120, and NYK leases berth 121 (Table 6.8). Because berth 122 has not been leased out in years, it has come into public hands.

In respect of the yard-operating systems adopted by the operators at CT4, rubber-tyred yard gantries are found in every berth. Tables 6.8 and 6.9 provide detailed information concerning the berths and the throughput at this terminal. CT4 is located on the seaside of Kaohsiung port; thus, containers moving between the interior and CT4 have to transit the cross-harbour tunnel. For security reasons, several types of cargoes are not allowed to transit the tunnel, including those that are dangerous or oversize. This restriction has limited the business opportunities of terminal operators at CT4. As a consequence, terminal operators at CT4 generally prefer to move landward when a container berth becomes available there. For example, Evergreen leased berths

Table 6.9:   Container volume handled by terminal operators in CT4 in recent years
(TEUs)

	1998	1999	2000	2001	2002
Evergreen	1,388,147	1,327,112	1,284,962	591,397	785,410
Tranship	646,491	654,963	682,232	251,914	336,993
Maersk Sealand	881,657	688,008	585,495	574,514	642,002
Tranship	517,618	461,934	378,677	421,730	422,211
Yang Ming	–	–	–	201,875	281,784
Tranship	–	–	–	48,232	65,301
NYK	236,779	300,990	261,566	271,969	328,582
Tranship	30,757	65,626	63,093	95,437	136,701

Source: Kaohsiung Harbour Bureau.

at CT5 for additional handling capacity, expanding the company's business opportunities and Maersk transferred container terminal operations from CT4 to CT5.

Not all terminal operators, however, have moved landside. Because container berths are valuable resources in Asia, terminal operators expand when there is a chance. For example, Yang Ming leased berth 120 to expand business. Evergreen keeps berths at both CT4 and CT5. After Maersk merged with Sealand, the berths leased by Sealand at CT4 were taken over by Maersk Sealand.

6.3.5   Container Terminal 5 (CT5)

Container Terminal 5, developed under the build-operate-transfer (BOT) scheme, is the most recent terminal in Kaohsiung. It was constructed between 1995 and 2000. The first stage of CT5 was completed in 1996; berth 75 was opened in May; and berths 76 and 77 were opened in October. In November 1998, the construction of berth 78 was completed, followed by berths 79, 80 and 81 in September 2000.

As mentioned above, Container Terminal 5 has seven container berths (berths 75–81), which are leased to four shipping lines: berth 75 to Hyundai, berths 76 and 77 to Maersk Sealand, berth 78 to Hanjin, and berths 79–81 to Evergreen (see Tables 6.10 and 6.11 for detailed information concerning the berths and throughput in recent years).

Unlike at CT4, the yard-operating systems at CT5 cover most major types of system. For example, Maersk Sealand and Hanjin use straddle carriers in the yard operation of container movements within the terminal. Hyundai uses rubber-tyred gantries in the yard, while Evergreen's yard-operating system is a rail-mounted gantry (RMG).

There are also huge differences in the throughputs achieved by the operators. For example, although Hanjin and Hyundai leased one container berth each,

Table 6.10:   Information about terminal operators in CT5

Operator	Berth no.	Quay length (m)	Terminal area (ha)	Storage capacity (TEUs)
Hyundai	75	320	10.0	n.a.
Maersk Sealand	76,77	675	23.3	11,817
Hanjin	78	320	19.0	11,354
Evergreen	79–81	815	40.1	27,500

Source: Kaohsiung Harbour Bureau.

Table 6.11:   Container volume handled by terminal operators in CT5 in recent years (TEUs)

	1998	1999	2000	2001	2002
Hyundai	223,564	251,340	285,898	192,121	172,447
Tranship	51,988	75,376	111,459	66,949	47,241
Maersk	795,922	946,749	787,526	781,556	789,121
Tranship	476,685	698,158	580,856	576,361	577,241
Hanjin		364,620	489,522	552,868	577,219
Tranship		72,218	185,600	306,323	279,797
Evergreen		156,185	313,870	1,090,859	1,246,973
Tranship		45,345	87,352	586,037	750,718

Source: Kaohsiung Harbour Bureau.

Hanjin handles around 600,000 TEUs per year, about three times the volume of Hyundai. The other two operators, Maersk Sealand and Evergreen, achieve about 400,000 TEUs per berth per year.

From the viewpoint of the volume of transhipment boxes handled, the berths operated by Maersk Sealand and Evergreen have been treated as hubs, with around 70 per cent of the containers handled being transhipped ones. The role of the terminal, however, is not limited to that of transhipment hub; for example, the Maersk Terminal is the company's repair and maintenance centre in Asia for damaged containers.

6.3.6   Future expansion

In the first decade of the twenty-first century, two developments in both the port and shipping industries have forced port authorities to provide container berths with deeper drafts and larger yards. The first is the development of the mega containership, which has a storage capacity of 8,000–10,000 TEUs; to accommodate these new ships, navigation channels must be dredged to a depth of at least 16 metres.[2]

Furthermore, container terminal operators have provided more value-added services, such as free-trade zones and logistics centres, which need larger container yards. To meet the demand from shipping lines for modern container terminals, Taiwan's central government approved the Kaohsiung port expansion project and has listed it as one of the major national development projects. The project covers one offshore mega container terminal and one petrochemical terminal. New terminals will be built on 512.7 hectares of reclaimed land located in the southern part of Kaohsiung port.

The container terminal is designed to handle container ships of 8,000 to 15,000 TEUs. There will be five container berths with a depth of 16.5 metres. The quay is 1,990 metres long, and the container yard covers 183 hectares of land. The terminal's annual handling capacity is expected to be 2.5 million TEUs.

When the construction of the new container terminal is completed, the outdated petrochemical berths (Nos. 59–61) at neighbouring CT2 will be moved to the new petrochemical terminal. Berths 59–61, with 544 metres of quay and 25.5 hectares of land, will be converted into two container berths. The terminal's annual handling capacity is expected to be 0.9 million TEUs. Together with five berths in the new terminal, the port expansion project will add seven container berths with a handling capacity of 3.4 million TEUs.

The project – covering both the container terminal and petrochemical terminal – is estimated to cost around US$3 billion (NT$92.4 billion), around 50 per cent of which will go towards infrastructure, with the rest going towards the operational facilities. According to government policy covering port projects, the terminal will be built under a BOT programme, which means the operational facilities will be built and paid for by the operators of the container berths.

In August 2004, however, because the financial feasibility of the offshore mega terminal is low, the Council for Economic Planning and Development (CEPD) added a new terminal into the mega terminal project, called 'phase one'. The major reason is that the construction of an offshore mega terminal needs the support of shipping lines or stevedoring companies; in comparison with a mega terminal, 'phase one' needs less time and lower investment. Another major difference is that the mega terminal will be able to expand easily to meet future demand, while 'phase one' could not. The mega terminal project will be held in abeyance until the demand is stronger and it becomes financially viable.

Project 'phase one' approved by the CEPD is a container terminal with four berths, 1,500 metres of quay, 75 hectares of yard, and 16 metres of draft. In 2006, the terminal will be opened up to bids from shipping lines or stevedoring companies. The construction of berths and facilities is scheduled to start in 2007 and completed in 2010. The estimated cost of the terminal is around NT$36 billion (US$1.1 billion), around 30 per cent of which will be paid by the lessee of the terminal.

6.4 Constraints and challenges

Because of fierce competition between container ports in Asia, together with the rapid development of Chinese ports, the world ranking of Kaohsiung port in respect of container traffic has dropped significantly in recent years, from third in 1999 to sixth in 2003. The future holds even more challenges for Kaohsiung port. In 2009, when the construction of container berths at Taipei port is completed, Kaohsiung is expected to lose at least 2 million TEUs of cargo, which may result in a further reduction in the volume of cargo handled by Kaohsiung.

Strategies implemented by Kaohsiung have also restricted the port's development. For example, poor co-operation between the Kaohsiung City government and port authority has limited the land available for the development of free-trade zones and new container berths. Furthermore, although Kaohsiung port played the role of landlord in respect of container terminal operations, the strategies of 'dedicated terminal' operators adopted in the 1980s have limited the opportunities of terminal lessees to obtain more berths to achieve economies of scale and reduce the cost of container handling.

In the meantime, the emergence of mega containerships has had an even greater impact on Kaohsiung port because new facilities and container terminals are needed to meet the demand of mega ships and provide better facilities to terminal operators.

In conclusion, Kaohsiung port must overcome many challenges. The next section examines these factors systematically and provides suggestions about what should be done given the constraints faced.

6.4.1 The development of Taipei port and its impact

Manufacturing in Taiwan is concentrated in the north of the island. Although the Port of Keelung has acted as the gateway for international trade in northern Taiwan, the limited land available for expansion there has restricted the efficiency of container handling and costs are relatively high, thus constraining the development of container transport at Keelung. As a consequence, Kaohsiung has become Taiwan's shipping hub, even for the north of the country. Kaohsiung provides efficient and cost-effective transoceanic transport service. Shippers and consignees in northern Taiwan use Kaohsiung as the gateway for their international business, though inland haulage between north and south Taiwan takes around eight hours and costs about US$400 per trip. Around 2 million TEUs per annum of local cargoes handled by Kaohsiung are transported to and from northern Taiwan, according to estimates by businesses in the sector and analyses by academics.

To provide efficient and cost-effective ocean transport service to importers and exporters in northern Taiwan, a 'northern port' has been proposed. Debate over the location of the port took more than ten years, with Taipei being selected. The goal of the Taipei port project is to provide an efficient and cost-effective gateway service for international trade in northern Taiwan and maintain the competitive advantage of industries in the region.

Taipei port will feature a container terminal with 2,366 metres of quay. It will have seven container berths with 110 hectares of land, with a 16-metre draft. The container terminal, to be constructed by a private consortium on the BOT model, will be operated by the Taipei Port Container Terminal Corporation, organised by three major Taiwanese container carriers. Evergreen controls 50 per cent of the investment, while Wan Hai holds 40 per cent and Yang Ming 10 per cent. The first phase of the terminal construction is expected to be completed around March 2008, with the completion of the last container berth set for no later than October 2014.

According to industry estimates, when the construction of container berths at Taipei port is completed, around 2 million TEUs of local cargo in northern Taiwan will no longer be transhipped by way of Kaohsiung port. In other words, Taipei port will handle some 2 million TEUs of basic cargoes, with Kaohsiung losing the same volume.

6.4.2 Constraints on development: Kaohsiung city vs. Kaohsiung port

The head of the Kaohsiung Port Authority is appointed by the central government, which is located in Taipei, in northern Taiwan. The central government also controls port development policies, shutting the Kaohsiung city government out of the decision-making process much of the time.

The Kaohsiung city and central governments have argued over the governance of Kaohsiung port for more than ten years. This chapter does not address which side should run the port but does seek to highlight the poor co-operation between the Kaohsiung Harbour Bureau and the Kaohsiung City Council. As a consequence, for the purpose of avoiding conflict between port and city, the development plan made by the port authority is limited to the port area only.

According to the 'Harbour Law', port areas are national property and cannot be sold. Most of the time, the port area is defined as the area 200–500 metres behind the quay, including the warehouses and marshalling yard. As a result, Kaohsiung port's development projects have always been limited.

Kaohsiung port's competitors – Hong Kong, Singapore and Shanghai – provide good examples of successful port development. Owing to the demand for integrated transport services, the function of the port is no longer limited to the interface between sea and land transport. More services are needed, such as warehousing and other value-added services. The emergence of free-trade zones is a good example. As a result, the huge tracts of land adjacent to the port should be covered by port-related services; moreover, a regional development plan covering both the port area and neighbouring land is needed.

Because of the conflict between local and central governments, development plans have not been made by Kaohsiung city. As a result, the plans have always been limited to the port land, constraining the opportunities for development.

The free-trade zone planned by Kaohsiung port (for completion in January 2005), for example, is limited to land within Kaohsiung port (Container Terminals 2–5). The argument is that given that most of the land in the container terminals is highly utilised for container loading and unloading, little land would be available for 'free-trade' facilities and operation. This author recommends that an ideal project should be put together by Kaohsiung city, which covers a wide-ranging area and encompasses a regional development plan. The development of the Shanghai Waigaoqiao Free-Trade Zone could serve as an example. Under the project, developed by the Shanghai city government, 1,000 hectares of land were assigned for free-trade related facilities and operation. Kaohsiung port would do well to learn from the success of this case.

Who should have the power to manage Kaohsiung port has been debated for more than ten years. Professionalism has been the reason for central government to keep control of Kaohsiung port – and the major reason to keep Kaohsiung city out of participation. The lack of integrated co-operation and development between the city government and Kaohsiung port has severely restricted Kaohsiung port's opportunities for expansion and is seen as a major weakness of the port. In short, although the strategies to strengthen the competitiveness of Kaohsiung port are clear, the political dispute between Kaohsiung city and Kaohsiung port make it unlikely the problem will be solved in the near future.

6.4.3   Strategy for terminal operation: from dedicated user to terminal operator

As mentioned above, Kaohsiung port has used a 'dedicated terminal' strategy to attract business. In the 1990s, however, the co-operation between shipping lines and the emergence of a 'hub-spoke' network have challenged this strategy. Meanwhile, container berth operators asked the port to lift the restriction on the shipping lines that could call at the berths. In response to these requests, Kaohsiung port has lifted the dedicated terminal restriction, allowing operators to handle boxes of all shipping lines. This has helped the lessees of the container berths to upgrade to 'terminal operators' and for Kaohsiung port to grow into a major shipping centre in Asia.

Though the lessees of container berths are free to attract the business of all shipping lines, most people do not think the lessees have actually upgraded to really become 'terminal operators'. The reason is that the differences between a 'terminal operator' and a 'dedicated terminal operator' are the size of the container yard, the length of the quay, and the number of shipping lines actually served. Though Kaohsiung port allows lessees of container berths to handle boxes of all shipping lines, most of them operate with only one or two berths, prompting the question of how many shipping lines could be served under current conditions.

The other factors to be considered are the time period leased and the economies of scale to be attained. Generally speaking, the break-even point between cargo volume and operating cost is around 150,000 to 180,000 TEUs per berth per year. To enjoy cost-effective service, the lessee must attract sufficient cargo volume over the long term (seven years, for example) to balance the cost. As a result, the cargo volume needed has become a barrier for lessees of berths. This barrier has also limited the opportunities for small to medium-sized shipping lines to lease container berths at Kaohsiung port, not to mention any other terminal operator without the support of major shipping lines. Though lessees face many challenges, Kaohsiung port's strategy seems to have been successful. From the data collected (as shown in the above sections), most lessees treat their container berths as an Asian hub. However, most of the boxes handled belong to the lessee (i.e. the shipping line that leases the berth) or its alliance.

Some of the operators, however, cannot become bigger and more competitive. The reason is that the container berths at Kaohsiung port are leased individually as and when they become available, making it difficult for terminal operators to obtain several berths at one time and to achieve economies of scale. As mentioned earlier, most operators managed only one container berth; few of them operate two or more berths. Although some operators succeeded in leasing several container berths, economies of scale could still not be reaped because the berths leased were in different container terminals. Maersk Sealand and Evergreen, for example, both lease four berths; but the berths are separated between Container Terminals 4 and 5. The expansion of Kaohsiung port has been treated as the only way to reorganise the lessees. Altogether there will be four berths available, and lessees with several berths – such as Maersk Sealand, Evergreen and Yangming – could be shifted to one terminal. Thus the expansion project has played an important role in whether lessees could become real terminal operators.

6.5 Conclusion

If the political disputes between Taiwan and China continue, the shipping links between Kaohsiung and Chinese ports may not open in the near future. The question of the role Kaohsiung is to play – hub or gateway – will not go away. For political reasons, central government will never stop trying to convince shipping lines to participate in BOT projects for new container terminals. However, shipping lines always make their choices based on self-interest, not politics.

From the perspective of the internal environment, Kaohsiung port faces challenges and constraints, with the construction of a new terminal a critical point. If the new container terminal is completed as planned, the lessees could be reorganised and Kaohsiung port will become more competitive. Major terminal operators in Kaohsiung, such as Maersk Sealand and Evergreen, would be able to move into one container terminal, reap economies of scale, and become medium-size terminal operators worldwide. Meanwhile, the other terminal operators, which operate two berths at different terminals, would also be able to move into one terminal. In addition, terminal operators with one berth would be able to move from old berths (such as CT1 and CT2) to modern ones. At the same time, the container yards of old berths could be converted into free-trade zones or international logistics centres.

However, there are uncertainties concerning the port-expansion project. This project needs close co-operation between the central government, Kaohsiung city and Kaohsiung port. Can they overcome their past differences and work things out this time?

Notes

1. The conclusion of the Council of Economic Planning and Development, Executive Yuan, on 5 August 2004.
2. In 2004, Cosco ordered a 10,000 TEU containership, with delivery expected in 2008.

References

Centre for Transportation Research (2000) *Mega-Containerships and Mega-Containerports in the Gulf of Mexico*, Austin: University of Texas Austin.

Chung-Hua Institution for Economic Research (2003) *The Study of International Logistics, Free Trade Zones and Industry Development*.

Division of Water Transport, Ministry of Transportation and Communications (2001) *Ways to Monitor Management Efficiency after Port Operations were Privatized*.

Economic Division (1995) *Study of Port Privatization and Liberation in Taiwan*, The Council for Economic Planning and Development, Executive Yuan, Taiwan.

ESCAP (2002) *Regional Shipping and Port Development Strategies*, UN.

Executive Yuan (2002) *Major Projects to Be Constructed During 2002–2007*.

Hsu, J.-Y. and Cheng, L.-L. (2002) 'Revisiting Economic Development in Post-war Taiwan: the Dynamic Process of Geographical Industrialization', *Journal of Regional Studies*, 36(8): 897–908.

Institute of Transportation (2002) *The Overall Development Project of Ports in Taiwan between 2002 and 2007*.

Institute of Transportation (2003) *Port Development and Its Impact on City Economy – the Case of Kaohsiung*.

Haynes, K. E., Hsing, Y. M. and Stough, R. R. (1997) 'Regional Port Dynamics in the Global Economy: the Case of Kaohsiung, Taiwan', *Maritime Policy and Management*, 24(1): 309–29.

Kaohsiung Harbour Bureau, Taiwan. www.khb.gov.tw.

Keelung Harbour Bureau (1999) *The Planning and Future Development of Taipei Port*.

Lirn, T.-C., Thanopoulou, H. and Beresford A. K. C. (2003) 'Transhipment Port Selection and Decision-Making Behaviour: Analysing the Taiwanese Case', *International Journal of Logistics: Research and Applications*, 6(4): 229–44.

Mainland Affairs Council, Taiwan. www.mac.gov.tw.

The Council for Economic Planning and Development (2002) *The Project of Generating World Trade Centre – Challenge 2008*.

7
Hong Kong: Asia's World Port
Peter Wong

7.1 Introduction: a blessed port in the Far East

Hong Kong, a small island located at the tip of southern China, began its modern history when the British took it as a colony in 1897 under the Treaty of Nanking. With its hilly topography and Victoria harbour, Hong Kong is well protected from natural perils and so it became a safe port for most coastal and ocean-going vessels within southern Chinese waters. Although Hong Kong became the most eastern port of the British Empire, it did not possess any significant commercial promise for future expansion. However, it did provide Britain with a strategically important position as far as naval power was concerned.

It was not until 1949, when the communists took power in China, that thousands of mainlanders flocked to Hong Kong to seek a better life. From that time onward, Hong Kong was blessed by various factors contributing to its significance for world shipping.

The immigrants from China brought with them their wealth and whole-hearted enthusiasm to turn Hong Kong into a major production area for the region. The hard work of the labour force was rewarded by orders received from many overseas customers. The industrial sector gradually took shape by evolving from simple assembly-line work to technology-related industries, such as toy moulding, fashion design and watch making. The Korean War in 1950 brought a golden opportunity to Hong Kong as the US declared an embargo on all Chinese exports and imports as a result of the direct involvement of the Chinese army in the war. The embargo of China trade funnelled all imports to, and exports from, China into Hong Kong through various channels, both legally and illegally.

With close links to Britain, Hong Kong was allowed to import advanced equipment for production uses which made Hong Kong superior in production technology to adjacent countries. Since then Hong Kong has maintained the function of an entrepôt vis-à-vis China. By combining, sorting, grading, semi-processing and storing commodities, Hong Kong was in a position at all times to meet the specific quantitative and qualitative requirements of buyers in other countries. The natural tendency of an entrepôt is outward-oriented, as it links two external entities – the hinterland and the world market.

7.2 Building up the foundation

In Hong Kong, there is no history of government direction in industrial developments. No explicit industrial or technology policies were implemented until the recent government took power after 1997. Initiatives to develop new products and create new industries have always come from entrepreneurs in a decentralised manner. The government has viewed its role as one of providing a suitable environment for industrial development. This refers primarily to the government task of ensuring the adequate provision of infrastructure. Plans for building infrastructure are not drawn with the express aim of servicing a particular industry, but are rather geared towards supporting all economic activities in Hong Kong.

The laissez-faire approach of the government allows local entrepreneurs to pursue any promising line of business and take the full risk as well as the first fruits in all sectors in order to advance themselves. However, this mode of operation has sometimes embarrassed the government. For example, when the first container terminal was set up at Kwai Chung in 1972, the government did not accurately assess how the service area of the port would extend into the adjacent transport network in an era of containerisation. Right from the beginning of the 1970s until the turn of this century, traffic congestion within the terminal has been the result.

7.3 Port management in Hong Kong

Endowed with a deep-water natural harbour and strategically located along a major sea route with close proximity to mainland China, Hong Kong became a regional sea transport hub. Advanced port facilities and efficient port services are complemented by extremely high trade volume to underpin Hong Kong's status as the tenth largest trading entity in the world. The port handles 80 per cent of Hong Kong's total external cargo volume. The shipping sector employs more than 25,000 people, and generates more than US$5 bn in revenues annually. Hong Kong is the world's busiest container port with most cargo coming from the Pearl River Delta (PRD) region. With its good sailing schedules, the majority of cargo passing through Hong Kong is ocean-going transshipment cargo.

Hong Kong's port facilities are financed, built, owned and operated by private firms. It is the only major port in the world that is not run by a port authority. Hong Kong is also a major shipowning and management centre. As of September 2004, there were 987 vessels (24 million gross registered tons) on the Hong Kong Shipping Register. In terms of tonnage, Hong Kong shipowners control more than 34 million tons (6 per cent) of the merchant ships in the world, ranking sixth after Greece, Japan, Norway, the US and China. According to the Hong Kong Shipowners Association, the total tonnage of ships owned or managed by its members is more than 60 million deadweight tons.

In the next section we discuss the significant measures that have influenced port development and contributed to Hong Kong's success in past decades.

7.3.1 Laissez-faire approach

A laissez-faire approach worked well in Hong Kong even without any democratic controls in the process. The danger that government might become wholly or largely subservient to powerful and dynamic private interests was avoided prior to the handover of sovereignty in 1997. The reasons were mainly due to the fact that:

- All senior civil servants were transferred from Britain. They were trained with higher moral and ethical standards than their local colleagues. The ultimate long-term goals or benefits of the colony always received a high priority in decision-making.
- The governor was appointed direct from Downing Street. He had no personal network or financial interest with local enterprises. Therefore, his policy was less biased and was fair to the community as a whole.
- As a developed country, Britain had encountered and solved many problems associated with policy implementation. A similar policy proposed and undertaken in Hong Kong benefited from lessons learned in Britain.

7.3.2 Land sales policy

Hong Kong's location and natural landscape have provided advantages in sea and air transport, as well as in the whole range of trade and investment-related activities involving mainland China and the region. The shortage of usable land and high land cost in Hong Kong has had a direct impact on industrial development and firm strategies. It has discouraged land-intensive, heavy manufacturing industries in favour of light manufacturing and services, and has led to the use of multistorey factories and to the relocation of production processes to low-cost sites in the Pearl River Delta and elsewhere. Lack of land has forced Hong Kong and its firms to use land efficiently providing Hong Kong with substantial strength in transport infrastructure. The sale of land, with usage explicitly indicated, became one of the major sources of income for the government and was frequently auctioned to the public. Overall land ownership gradually became dominated by several property tycoons and the land price has remained high over the past 50 years. For example, the first berth of the container complex at Kwai Chung, owned and operated by Modern Terminals Limited, represented an investment of $155 million for berth 1 in 1972.

Hong Kong's port operators are private entities that have purchased the right by public auction or private tender to reclaim land, develop the facilities, and operate them. Three main terminal operators dominate the operations of the container terminals. The mode of terminal operation under private management in Hong Kong's port is supported by the government as it ensures efficiency in container handling and the optimum allocation of resources.

7.3.3 Trigger point system

The influx and departure of immigrants made the overall planning in society a difficult task for the Hong Kong government. In order to cater for the vast daily necessities of the immigrants, the government took a liberal view in running society. One of the effective tools used to run society was to apply a trigger point system to every project under consideration. This trigger point mechanism applied to sectors like housing, education, transport and port development. Under the laissez-faire approach, the trigger point mechanism is usually initiated by private enterprises.

The advantages of the trigger point system are that:

- it avoids over-investment in the project so that limited resources can be fully utilised;
- the provision of the infrastructure/services is flexible and projects can be easily altered even beyond the construction period;
- the trigger point mechanism was mainly executed by commercial enterprises which by-passes bureaucracy at the initial stage. The project could then be implemented in a timely fashion.

7.3.4 Customs regulation

The only dutiable items in Hong Kong are alcoholic beverages and cigarettes. The simple structure of duty levied allows the Customs and Excise Department of Hong Kong to concentrate on drug trafficking, instead of on inspecting cargoes in and out of Hong Kong. Eventually, this will facilitate the speedy movements of goods that are transhipped in Hong Kong.

7.3.5 The labour issue

In the past few decades, workers in Hong Kong have devoted themselves wholeheartedly to their work. The only reason that explains this phenomenon is that they are largely refugees that fled from mainland China and, therefore, they perceive themselves as very lucky to be employed here. With this background and strong lobbying from the employers, the government is reluctant to pass any bills either on collective bargaining or minimum wages. Without any legal protection for the workers, Hong Kong seldom sees any large-scale strikes in any sector. Industrial relations in Hong Kong can be described as very harmonious.

7.4 The policy-makers

In the early 1980s, the Director of Marine was charged with the responsibility for the administration of the port. Currently, the Director of Marine is

Table 7.1:   Policy-makers (before 1997)

Year	Policy-maker/adviser	Report to	Duties
Before 1980	Port Executive Committee	Director of Marine	Shipping, commercial and port needs
	Port Committee	Governor	Shipping, commercial and port needs
Before 1990	Director of Marine	Governor	Administration of port
April 1990	Port Development Board (PDB)	Governor	• Identifying strategic port needs • Monitoring plans to meet these needs • Listening to and gathering views of the port industries and services • Following up on those views as necessary • Maintaining the port's competitiveness in the region • Linking government and private sector involvement in port planning and development

responsible for all navigational matters in Hong Kong and the safety standards of all classes and types of vessels. The policy-making process was transferred to the hands of related parties from 1990 when the Port Development Board was formed.

The policy-makers related to port development are shown in Tables 7.1 and 7.2 for easy reference. The membership of the advisory committee is mainly drawn from relevant industries. The advisory committee will merely formalise the interests of the port industry.

In order to strengthen Hong Kong's position as an international shipping centre, the government has reduced merchant shipping registration fees and annual tonnage charges by 50 per cent. Other improvements include simplifying ship survey requirements, computerising ship registration procedures, negotiating double-taxation agreements with major trading partners and reducing the tax burden on Hong Kong shipping companies. These measures not only aim at building up Hong Kong's register of tonnage, but also to attract shipping companies to set up operations in Hong Kong to manage their ships. After 28 January 2000, Hong Kong-registered ships paid lower dues when they call at mainland ports.

The following schematic diagram (Figure 7.1) indicates container cargo flow in Hong Kong. Most of the line-haul operators prefer to load their cargoes in

Table 7.2: Policy-makers (post-1997)

Year	Policy-maker/adviser	Report to	Duties
June 1998	PDB renamed and reorganised as the Hong Kong Port and Maritime Board	Chief Executive	• Promoting the Hong Kong shipping industry • Developing Hong Kong into an international shipping centre
June 2003	Hong Kong Port Development Council	Chief Executive	• Assess Hong Kong's port development needs taking account of changing demand for port facilities, productivity and performance; and promote the competitiveness of Hong Kong relative to major regional ports; • Co-ordinate the involvement of government and private sector agencies in the planning and development of port services; • Provide a forum for consulting parties involving, or affected by, Hong Kong's port; • Conduct publicity campaigns to publicise and promote the port of Hong Kong; • Devise and recommend optimum planning and disposal strategies for port facilities; • Form specialist sub-groups as deemed necessary; and • Undertake any other tasks relevant to the above as may be referred to it by the government.
	Sub-com: Maritime Industry Council a dedicated, high-level advisory body made up of private sector and government officials	Chief Executive	• Advise the government on the formulation of measures and initiatives to further develop Hong Kong's maritime industry; • Assist the government to promote the comprehensive maritime services provided and the edges of operating maritime business in Hong Kong.

Source: Compiled by the author from various HKSAR Government publications.

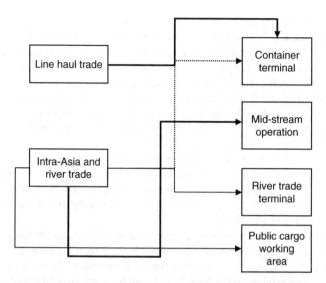

Figure 7.1:   Schematic diagram of parties involved in loading and discharging containers in Hong Kong

the container terminal due to a tight sailing schedule and the high performance offered by the operators. However, these line-haul operators may also use mid-stream operators for unloading their empty boxes.

For intra-Asian trade, most liner operators will be using mid-stream operations due to their low terminal handling charges (THC). The establishment of the River Trade Terminal in 1998 was aimed at catering for feeders (river trade operators) serving the PRD region. However, due to a lack of cargo for the return leg, many river trade operators still favour public cargo working areas (PCWAs) for their daily operation. With the demise of a number of PCWAs around Hong Kong, this type of operation will become gradually eliminated.

7.5   The players in Hong Kong

7.5.1   Terminal operators

Container terminals (CTs) in Hong Kong are situated in Kwai Chung basin. There are eight terminals under the operation of four different operators, namely Modern Terminals Ltd. (MTL), Hongkong International Terminals Ltd. (HIT), COSCO-HIT and Dubai Ports International (owner of CSX World Terminals Hong Kong Limited and Asia Container Terminal Ltd.). They occupy 217 hectares of land, providing 18 berths and 6,592 metres of deep-water frontage.

Among all these operators, HIT is the most influential player in global container operations. The parent company of HIT, Hutchison Port Holdings Group

(HPH) now owns, manages and operates container terminals in the Chinese mainland, the UK, Netherlands, Panama, Bahamas, Indonesia, Myanmar etc. It is the biggest independent port operator in the world, handling around 10 per cent of global container traffic. As a subsidiary of HPH, HIT holds a strategic position for HPH, as many initiatives in container handling have been installed, tested and implemented in various locations within the group after having been tested in Hong Kong. HPH also holds shares of various port service providers in Hong Kong. These include: Asia Port Services (APS) – a mid-stream operation, and the River Trade Terminal.

The fourth of the six-berth container terminals, CT9 (see Figure 7.2), situated on the southeast of Tsing Yi Island opposite the existing terminals, started operations at the end of 2004. For the new terminal, CT9, both MTL and HIT have invested over US$66 m and US$429 m respectively in the infrastructure, equipment and IT installation.

Under the banner of 'promoting the Port of Hong Kong as the key container hub port of the region providing premier service to the container shipping industry', the Hong Kong Container Terminal Operators Association Limited (HKCTOA) was established in June 1999 by all the container terminal operators of Kwai Chung. This form of cartel is allowed in Hong Kong as there is no existing law that prohibits this practice. Table 7.3 summarises the total hardware available in Hong Kong for container handling.

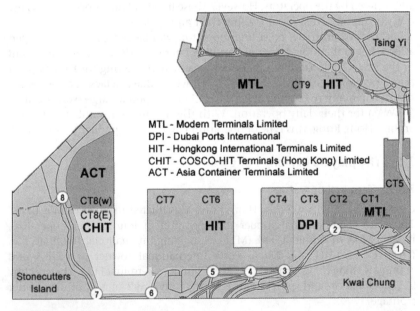

Figure 7.2:   Kwai Chung Terminal
Source: Drawn by the author.

Table 7.3: Facilities in Hong Kong container terminals

	Modern terminals 1,2,5,9 (south)	DPI Hong Kong	HIT terminals 4,6,7	HIT terminal 9 (North)	COSCO-HIT terminal 8 (East)	ACT terminal 8 (West)	Total
Numbers of berths	7	1	10	2	2	2	24
Total areas (hectares)	93	17	92	19	30	29	279
Length of main berths (m)	2,322	305	2,987	700	640	740	7,694
Length of lighter berths (m)	–	–	305	–	448	–	753
Minimum depths alongside (m)	15.50	14.00	12.5–15.5	15.50	15.50	15.50	–
Quay gantry cranes	30	4	34	8	9	8	93
Rail mounted gantry cranes	–	–	24	–	–	–	24
Rubber tyred gantry cranes	106	8	90	21	32	20	277
Rail mounted jil crane	–	–	4	–	–	–	4
Waterhouse storage area (sq m)	112,585 (gross leaseable area)	620,000	277,741	–	–	–	–
Stacking capacity (TEUs)	85,000	10,872	–	–	–	36,414	–
Reefer power points	3,480	378	1,356	300	696	750	6,960

Source: Compiled by the author from various sources.

7.5.2   The player with potential: the River Trade Terminal

With Hutchison Port Holdings (HPH) Group as one of their shareholders, the River Trade Terminal (RTT) started operation in 1998 and is a common-user facility for container and cargo handling in Hong Kong. It was built to cater for the growth of trade movements related to the Pearl River Region, to enhance port productivity and to enable better utilisation of social resources. In their proposal submitted to the government, the RTT recommended the use of marine shuttles to transfer containers between the RTT and the main container terminals. However, since it started operation, most container transfer is done via road instead.

Even the company name indicated that the RTT should cater solely for river trade traffic, but it started to handle intra-Asian trade in 2001. The government has taken the case to court claiming that the RTT has altered the land use of the terminal. The final ruling was in favour of the government's argument.

7.5.3   The small one: mid-stream operations

Besides the highly efficient terminal operators, shipping lines can discharge their cargo via mid-stream operations in Hong Kong. This is a very common loading method that is extensively used in river mouth approaches throughout the world. However, there is no other place like Hong Kong where mid-stream operations handle over one-sixth of the container throughput of Hong Kong (Table 7.4).

The growth rate for mid-stream operations was high during the period 1987–93, but slowed quite a lot to single-digits in 1994–6. The business environment for mid-stream operations in the past few years has been increasingly difficult due to large investments in computerisation, the refurbishment of facilities, additional workforce, and the extension of service hours and staff training to raise service standards. These have resulted in an acceleration of operational flow, improvement of yard safety and a reduction of tractor waiting time. However, mid-stream operators are at the same time under continuous pressure to reduce their tariffs, a situation brought about by the keen competition among operators.

Table 7.4:   Hong Kong container throughput (000 TEUs)

	1990	1997	2000	2003
Terminals	3,831	9,564	11,603	11,736
Mid-stream	1,198	2,900	3,033	3,131
PRD	71	1,922	3,462	3,858
Total	5,101	14,386	18,098	18,726
Transhipment	760.2	2,983	6,334	

Source: Ocean Shipping Consultants.

Loan Receipt
Liverpool John Moores University
Learning and Information Services

Borrower ID: 21111140572116
Loan Date: 10/10/2008
Loan Time: 8:37 pm

Container port production and economic
efficiency /

31111011841366
Due Date: 31/10/2008 23:59

Asian container ports :
31111011849997

Due Date: 31/10/2008 23:59

Please keep your receipt
in case of dispute

7.5.4 The loser: PCWAs

The operation of Public Cargo Working Areas (PCWAs) involves the short-term allocation of berths and waterfront working areas for the purpose of handling general cargo, bulk and containerised cargo transferred from lorries to barges and vice versa. PCWAs are managed by the Marine Department and currently situated at eight different locations, comprising a combined total quay length of some 7,020 metres. In his 1999 policy address, the Chief Executive indicated that:

> PCWAs should be relocated to more appropriate sites. The current location of PCWAs in the inner harbour area is at odds with proclamations from government and its agencies to transform Hong Kong into a world city. Within government, the Economic Services Bureau is seen to continue to resist popular opinion to phase out PCWAs citing the need to prevent the loss of jobs. The Chamber feels that the economic benefits that accrue from other activities such as tourism, entertainment and the restaurant trade should far outweigh any likely drawbacks from the displacement of PCWAs from the inner harbour.
>
> The presence of PCWAs in the inner harbour is regarded as being incompatible with Hong Kong's knowledge-based world class ambitions. As such, government should look into eliminating this misappropriation of space and resources for utilitarian use. Within the meaning of this, government should consider zoning the central/inner harbour for tourism and other service-based activities that are of a more aesthetical appeal with existing PCWAs relocated to sites beyond the inner harbour should the need exist.

With reduced locations for PCWAs, the mid-stream operators will find it difficult to find a suitable quayside for them to load/discharge containers. In the long run, only those mid-stream operators with their own waterfront can survive in this increasingly competitive environment.

7.6 Competition

7.6.1 External situation

Despite Hong Kong maintaining its position as one of the world's top container ports in the past few decades, the total cargo volume within the PRD region is diluted between Hong Kong and adjacent mainland China ports as indicated in Table 7.5.

When we compare the growth rate of container throughput between Hong Kong and its adjacent ports in Shenzhen we may find that the situation in Hong Kong is not as good as we might expect (see Tables 7.5 and 7.6). With the close proximity of Shenzhen ports to Hong Kong, a steady flow of container

Table 7.5:   Container throughput (million TEUs)

	1994	1995	1996	1997	1998	1999	2000	2001	2002	2003
HKG	11.05	12.55	13.46	14.39	14.58	16.21	18.10	17.83	19.14	20.45
SHZ	0.18	0.28	0.59	1.15	1.95	2.99	3.99	5.08	7.61	10.65
HKG growth rate		13.6%	7.3%	6.9%	1.4%	11.2%	11.6%	−1.5%	7.4%	6.8%

Base Year = 1994
Source: HKSAR Marine Department.

Table 7.6:   Container throughput in TEU – growth rate

	1995	2003	Growth rate
HKG	12,549,746	20,449,000	6.3%
SHZ	28,400	10,649,900	57.3%

Base year = 1995
Source: HKSAR Marine Department.

trade has been diverted into Shenzhen ports where there is an advantage of lower transport cost compared to Hong Kong. If the container throughput situation between Hong Kong and Shenzhen ports continues, the dominant position of Hong Kong will be replaced by Shenzhen within the next decade. To worsen the situation, many shipping lines have recently increased their frequency of port calls to Shenzhen and have reserved more slots in their ships to pick up containers in Shenzhen.

7.6.2   Internal consolidation

The current container terminal configuration indicates a concentration of ownership amongst terminal operators. The public is concerned that this might result in insufficient competition in the service and create an oligopoly or cartel situation. Persistently high terminal handling charges (THC) have sparked off a complaint filed with the Hong Kong Consumer Council by the local Shipper Councils in 2002.

The concentration of terminal ownership in Kwai Chung should be of some concern, but this alone does not imply that there is either insufficient competition or the presence of collusion. Under the 'trigger point mechanism' agreed between the government and the terminal operators, additional terminals will only be built if forecasts of future demand for terminal services exceed available capacity. Since the amount of excess demand is determined in part by the level of handling charges set by terminal operators, this mechanism provides existing operators with a tool to limit competition by reducing the rate of entry.

Table 7.7: Ownership of Shenzhen ports

Hong Kong Port		Major PRD port		
	Shareholders of HKG terminals	*Shekou*	*Yantian*	*Chiwan*
HIT	Hutchison Port Holdings (HPH) Group (100%)		48%	
MTL	The Wharf (55%)			
	China Merchants Holdings (International) Co Ltd (22%)	Phase I – 32.5% Phase II – 51%		20% JV with MTL
	Swire Pacific Limited (18%)	Phase I – 25%		
	Jebsen Securities Ltd (5%)	Phase II – 9.67%		
	MTL Shekou Holding Ltd	19.33%		

The ownership of Hong Kong container terminals has been extended to Southern China as both HIT and MTL also hold shares in adjacent China container terminals (see Table 7.7). The ownership of ports around southern China by Hong Kong terminal operators will create a situation where all shippers in southern China must use one of their terminals, despite there being a choice in location. The high port charges in Hong Kong will allow ample margin for port charges in southern China to increase. Obviously, handling charges in Hong Kong will not fall in the near future. With persistently high handling charges, the annual growth rate of Hong Kong throughput will remain low and the trigger point will never be reached. Even if the government determines to build terminal 10, the new terminal will be located in an area which is far away from Kwai Chung. Additional transport costs may be incurred, therefore, in delivering containers to or from the new terminal.

7.7 Conclusion

Hong Kong has been blessed with all the ingredients required to build up a port gradually over the past few decades. The laissez-faire approach of the government gave Hong Kong port industries a free hand to invest and expand at will without any legal impediments to their developments. The operations of the port being in private hands ensured quick responses to any external changes. The political changes in China during the 1950s and 1960s offered Hong Kong a unique time frame to capture overseas cargo channelled via Hong Kong.

With China's open door policy in 1978, the Port of Hong Kong extended its hinterland into China and offered its services and assistance in developing coastal ports around southern China. Hong Kong enjoyed the outcomes of this inward expansion into China with a remarkable growth in volume. However, as from 2000, the overlap of the same hinterland with adjacent ports backfired and the growth rate of container volume in Hong Kong through-put declined as indicated in Table 7.6. With the abolition of the USA/Europe textile quota starting from 2005, Hong Kong will face yet another challenge in maintaining the cargo volume coming out of the PRD area.

Fortunately, the local terminal operators, namely MTL and HIT, also own shares in these adjacent ports. They will probably adjust the slot allocation internally so that they can obtain maximum benefits from the rapid economic growth in China.

References

Cheng, L. K. and Wong, Y. C. (1997) *Port Facilities and Container Handling Services*, Hong Kong: City University of Hong Kong Press.

Drewry Shipping Consultants Ltd. (1998) *World Container Terminals*, London: Drewry Publications.

Enright, M. J., Scott, E. E. and Dodwell, D. (1997) *The Hong Kong Advantage*, Hong Kong: Oxford University Press.

Geiger, T. (1973) *Tales of Two City-States: the Development Progress of Hong Kong and Singapore*, Washington: National Planning Association.

Hong Kong Annual Reports (1965–2002) Hong Kong Government Publications, Hong Kong.

Kwong, K.-S. (1997) *Technology and Industry*, Hong Kong: City University of Hong Kong Press.

Lewis, D. K. (1992) *Hong Kong, a Completely New Port,* Government Publication, Hong Kong.

Ocean Shipping Consultants (1998) *Opportunities for Container Ports*, Ocean Shipping Consultants Ltd., UK.

Ocean Shipping Consultants (1999) *World Container Port Markets to 2012*, Ocean Shipping Consultants Ltd., UK.

Ocean Shipping Consultants (2003) *World Containerport Outlook to 2015*, Ocean Shipping Consultants Ltd., UK.

Robinson, R. (1999) *Measurements of Port Productivity and Container Terminal Design*, London: Cargo Systems.

Stamford Research Group (1996) *Study on the River Trade Cargo Movements and Port Facility Requirements*, Hong Kong Government Planning Department.

Wong, Y. C. (1992) *Competition in Container Terminals*, HKCER Letters, 16, September, http://www.worldcargonews.com/htm/n20040501.368224.htm

Official websites

http://www.asiacontainerterminals.com/default.htm
http://www.asiacontainerterminals.com/default.htm
http://www.csxwthk.com/
http://www.cwcct.com/cct/cct_en/publicinf/main/index.aspx
http://www.hit.com.hk/index.html
http://www.hkctoa.com/
http://www.hph.com.hk/
http://www.mardep.gov.hk/
http://www.modernterminals.com/
http://www.pdc.gov.hk/
http://www.sctcn.com/english/index.htm
http://www.yict.com.cn/english/index.asp

Part IV
Ports in Southern Asia

8
Singapore: the Premier Hub in Southeast Asia

Jose Tongzon

8.1   Introduction

Singapore is no doubt one of the most economically successful economies in Southeast Asia. As one of the miracle economies over the past decades prior to the 1997/8 Asian crisis, Singapore has not only managed to maintain high growth rates but has also made significant progress particularly in the area of poverty alleviation, preservation of the quality of the environment and social cohesion. From a low per capita income (in terms of GDP) of around US$512 at the time of its independence in 1965, it now enjoys one of the highest per capita incomes of around US$21,825 (as of 2003). It has also eliminated absolute poverty.

Singapore as a city state presents a unique case. It has no agricultural sector and thus is free from the problems arising from economic dualism which characterises most developing countries in Asia. Although the government is highly interventionist at the macroeconomic and microeconomic level, its nature of interventionism with regard to poverty alleviation and income inequality reduction is quite unique.[1] To address the issue of poverty alleviation and equity, it has only intervened in certain specific sectors that are deemed important to the development of human skills and human wealth such as education, health and housing provision by way of subsidies. Unlike other high-income countries, however, these subsidies are granted directly to the providers or suppliers of these selected sectors to ensure that the subsidies are not spent on the 'wrong' goods. These subsidies are also not means-tested but are available to all Singaporeans regardless of their income as long as they meet certain criteria. In addition, the sense of social responsibility and citizenship has been actively promoted by the government. Individuals are urged to volunteer for social responsibility and the importance of the family is promoted as one of the pillars of Singapore society. Secondly, there is great emphasis on economic growth and corporate profitability, and the enhancement of international competitiveness based on the philosophy of individual responsibility. Underlying this growth-oriented and government-led approach is the belief that the needs of the poor can be better served by providing them with more access to education and more employment opportunities instead of providing them with hand-outs and direct welfare payments as is being done in most developed countries.

Singapore's transportation and, in particular, its sea port have played a significant role in its economic development process. The economic development model adopted by Singapore has been based on an outward-looking industrialisation strategy with a heavy reliance on foreign direct investment and exports, constrained by a limited domestic market, lack of natural resources and low domestic savings at the initial stage of its economic development. By developing a world-class sea port and an environment conducive for business, it has successfully attracted several multinational corporations (MNCs) to base their production, regional headquarters and distribution base in Singapore, making Singapore an important hub in Southeast Asia. Its efficient port has also contributed to the competitiveness of its exports in the international market – a major source of Singapore's continued growth and economic stability.

Because of the importance of its port in the process of Singapore's economic transformation, the main objective of this chapter is to discuss the strategies adopted by the government of Singapore during the economic transformation process and, in particular, the role of the government in achieving and maintaining its status as a hub in Southeast Asia. The role of the government will be discussed together with other key factors responsible for making the Port of Singapore a hub port. Before discussing the key factors behind the success of Singapore port as a hub and the role of the Singapore government, it is useful to first evaluate briefly the economic contribution of the transportation sector and the port in particular to Singapore's economy.

8.2   Singapore as a hub

Singapore is the premier hub of Southeast Asia, attracting from all over the world a number of international manufacturing firms operating as distribution centres and international logistics service providers. There are over 6,200 businesses in Singapore's logistics industry, employing about 97,000 people with gross receipts totalling S$28 billion. Many of these logistics companies are transnational with their parent companies located in the United States, Northeast Asia and Western Europe, and are operating in Singapore to serve the local and multinational manufacturing companies based in Singapore. Most of the international manufacturing firms have chosen Singapore as their regional headquarters and production base for their high-valued manufactured products.

Transportation has played a very critical role in the economic development of Singapore. Over the years Singapore has built on its strength as a transportation and distribution hub to become one of the leading logistics centres in the world. The transportation sector is vital to the Singapore economy. It has been a major contributor to national income and employment. As Table 8.1 shows, transportation accounted on average for 11 per cent of Singapore's GDP over the period 1997–2001, which is almost as important as Singapore's financial services sector, accounting for about 13 per cent in 2001. In terms of employment, this sector has also generated substantial job opportunities for the economy. With a population of around 3 million, the number of employees employed in the transportation sector (114,794 persons) certainly constitutes a significant portion of its total employment in 2001 (5.6 per cent), as can be gleaned from Table 8.2.

Apart from its direct contribution to the national economy in terms of output and employment generation within its sector, it also has contributed indirectly by facilitating international trade and serving the trading and manufacturing sectors. Since the transportation industry is closely linked to many industries, the cross-industry effect as a result of an expansion or development of the transportation industry can lead to many positive effects in other related industries. Transportation can extend the market reach of raw materials and supplies for manufacturers and provide consumers with a wider range of goods and services produced locally or overseas.

Efficient transportation reduces waste and promotes efficiency by exploiting economies of scale and scope to spread this advantage via a multiplier effect throughout the economy. It further lowers operating costs which improves a country's international competitiveness and its attractiveness to multinational companies to set up a regional base in Singapore. The inflow of foreign direct investment into the economy has brought with it capital, technology and international marketing networks and thus contributed to the maintenance of Singapore's international competitiveness and sustained economic development.

Singapore's attractiveness as an international trading and logistics hub has been strengthened through the development of a world-class hub port and airport (Trade Development Board, 1999). The Port of Singapore is a major port of call for over 4,000 shipping lines from more than 740 ports worldwide. Singapore's Changi International Airport has the most links in the Asia Pacific region and both ports have received numerous international accolades in terms of efficiency and high quality of service. Thus, international manufacturing firms have been attracted to Singapore as the demand for quick and safe delivery requires a high level of both efficiency and frequency of services both by sea and air (Working Group on Logistics, 2002).

8.3   Port facilities

The ability of Singapore to achieve and maintain its status as a hub has greatly hinged on its superior infrastructure both in sea and air transport. Its port infrastructure has defined its capacity to handle vessels and container

Table 8.1: Relative importance of transportation in Singapore's economy

	Values (S$million)					Percentage shares (%)				
	1997	1998	1999	2000	2001	1997	1998	1999	2000	2001
Goods-producing industries	47,950	48,336	48,208	55,614	48,611	23.053	23.639	24.58	26.84	23.44
Manufacturing	32,339	32,532	34,433	42,921	35,975	9.0655	9.368	7.987	6.223	6.134
Construction	12,717	12,892	11,187	9,950	9,413	1.8827	1.9598	1.697	1.588	1.977
Utilities	2,641	2,697	2,377	2,539	3,034	0.1811	0.157	0.151	0.128	0.123
Other goods industries	254	216	211	204	189					
Services-producing industries	95,600	92,811	95,797	107,296	108,790					
Wholesale & retail	21,691	20,010	21,922	26,663	25,407	15.463	14.54	15.65	16.68	16.56
Hotels & restaurants	4,148	3,810	3,801	4,195	4,194	2.957	2.7685	2.714	2.624	2.733
Transportation	15,804	15,733	16,555	17,757	17,290	11.266	11.432	11.82	11.11	11.27
Financial services	18,189	18,571	18,613	19,354	20,119	12.966	13.495	13.29	12.1	13.11
Business services	20,308	19,015	18,796	21,556	22,463	14.477	13.817	13.42	13.48	14.64
Other services	1,460	15,673	16,111	17,771	19,318	11.021	11.389	11.5	11.11	12.59
Owner-occupied dwellings	4,700	4,995	5,116	5,379	5,666	3.3505	3.6296	3.652	3.364	3.692
Gross Domestic Product	140,279	137,618	140,070	159,888	153,455					

Source: Singapore Department of Statistics (2001).

Table 8.2:   Employment aspects of transportation, 2000

	Number of establishments	Number of employees
Land transport & supporting services	3,691	32,930
Water transport & supporting services	1,707	23,069
Air transport & supporting services	98	24,080
Services allied to transport	2,584	29,749
Storage & warehousing	220	4,966
Total	8,300	114,794
Total employment (2001)		2,046,700 (5.6%)

Source: Singapore Department of Statistics (2001).

Table 8.3:   Singapore's container terminal facilities

Terminal	Area (hectares)	Draft (metres)	Berths	Cranes	Ground slots	Reefer (points)
Tanjung Pagar	80	11.0–14.8	6 main 2 feeder	29 QC 95 RTG	15,940	840
Keppel	96	9.6–14.6	4 main 10 feeder	36 QC 106 RTG 13 RMG	20,230	936
Brani	79	12.0–15.0	5 main 4 feeder	29 QC 105 RTG 5 RMG 2 BC	15,424	1,344
Pasir Panjang	84	15.0	6 main	24 QC 44 BC 15 RMG	14,020	648

Source: PSA website (http://www.psa.com.sg/).

flows. It is generally divided into physical and soft elements. Physical infrastructure includes not only the operational facilities (such as the number of berths, the number of cranes, yards and tugs, and storage area) but also intermodal transport[2] (such as roads and railways). The soft infrastructure refers to the manpower employed. Maximum deployment of both types will assist in reducing vessel turnaround, thereby increasing the port's capacity to accommodate more vessels and container flows.

The Port of Singapore has a well-developed port infrastructure, not only in terms of the number of container terminals, container berths, cranes and adequate storage facilities, but also in terms of the quality of the cranes, quality and effectiveness of the port/inter-port information systems, approach channel provided, preparedness of port management and a wide range of port-related and ship-related services offered. Table 8.3 presents Singapore's container

Table 8.4:   Adequacy of port infrastructure: comparative study of selected ports

Port	Number of container berths	Number of container shipcalls	Delays (hours)	Number of along the shore cranes
Port of Singapore	37	24,015	2.3	118
Port of Klang	13	4,889	–	31
Port of Bangkok	20	2,415	–	–
Port of Manila	10	5,463	22.0	19
Port of Tanjung Priok	25	3,239	50.0	10
Port of Rotterdam	30	5,544	1.7	66
Port of Melbourne	12	823	8.0	16
Port of Auckland	3	2,381	–	7
Port of Felixstowe	13	2,677	0.6	29

Source: Taken from interviews, and port publications.

terminals and their facilities. Table 8.4 compares the Port of Singapore with similar ports and other rival ports in the region in terms of physical infrastructure and average ship delays.

To be a hub port requires, in particular, an adequate number of berths and other required port facilities to deal with significant volumes of cargo traffic, high frequencies of ship visits and very large ships. It also requires a well-motivated, skilled and co-operative workforce to handle the high level of co-ordination required as a hub port. To meet these requirements, the Port of Singapore has ensured that its port facilities are adequate to handle future increases in cargo traffic and ship visits by investing in port expansion and upgrading. It has also adopted a remuneration system that encourages high productivity and co-operation, rather than confrontation, from port workers. By tying remuneration to performance, the system encourages high productivity and dedication. The harmonious and constructive relationship between the management and port workers' unions has also played an important role in helping port employees adapt to the fast-changing and competitive business environment, as well as in maintaining constructive communications to avoid any violent and disruptive confrontations.

The newly completed development of the Pasir Panjang terminal, which first opened in 1998 (after completion of the first phase of the project), will give an extra handling capacity of 18 million TEUs. Once this terminal becomes fully operational, the port's total container handling capacity is expected to be roughly 36 million TEUs per annum. In addition, the port's terminals are supported by a number of district parks, providing over half a million square metres of warehousing in total. A district park is a large covered warehouse, which provides automated storage facilities. Customers can process their documents, pack and unpack, mark, label and assemble their goods for distribution to other distribution centres.

Table 8.5: Contribution of PSA to the GDP of Singapore (S$ million)

Description	1999	1998	1997	1996	1995	1994
GDP at 1990 market price	127,250	120,206.9	119,835.3	110,699.2	102,859.4	95,229.3
PSA's operating income	2,541	2,212*	1,972.0	1,873.7	1,765.6	1,519.7
Percentage of GDP	2	1.84*	1.65	1.69	1.72	1.60
PSA's operating surplus	1,445	1,356.8*	982.4	896	804.2	646.6
Percentage of GDP	1.14	1.13*	0.82	0.81	0.78	0.68

* Estimated figures
Source: Compiled from various PSA annual reports and Department of Statistics website.

PSA plans to expand its cargo-handling capacity from the present capacity of 20 million containers per annum to 32 million by 2011. This is based on the assumption of a continued growth in the global economy underpinned by the economic rise of China, India and the Southeast Asian economies. This will result in the positive growth of container throughput through the Port of Singapore, even though it might lose some share in the overall maritime business market.

The Port of Singapore has now established itself as the region's premier port and holds an enviable position as one of the busiest container ports in the world. For many years the Port of Singapore was lagging behind that of Hong Kong in terms of container throughput, but in 1998 its container throughput grew by about 7 per cent to 15.3 million TEUs, surpassing that achieved by the Port of Hong Kong. In 2000 the port's container throughput grew by 6.5 per cent to reach a record 17.086 million TEUs (*The Straits Times*, 2001). In 2003 its container throughput increased to 18.411 million TEUs. In terms of shipping tonnage, the Port of Singapore has consistently ranked as the world's busiest port. In 2000 there were more than 140,922 ships that called at the port of Singapore, equivalent to 910.1 million gross registered tonnes (GRT). It has been said that at any one time 800 ships are waiting to berth at the port. It is also the largest bunkering port in the world, with 18.6 million tonnes of bunkers sold in 2000. It has the eighth largest shipping fleet behind Panama, Liberia and Greece.

In the national context the port has been a major contributor to national income and employment, and despite the Asian economic crisis of 1997/8, has shown a certain degree of resilience and determination to maintain its premier port status. In 1999, PSA recorded an operating income of S$2,541 million, accounting for 2 per cent of Singapore's real GDP and an operating surplus of S$1,445 million, representing about 1.14 per cent of Singapore's real GDP. As seen from Table 8.5, this percentage contribution has been increasing steadily over the years and is likely to rise further in the future. However, as

Table 8.6:   Income, output and employment multipliers for
the Port of Singapore

	Income	Output	Employment
a. Direct	0.78	1.00	11.99
b. Indirect	0.14	0.27	2.49
Total (a + b)	0.92	1.27	14.48
c. Induced	0.28	0.49	5.75
	1.20	1.76	20.23

Source: Toh et al. (1995).

Table 8.7:   Value added dependency per S$m of change in final demand

Industrial sector	VA multiplier	Impact on			
		Itself	Others	Itself	Others
	$ million	$ million		%	
Agriculture & quarrying	0.677	0.474	0.203	70	30
Manufacturing (non-oil)	0.396	0.302	0.094	76	24
Manufacturing (oil)	0.105	0.068	0.037	65	35
Utilities	0.730	0.647	0.083	89	11
Construction	0.667	0.498	0.169	75	25
Commerce	0.818	0.567	0.251	69	31
Transport & communications	0.667	0.566	0.101	85	15
Seaport & related services	**0.609**	**0.507**	**0.102**	**83**	**17**
Financial services	0.892	0.747	0.145	84	16
Business services	0.881	0.771	0.110	88	12
Other services	0.732	0.579	0.153	79	21

Notes: Transport & communications figures exclude seaport & related services. Seaport & related services refers to water transport, ports services, forwarding & warehousing services and crane & container services.
Source: Singapore Input–Output Tables (1990).

impressive as these figures are, they merely serve to illustrate that there is indeed an impact of PSA on the national economy but that the figures do not truly reflect the total multiplier effects of port activities on the entire local economy.

To account for the indirect impacts of port activity, the direct, indirect and induced multiplier effects of the Port of Singapore were calculated and are presented in Table 8.6.

The results from Table 8.6 show that the income multiplier for port activities is S$1.20. In the case of the output multiplier, every dollar of port revenue generates S$1.76 of output. The port employment multiplier is 20, smaller compared to the more labour-intensive tourism industry, which has an employment multiplier of 25. This is because the PSA workforce has been progressively declining from a peak of 12,500 in 1965 to a low of 7,000 in 1999, despite an accelerating throughput. This indicates the increased capital intensity of port operations in Singapore.

Multiplier analysis can only give the impact at the level of the overall economy. It is also important to know the impact of port activities on specific sectors, especially for policy-making purposes. Dependency analysis can be used to show how the multiplier effect is spread among the various sectors of the economy.

With reference to Table 8.7, a dollar increase in the final demand of the seaport and related services sector would lead to other sectors benefiting from 17 per cent of the increase in the value added (VA) generated in the total economy. Although the seaport and related services sector did not have the highest impact on the VA of other sectors, its impact can still be considered rather substantial. This figure is likely to increase in the present age of integration and globalisation, where transport will indisputably be vital to the economy.

8.4 Other key success factors

Other key factors are responsible for Singapore's success as a hub port, including a strategic location that allows coverage of a large number of countries, a high level of efficiency, high connectivity, internationalisation and language skills, strong government support with transparent policies, and the availability of logistics professionals and harmonious management–labour–government relations.

8.4.1 Strategic location

To become a hub, a country must be strategically located. A country is strategically located if it has at least one of the following characteristics: being situated on the main trade lanes and/or situated in or near production and/or consumption centres. Moreover, a good geographical location should also be one where favourable climatic conditions prevail. Harsh weather can obstruct daily logistics operations and hinder development. Fleming and Hayuth (1994) have stressed the importance of location advantages to load centring, and Fleming (1997) has further observed that the world's top container ports are endowed with such location attributes as centrality and intermediacy, in various and varying proportions. They are all central to something and en route to something else, which is, as one might expect, true of any large seaport gateway.

Singapore is located along the Straits of Malacca, which is a main shipping route between east and west. It was estimated that over 600 ships transit the Straits every day (*The Business Times Shipping Times*, 1997). It is also fortunate in enjoying natural deep waters and harbours, which allows it to service ships with deeper drafts without necessarily resorting to extensive and expensive dredging operations. The waterways serving as entrances to Singapore allow even the largest ships to use them. Singapore does not have typhoons and other natural calamities. Hence, port operations and freight movements are safe and reliable.

Singapore is located close to some of the world's most dynamic economies. Even before rapid economic development of these economies started, Singapore has already played an entrepôt role, serving as a gateway to Singapore's hinterland. The remarkable economic development and growing trade orientation of its close Asian neighbours have only heightened its entrepôt role. Although the 1997/8 economic crisis has adversely affected its logistics business, the long-term future for the region is bright and it will remain one of the most dynamic regions in Asia.

8.4.2   A high level of efficiency

Although geographical location is an important factor behind Singapore's success as a hub, Singapore has taken advantage of its location and maintained its status by achieving a highly efficient infrastructure. In a survey conducted by UNCTAD, 'on-time delivery' was cited to be a major concern by most cargo owners (UNCTAD, 1992). In fast-paced industries where products must be moved to the markets on time, service providers as vital nodes in the logistics chain must be in a position to guarantee customers very fast and reliable service levels at every node.

Singapore's adequate and highly efficient infrastructure is particularly manifest in its sea-air transport and telecommunication sectors. For example, in the case of port infrastructure, Tongzon and Ganesalingam (1994) and Tongzon (1995) have shown the Port of Singapore to be in the same league (similar in contexts) as the Ports of Rotterdam, Hong Kong and Kaohsiung, and that the Port of Singapore has outshone all other similar ports in the area of ship turnaround time, labour efficiency, crane efficiency and in the utilisation of other port assets. Singapore's high level of efficiency has made it more economical for shipping lines to call at the port, despite its relatively high port charges. As Table 8.8 shows, compared to its regional rivals and like-for-like ports, Singapore's port charges are much higher, but its ship turnaround time is one of the lowest.

8.4.3   High connectivity

While waiting to be transported at a logistics hub, cargoes are costly and counter-competitive in terms of transit time. Whenever possible, operators should strive for tight connections between feeder and mother carriers. A country that provides an exhaustive and fast connectivity to other destinations is capable of assuming the role of a logistics hub for a defined region. The Port of Singapore is linked by 400 shipping lines to practically 740 ports worldwide. Practically all the major international carriers and shipping lines, 400 of them,

Table 8.8: Like for like comparative performance of Singapore based on selected indicators (2000)

	Port charges[a] (US$)	Ship turn-around time (hours)	Connectivity to other ports
Port of Singapore	155.0	12	740
Port of Klang	50.0	12.5	500
Port of Bangkok	23.37	15	–
Port of Tanjung Priok	–	–	–
Port of Manila	24.74	–	–
Port of Rotterdam	–	–	1,000
Port of Melbourne	23.28	–	200
Port of Auckland	26.52	14.9	160
Port of Felixstowe	108.51	–	365

Notes:
– not available; ranks from 5 (highest) to 1 (lowest);
[a] Represented by container handling rates per FCL;
Exchange rates used: US$1 = S$1.74, US$1 = RM3.80, US$1 = THB42.8, US$1 = 48.50 pesos; US$0.49 = AUD$1; US$1 = NZ$ 2.47; US$1 = 0.6912 pounds
Source: Fairplay Port Guide (1999/2000); www.cosco.com.au/ports.htm.

Table 8.9: Connectivity and frequency of calls at the Port of Singapore

Country/Region	Number of shipping lines	Average number of daily sailings
Europe	68	5
West Asia	52	3
South Asia	74	4
Africa	59	2
Central & South America	35	1
Australasia	70	1
US	53	3
China	68	4
Hong Kong	76	7
Japan	62	4
Korea	59	4
Taiwan	60	5
Indonesia	156	7
Malaysia	105	9
Philippines	41	1
Thailand	74	3

Source: PSA website (http://www.psa.com.sg/).

call at Singapore. As can be gleaned from Tables 8.8 and 8.9, its high port connectivity and ship frequencies cover all parts of the globe, with concentration in Southeast Asia. This wide-ranging port connectivity allows shipping lines to maximise slot utilisation on their mother vessels by offering more choice of feeders to various trade routes.[3] Shippers are also able to move their products to and from the markets faster and at lower inventory costs.

Reduced connection times are made possible with the introduction of FastConnect.[4] Hailed as the new transhipment system, it aims mainly to cut down the cumbersome procedures involved in shipping transhipment containers while making possible tighter connection times within the terminals.[5] Thus, in addition to providing comprehensive connectivity, the port is able to expedite the connections, which helps reduce a ship's stay at berths leading to lower charges to shippers.

8.4.4 Internationalisation and English language skills

Singapore is one of the most open economies with an international trade component much greater than the value of its GDP. This openness, brought about by its highly liberal trade and investment policies, has made the economy attractive for logistics and export-oriented companies.

English is Singapore's official language and means of communication in business and at the government level. The ability to speak and write English is useful since English is an international language used in many business transactions. Knowledge of the English language also allows easy access to information and new ideas available in international organisations and other foreign sources, which may be required for business operations. Since Singapore's laws, rules and regulations are written in English, foreigners have found it easier to understand and interpret them. Doing business in Singapore is therefore much easier and more convenient for foreign businessmen.

8.4.5 Strong government support with transparent policies

The government of Singapore has played a critical role in achieving hub status for Singapore. The government of Singapore, in particular, has formulated and effectively implemented policies and strategies to create an environment that nurtures openness, efficiency and accountability in its transport operations and services.

Singapore's type of government intervention is a combination of no distortion and *dirigism*. It encourages competition and operational efficiency by adopting a policy of openness (no import restrictions, price controls or subsidies). On other hand, it intervenes in the economy directly (i.e. running government enterprises) and indirectly by way of regulations and other policies affecting the private sector.

The Port of Singapore is a good example of this type of government intervention. The port is run on a commercial basis, is self-financing, and is expected to compete with other ports on an equal footing. However, this is also a public port and it is expected to operate with objectives consistent with the national development agenda and priorities of the government of Singapore. The Port of Singapore Authority (PSA), operating on 1 April 1964 and later renamed as the Maritime and Port Authority of Singapore (MPA) with the corporatisation of PSA in 1997, is a statutory board whose main task is to regulate and control navigation and shipping in the port area and is under the Ministry of Communications.

The Ministry of Transport (MOT) oversees the development and regulation of land, sea and air transport. MOT sets the strategic and policy direction, with operations and regulatory functions being carried out by a number of statutory boards established under Acts of Parliament, including: the Civil Aviation Authority of Singapore (CASA); the Land Transport Authority (LTA); the Maritime and Port Authority of Singapore (MPA); and the Public Transport Council (PTA). Organisationally, these boards operate under the aegis of the MOT.

The Maritime and Port Authority of Singapore (MPA) operates under the Maritime and Port Authority of Singapore Act (Chapter 170A)(1996). It was formed by the merger of the Marine Department, the National Maritime Board, and the regulatory departments of the former Port of Singapore Authority (PSA). The MOT is responsible for overseeing the activities of the MPA.

The MPA's key roles are as follows[6]:

- As port authority, the MPA controls vessel movements, ensures navigational safety and regulates marine services and facilities.
- As port industry regulator, the MPA regulates marine services, notably pilotage and tugboat services, as well as the port industry's economic behaviour.
- As port planner, the MPA draws up the national port master plan and determines where and when future port development should take place.
- As port developer, the MPA works with other agencies to ensure the continuing strength of Singapore's maritime sector.
- As national sea transport policy developer and government adviser on matters relating to sea transport, the MPA represents Singapore at regional and international meetings.

Following the formation of the MPA, the former Port of Singapore Authority (PSA) was corporatised to form the Port of Singapore Corporation (PSC). PSC is the operator of the Port of Singapore. Before the Port of Singapore was corporatised in 1997, it was a statutory board created under the PSA Act of Parliament. As a statutory board, its mission was primarily to build the port infrastructure for the enhancement of Singapore's economic development. The motivation of the port corporatisation was to make the port more flexible and more able to take advantage of the growing market opportunities emerging in Asia after the region had witnessed tremendous growth in trade driven by economic dynamism and the increasing trade orientation of the development objectives of countries in the region. By the Companies Act, PSA became the sole port operator while the regulatory function was taken over by the Maritime and Port Authority (MPA) – a government-body created to regulate the port and shipping business. In particular, MPA sets guidelines on port charges, maritime safety and other policy areas. As a corporatised port, PSA is fully independent from the government in terms of investment and financing decisions, although it still has to comply with the general policy orientation of the country.

PSA port pricing is subject to the guidelines set out by the MPA. Stevedoring charges are subject to a ceiling imposed by the MPA which also collects the port dues. This is to ensure that the charges are not too excessive, as the terminals are all owned and managed by PSA. The only terminal managed and leased by a private shipping line – COSCO's dedicated terminal – and those terminals owned by Jurong port can provide internal competition for PSA in the stevedoring business. In relation to the other parts of the port operation there is more competition. In pilotage, there is more than one provider, including PSA Marine. There are no special privileges given to this PSA-owned towage company except for the networking services that the PSA can provide. There is also a level playing field in towage as there is more than one private player.

The government of Singapore has long subscribed to the philosophy that competition, both international and domestic, is desirable for the health of the economy. Singapore regards the world as its marketplace, and international competition is thought of as an 'invisible hand' disciplining the domestic economy.[7] Singapore passed legislation to ban certain anti-competitive practices in 2004, although the legislation will not come into effect until 2006.

Singapore's new Competition Law passed through Parliament in October 2004. It focuses on three areas: anti-competitive agreements, decisions and practices; abuse of a dominant market position; and mergers and acquisitions which are likely to substantially reduce competition. Whilst the Competition Commission, a statutory board, was created in January 2005, there was a transition period of 12 months before the provisions of the Competition Law came into effect on 1 January 2006.[8]

The government has been responsible for designing and implementing appropriate strategies to meet its objectives. Over the years it has shown its effectiveness in ensuring that the Port of Singapore can respond efficiently to new business opportunities and cope with challenges in a changing global trading environment. For example, in achieving the objective of making Singapore a world-class transhipment port, the government has adopted a number of incentive schemes apart from ensuring that port capacity and infrastructure are adequate to deal with future demands for port services. The 'China Cargo Scheme' was introduced in 1975 to increase trade with China. Since 1979, the berth appropriation scheme has been adopted for certain major shipping lines. Under the scheme a shipping line is given priority in berthing its vessel at a designated berth and has exclusive use of the go-down behind it. This enables the shipping line to schedule its vessel calls and plan its operations more efficiently. On its part, the shipping line has to guarantee a minimum cargo throughput and the use of its own stevedores and gear.

To attract more shipping lines to its port, the government has adopted a strategy of function diversification. Apart from the standard role of handling cargoes between ship and shore, ship repair, bunkering and distribution, other roles such as offering ship finance and insurance have been promoted for the Port of Singapore so that it would become a one-stop shop for shipowners. Deregulation in bunkering has also made it easy for foreign companies to set up their own agents in Singapore, instead of having to operate through Singapore agents or foreign–local joint ventures. It has also promoted the Singapore flag. As a result, the Singapore Registry of Ships has grown rapidly in recent years and today ranks as the seventh largest in the world.

To attract shipowners to set up base in Singapore, since 1991 the Trade and Development Board has implemented an attractive incentives scheme called the Approved Shipping Enterprise Scheme (AIS). Companies under this scheme enjoy a tax exemption of up to 10 years on income earned from qualifying shipping operations. To qualify for the scheme, 10 per cent of the company's fleet has to be registered with the Singapore flag. The scheme has proved a strong draw for some of the world's top shipping companies, with 36 AIS companies operating a total of more than 500 vessels using Singapore as a base. Singapore now has a thriving ship financing community with shipping banks such as ING, Christiana Bank and MeesPierson joining the local player – the Development Bank of Singapore. Progress has also been made in building up the local insurance industry. Two P&I Clubs, the Standard Club and the UK Club now have regional offices in Singapore. Lloyd's of London has negotiated to set up an underwriting presence in the republic.

8.4.6 Availability of logistics professionals

The importance of developing a ready pool of skilled logistics professionals to manage increasingly complex logistics operations is vital. A wide variety of courses are available at training institutes, polytechnics and universities. These range from certificate and diploma level to fully-fledged graduate and post-graduate degree programmes. A multi-agency effort by TDB, EDB, CAAS, MPA and NSTB, the Logistics Institute-Asia Pacific was established in 1999 to provide world-class training to meet the demands of the dynamic global logistics industry. TDB will also work closely with the Ministry of Manpower to formulate a logistics manpower road map to develop manpower capabilities in the logistics industry.

8.4.7 Harmonious government–labour–management relations

As mentioned earlier, the transportation business requires a well-motivated and co-operative workforce to handle the high level of co-ordination required. Singapore's remuneration system helps to ensure high productivity and co-operation, and discourages confrontation, from transport workers. This strategy also ties remuneration to performance, thus leading to high product-ivity and peaceful and constructive relations between the government, man-agement and unions. This has helped the workers adapt to a modern and dynamic working environment, and to develop a commitment to dialogue and communication for the settlement of any disputes.

In a nutshell, the success of Singapore as a hub is attributable not so much to its geographical location as to the determined effort to build world-class infrastructure with a highly efficient transportation system and to create an environment conducive to doing business for domestic and foreign investors. In particular, its sea, air and land sectors have achieved world-class standards – its air and seaports have remained major hubs with excellent facilities and efficient operations.

But behind all these other factors lies the crucial role of the Singapore gov-ernment. The involvement of the government through agencies such as the Trade Development Board (TDB), the Port of Singapore (PSA), the Civil Aviation Authority of Singapore (CAAS) and the Maritime and Port Authority (MPA) is critical to its success. As a facilitator, initiator and provider of structure, the government of Singapore has been involved in a range of joint government–private sector activities such as financing of private sector initiatives, employ-ment of IT, development of skilled and appropriate manpower and provision of hard infrastructure such as congestion-free roads, efficient sea and airports.

8.5 Conclusion

The volume of container cargo handled by container ports in the world has grown significantly. For example, over 1990–8 it grew on average by roughly 9 per cent per annum. However, because of the rapid rise in transhipment volumes through the key hub ports, the growth rate for containerised trade is slightly less than the growth of containers handled at ports. Containerised trade grew on average by around 7 per cent over the same period, whereas the average growth in total trade tonnage was only 2.8 per cent (Avery, 2000: 15). Figure 8.1 further illustrates this growth, showing a consistent increase from roughly 46 million TEUs in 1983 to 225 million TEUs in 2000, despite the 1997 and 1998 Asian crisis.

This robust growth in container traffic is expected to continue into the future due to the following major factors: continued growth of the world economy; continued rise in world trade; the growing industrialisation of developing countries; and the economic rise of newly emerging economies such as China and India. When there is an increase in economic activity as manifest in increased gross national output, there will be an increase in imports and thus world trade. Over the past decade the world has been growing consistently. Moreover, the world economy has become increasingly dependent on trade, with each major regional trading bloc rapidly accelerating the level of goods transferred both between economies in the region and also between major

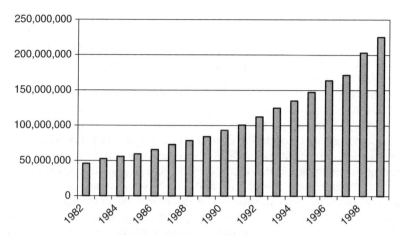

Figure 8.1: Total world port volumes 1983–2000 (million TEUs)
Source: *Container International Yearbook* (various issues).

trading blocs. For example, the formation of regional trading arrangements such as the European Union and the North American Free Trade Area has resulted in a greater amount of goods traded in the world as it spurred the world towards regionalism. Containerisation has also facilitated the transfer of manufactured goods between nations. As developing nations continued to industrialise resulting in more production of manufactures and higher value-added goods, demand for containers has grown.

Against this backdrop of tremendous business opportunities, more and more countries in Asia are positioning themselves to become the preferred hubs in the region. The increasing regional competition for foreign direct investment (ASEAN Secretariat, 1999) and to take a slice in the growing logistics market make it imperative that ports in Asia develop an effective hub policy and strategy to become internationally competitive.

Operational efficiency is very important for policy-makers and operators to gain a competitive advantage and win in the competition. This also implies that the customers of logistics services pay more attention to operational efficiency when selecting services. The results show that another most important factor determining competitiveness is adaptability to customer demand. Since logistics is a service industry, it is reasonable that operators should well understand the requirements of their customers and make efforts to meet and exceed their expectations.

Countries in Southeast Asia should therefore focus on improving their product and service quality through innovation and improved technology, efficiency and reliability. To improve their level of technology, they should invest in strengthening the scientific and technological capability of their citizens. This is an area where more ASEAN co-operation can bring about more technological progress throughout the region. In the case of the CLMV (i.e. Cambodia, Laos, Myanmar and Vietnam) countries, the provision of technical assistance and other capacity-building measures from the more developed member countries should be intensively pursued so as to expedite their catching up in terms of human skills and technological development and thus expedite the process of economic integration within the region.

While joint technology enhancement (especially in the area of information technology) is important to improve their level of competitiveness, there is also some scope for co-operation instead of engaging in competition to become the logistics hub of Southeast Asia. Further co-operation and win–win alliances among the major seaports and airports in the region should be explored to make the region more competitive and attractive for foreign manufacturing and logistics firms. For example, in the area of sea and air transport, regional alliances in the form of marketing, cargo handling, training and research which lowers overhead and operational costs would be desirable and feasible and would make the region more attractive as distribution centres for logistics companies. However, alliances in terms of price fixing and profit sharing would be difficult, if not impossible, especially when these ports are government-owned; due to nationalistic and political factors, quite apart from the tendency for countries to try to capture the largest slice of the logistics market.

Singapore and the rest of ASEAN have followed different industrialisation paths and adopted different policy orientation due to their differences in market size and factor endowments. Thus, since its political separation from Malaysia, Singapore has adopted an export-oriented industrialisation strategy with heavy reliance on foreign investments. This is in contrast to other ASEAN countries' import-substitution strategy in the early stages of their economic development.

However, the experience of Singapore as a logistics and distribution hub can be of relevance to other ASEAN countries which also aspire to strengthen their logistics sector to take advantage of its growing economic opportunities. Especially for the less developed countries of the region, a number of institutional and non-institutional changes must be undertaken individually before economic opportunities can be realised amidst increasing regional competition, as follows:

- To make a freer trading and investment environment, they should be more outward-looking and welcoming to foreign investors by liberalising markets, improving customs clearance and treating foreign and large businesses on the same footing as local small and medium-size firms (SMEs).
- To improve the level of English proficiency and increase the number of logistics professionals. English proficiency needs to be further improved to make it easier for foreign investors to operate their businesses. Greater variety of short- and long-term English and logistics courses may be established in various universities and non-profit educational organisations.

- To improve the consistency and the transparency in government policy towards industry. Foreign investors need to have a sense of security from consistent and predictable policies since their investment is usually bulky and requires a long gestation period. Transparency also implies that the rules must be open so that they know what they can do and cannot do at the time of investing. Since the government plays a significant role in economic development and other economic initiatives, transparency of government policy is critical.
- To have a clean government with efficient and simplified administrative processes. Clean government and efficiency in bureaucracy is one of Singapore's unique features which made the island attractive as a base for the regional and global operations of multinational corporations.
- To foster harmonious relations between the government, management and labour unions. No doubt, harmonious labour–management relations are vital to the smooth functioning of transportation, distribution and other aspects of logistics operations, as shown by the 2002 long-shore labour strike at the 29 ports on the US West Coast, which cost the US economy US$2 billion a day and had damaging ripple effects rolling into the Pacific and resulted in international trade disruption and failed just-in-time delivery of goods (*The Straits Times*, 2002). Singapore is well known for its tripartite peace of government–union–management and political stability. Singapore has not had any labour strikes since the mid-1980s.
- To foster good partnership between the government and the private sector. Although the government sector is important for the formulation and implementation of appropriate policies, it needs the private sector to carry out and translate the overall policy direction into action. Thus, a good partnership between the government and the private sector is an important ingredient to the success of a logistics hub strategy. Based on Singapore's experience, the government of Singapore has always been pro-active and supportive to logistics providers by providing world-class infrastructure and a broad range of logistics solutions and services, including the establishment of efficient customs procedures and a pro-business environment.

Notes

1. Singapore belongs to the 'Teach them to fish rather than give them fish' school of social policy, emphasising education and skills training.
2. Intermodal transport refers to the transport of unit loads by the co-ordinated use of more than one transport mode.
3. In terms of connections, at the Port of Singapore there are three daily sailings to the US, four to Japan, five to Europe and 22 to South and Southeast Asia.
4. FastConnect has a range of features, from recommending to lines the earliest connectible carriers based on their interline agreement, to auto-paging them for a re-nomination when the approved connection cannot be effected due to the vessel's delay or early arrival. After the lines have arranged shipment with their respective connecting carriers and when they submit import status, the system will approve

or reject the application at the point of nomination to enable lines to take alternative actions early.

5. The advanced information and automation structure adopted by the Port of Singapore allows them to monitor and manage transactions quickly and effectively. This system consists mainly of electronic data communication systems (PORTNET), integrated maritime information system (MAINS), computer integrated terminal operations system (CITOS) and financial electronic data interchange (EDI). This will be discussed again when we get to the issue of infostructure.

6. This section relies on Almec Corporation, *ASEAN Maritime Transport Development Study*, Final Report, G-1 to G-3.

7. APEC Competition Policy and Law Database (http://www.apeccp.ord.tw).

8. See *Business Times* (Singapore), 20 October 2004.

References

ASEAN Secretariat (1999) *Investing in ASEAN: a Guide for Foreign Investors*, Jakarta: ASEAN.

Avery, P. (2000) *Strategies for Container Ports, Cargo Systems Report*, London: Informa.

Fairplay Port Guide (1999/2000), London: Fairplay Publications.

Fleming, D. K. (1997) 'World Container Port Rankings', *Maritime Policy and Management*, 24(2): 175–81.

Fleming, D. and Hayuth, Y. (1994) 'Spatial Characteristics of Transportation Hubs: Centrality and Intermediacy', *Journal of Transport Geography*, 2(1): 3–18.

Singapore Department of Statistics (2001) *Statistics Singapore*, http://www/singstat.gov.sg.

The BusinessTimes Shipping Times (1997) 'Accidents in Straits of Malacca', 16 October, p. 1.

The Straits Times (2001) 'PSA Anchors Year 2000 with Record 17 m Boxes Moved', 10 January, p. 10.

The Straits Times (2002) 'Just-in-Time Philosophy Takes a Beating', 26 October, p. 29.

Toh, R. S., Phang, S. Y. and Khan, H. (1995) 'Port Multipliers in Singapore: Impact on Income, Output and Employment', *Journal of Asian Business*, 2(1): 1–9.

Tongzon, J. (1995) 'Systematizing International Benchmarking for Ports', *Maritime Policy and Management*, 22(2): 171–7.

Tongzon, J. and Ganesalingam, S. (1994) 'Evaluation of ASEAN Port Performance and Efficiency', *Asian Economic Journal*, 8(3): 317–30.

Trade Development Board (1999) *The Next Frontier for Singapore's Logistics Industry*, Press Release PR No. 067/99, 29 December.

UNCTAD (1992) *Strategic Planning for Port Authorities*, Geneva: United Nations.

Working Group on Logistics (2002) *Developing Singapore into a Global Integrated Logistics Hub*, September.

9
Tanjung Pelepas: the Future Regional Hub Port

Choon Heng Leong

9.1 Introduction

Unlike the ports in Shenzhen, the Port of Tanjung Pelepas (PTP) at the southern tip of the Malay Peninsula, across from the island of Singapore, did not emerge to serve a massive number of industries relocated in its hinterland. The relocation of small and medium-sized factories in Johor by Singapore investors has been ongoing since the 1980s due to rising labour costs and a labour shortage in Singapore and there were no indications in the 1990s that this trend was going to accelerate. Both foreign and domestic investments continued to come into Johor in the 1990s but not at a steady rate and certainly not at rates which would have a drastic impact on port activities (see Figure 9.1). At the same time, there were also investments which were closing down, obviously with some moving to China (Figure 9.2). Economic and industrial activities in the state of Johor in the 1990s would not have justified the creation of a new port with the kind of ambition expressed by PTP. Johor port already existed at

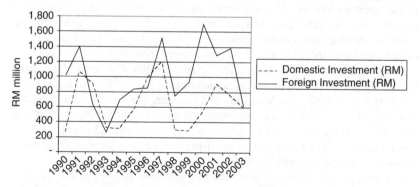

Figure 9.1: Domestic and foreign investments in Johor, 1990–2003 (RM million)
Note: The data are based on actual investments in approved projects.
Source: Data provided by the Malaysian Industrial Development Authority.

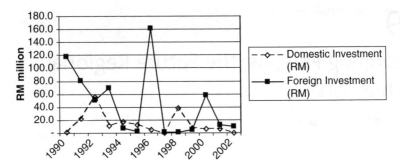

Figure 9.2:   Closing down of foreign and domestic investments in Johor, 1990–2002
Source: Data provided by the Malaysian Industrial Development Authority.

Pasir Gudang to cater to the international trading needs of these industries. Many of the exports and imports of these industries were also using the Port of Singapore.

PTP was therefore intentionally created to cater primarily to transhipment cargo and not to serve the Johor industrial hinterland at the southern end of the peninsula. Having been established, however, this would not exclude it from serving the Johor industrial hinterland or even the larger Malaysian hinterland, especially for container cargo. As a transhipment container port, it would only compete directly with the Port of Singapore which was already endowed with all the necessary conditions that made it the second busiest container port in the world. The strength of the Port of Singapore was known prior to the decision to create PTP. It was nevertheless created on the doorstep of Singapore.

This brings to mind several questions about port emergence which are rather puzzling. What is the interplay of forces which leads to the emergence of ports? Which carries more weight – domestic cargo from the immediate hinterland or international transhipment cargo from the region? Or do ports emerge when national ambitions meet international shipping needs, particularly as defined by large shipping lines? One may think that it would be foolish to develop a port without sufficient base cargo. Similarly, it would be equally foolish if there were already excess capacity in the region. In the arena of port competition, however, the importance of base cargo and regional port capacities could be eclipsed by the combined effect of national ambition, global strategic moves and the lure of non-core port businesses. The logic of PTP's emergence and its subsequent survival provides a case for discussing these issues as the subject of this chapter.

This chapter will discuss in depth the transhipment strategy of PTP, explaining why and how the strategy developed and its consequences. It will also show the contradiction of this strategy with existing national port policies and the difficulty of resolving the contradiction under the existing structure of port administration. The management and ownership of the port, manner of financing, and government support will be apparent from the discussion. Finally, this chapter will draw some useful lessons from the PTP experience and identify the essence of its transhipment strategy.

9.1.1   Born into a crowded world of ports

On the important Far East–Europe shipping route, there were already a sizeable number of large-scale hub ports as well as ports which functioned as terminal points, minor hubs and load centres. These included Hong Kong, Kaohsiung, Busan, Yokohama, Singapore and Port Klang. These ports have developed the capabilities and efficiencies to function as hubs, thus ensuring that ships continued to call at them. At the same time, ports were emerging along the coast of China, namely Shenzhen, Shanghai, Tianjin, Qingdao, Yantian, Ningbo, Xingang, Chiwan and Xiamen, not to mention Southeast Asian ports, such as Laem Chabang and Tanjung Priok which were also aspiring to build themselves into regional hub ports. Port development was also taking place along the coast of India given its growing economy and rising exports and imports. The Asian port scene seemed to be getting crowded.

The growth of ports in China was a consequence of increasing exports. Trade between the Far East and Europe has largely gravitated towards China as the fastest growing economy in the Asian region. Exports originated from China and would end up in developed country markets in Europe and the United States. High volume shipping would therefore converge in China, necessitating the development of ports there. Having reached a certain size, several of these ports may become hubs for the region. Shanghai was already seen to be the most likely candidate. Ports and hubs were increasing in number.

For intra-Asian trade, including between China and Southeast Asia, cargo could be transported through short-sea shipping or direct port-to-port calls between existing ports, such as Port Klang, Laem Chabang, Tanjung Priok, Singapore, Hong Kong, Shenzhen, Shanghai and so on, and need not go through the hub-and-spoke transhipment system. Cargo movement between Asian ports certainly need not be a part of the Far East–Europe long haul. It could be served by shuttle services and short-sea rotations. If a second transhipment hub were to be created in Southeast Asia it would not be clear as to which cargo it would carry. The ambitious plans and announcements of PTP to be a Southeast Asian transhipment hub adjacent to Singapore therefore came as a surprise to many in Malaysia and internationally.

If the immediate Malaysian hinterland could not generate enough cargo to support a large-scale hub port right next to Singapore while the number of ports in the region continued to rise steadily, where then lay the source of cargo for PTP to be a major international hub port? When PTP was initiated as a privatised project in 1995 through a 60-year concession privatisation agreement between the Malaysian government and Seaport Terminal (Johor) it was meant to solve the anticipated capacity bottleneck in the existing Johor port in Pasir Gudang.[1] It was therefore intended to cater to a projected growth in base cargo in the Johor industrial hinterland. However, by the time the first-phase construction was completed in January 2000, it was clear that it was to be a major international hub port and not just a platform for Johor.

A study conducted by the Transport and Tourism Division of the United Nations Economic and Social Commission for Asia and the Pacific (UNESCAP) in 2001 forecasted increasing demand for container shipping and container port activities throughout the first decade of 2000 until 2011 as a result of growing trade.[2] Maybe the conditions were not as bleak as described earlier. In fact, the study predicted an increase in transhipment activities; hence, a demand for hub ports in the Asian region. The prediction was one of a greater number of ports along with more shipping and larger vessels to accommodate the growth of trade. In a crowded world of ports, based on the UNESCAP forecasts, there was still a need for more ports.

The UNESCAP study predicted world container trade to grow by between 6 per cent and 6.5 per cent annually from 1999 to 2011 (UNESCAP 2001). Asia's share of this trade would increase to 51 per cent, with China becoming the world's largest container market by 2011. Intra-Asian trade would grow by an average of 7.6 per cent a year in the same period. UNESCAP envisaged two scenarios in the shipping arena to meet demand. In the first scenario, i.e. a 'base case' scenario, in which ship size would grow slowly, there would be an increase in mid-sized post-panamax ships of 4,000 to 6,000 twenty foot equivalent units (TEUs) deployed on existing major routes. The number of services on these routes would increase and would entail direct and multiple port calls. Co-existing with this would be a smaller number of larger ships of around 8,000 TEUs providing long-haul services on streamlined routes and calling largely at hub ports. The second or 'big ships' scenario was one dominated by very large ships of above 10,000 TEU that called only at major hub ports in each region. Smaller vessels would provide feeder services to these major hub ports, resulting in a clear demarcation between hubs and secondary feeder ports in this second scenario.

Under both scenarios, UNESCAP predicted an increase in transhipment cargo and in the demand for transhipment hub ports. Even under the more modest 'base case' scenario, transhipment as a share of total port volume was expected to increase from 28 per cent in 1999 to 30 per cent in 2011 in the ESCAP region, which comprises largely East, South and Southeast Asia (UNESCAP, 2001: 51). The amount of containers transhipped would be around 64 million TEUs in 2011. Assuming the hubs of Hong Kong, Singapore and Kaohsiung would tranship around 35 million TEUs, this still left a sizeable 29 million TEUs transhipment cargo for the other emerging transhipment hubs. According to UNESCAP: 'There is a considerable potential for the development of a substantial transhipment business at several new regional hubs: Busan, Gwangyang, Port Klang, Tanjung Pelepas and Shanghai' (UNESCAP, 2001: x). But still, why would any increase in cargo go through PTP?

Table 9.1: Container throughput in the Port of Tanjung Pelepas (TEU), 1999–2004

	1999	2000	2001	2002	2003	2004
Throughput TEU	20,696	423,710	2,049,487	2,668,512	3,487,320	4,020,421

Source: Compiled from the website of PTP.

With regards to PTP, the UNESCAP study revealed that:

> The modelling work undertaken for the present study suggests that Tanjung Pelepas has the potential to build a very strong transhipment business, although it is unlikely to pose a major threat to the dominance of Singapore within the forecast period. Under the assumptions of the 'base case', throughput at Tanjung Pelepas is expected to grow to 4.5 million TEU by 2011, over 80 per cent of which will be transhipment cargoes.
>
> The positioning of Tanjung Pelepas as a head-to-head competitor of Singapore is underscored by similarities in the composition of their transhipment cargoes. Tanjung Pelepas is also very heavily dependant on the South-East Asian market – even more so, in fact, than Singapore. It is estimated that South-East Asian traffic will account for 86 per cent of Tanjung Pelepas total transhipment traffic in 2011. (UNESCAP, 2001: 59)

It seems that the UNESCAP study has assumed that there would be a natural spillover of traffic from Singapore to PTP as a result of the general increase in container movement in the Southeast Asian region, and that the bulk of this would be transhipment traffic. Congestion in Singapore also provided an opportunity for a gradual increase in container cargo using PTP. The UNESCAP study underestimated the impact of PTP. Rather than gradual, the increase in container traffic through PTP was quite drastic as can be seen from Table 9.1 and Figure 9.3, suggesting that there was more than a spillover effect.

In January 2005, PTP announced that in 2004 it had broken the 4 million TEU barrier, handling 4,020,421 TEUs compared to 3,487,320 TEUs in 2003 (*New Straits Times*, 24 January 2005, p. 27). More than 95 per cent was transhipment cargo. To have achieved such growth in such a short time without the prerequisite local base cargo, the PTP phenomenon could not have been just a spillover from Singapore and a by-product of the general growth of container trade and transhipment cargo in the Asian region. It also would have been influenced by changes in the configuration of the container shipping network, the routeing of ships, and the positioning of facilities.

9.2   Weighing the opportunities for hub port development

Deciphering whether the people who decided to embark on the PTP project ever correctly weighed up all the pros and cons of the project beforehand

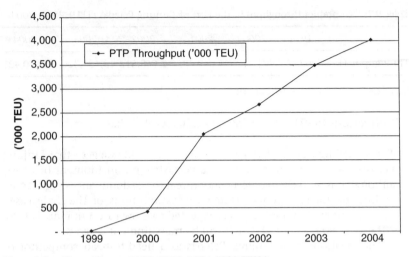

Figure 9.3:   Throughput of PTP, 1999–2004 ('000 TEUs)
Source: Table 9.2.

would be a difficult task. It was probably impossible to weigh up all the pros and cons in the first place. Nevertheless, some of the trends in container shipping and handling at ports would not have been missed. Several of the major trends can be summarised as follows:[3]

- Container traffic grew consistently throughout the 1990s and slowed down after 2001. Nevertheless, the trend towards greater containerisation would persist and more general bulk cargo, such as grain, would be converted to container cargo. Cargoes which had begun as container cargoes, such as manufactures and especially electronic equipment, would continue to increase. There would not be any foreseeable downward trend in the demand for container shipping and container terminal facilities. Container cargo has generally grown faster than maritime trade.
- The container shipping fleet would continue to increase and so would the size of vessels. The debate lay in whether the size increase would be slow or rapid, considering that the benefits of economies of scale diminish with larger vessels. Periodic excess capacity would be seen as cyclical, thus, not putting any halt on vessel expansion.
- The increase in container fleet and rise of very large super post-panamax ships would put pressure on ports to upgrade and expand facilities. It might also lead to demand for more regional hubs, transhipment and feeder services. More ports were expected to appear along the major shipping routes, especially along the Far East–Europe route. With more ports, there would be more strings on the major routes. At the same time, there would be a

growth in transhipment container traffic using the hub-and-spoke system, accounting for about 30 per cent of total container traffic.

- The persistent low-profit environment for container shipping would force shipping lines to rationalise their operations. This, together with new logistics and supply chain demands, put pressure on shipping lines to reorganise shipping network configurations and the global positioning of port infrastructures in order to cut costs. Ports were also pressured to lower charges, increase throughput and shorten turn-around time. Major carriers would continue to get bigger through fleet expansion, acquisitions and mergers, leading to greater market control and bargaining power vis-à-vis ports. Shipping lines would demand dedicated terminals or exclusive berthing and better port services. There would be a greater readiness to switch ports.
- The trend of large carriers owning and managing ports and terminals would continue. Concurrently, many ports would undergo privatisation, relegating control, and even ownership, to global terminal operators, such as Hutchison Port Holdings (HPH), Port of Singapore Authority (PSA) and AP Moller. Partnerships and co-operative arrangements between ports and shipping lines were the new strategies.

Given these global trends, the switch around the late 1990s by PTP to become an international transhipment hub port was strategic as well as opportunistic. PTP could exploit a combination of these trends, or miss them altogether and choose to remain a port serving primarily the Johor hinterland. Besides having a strategic geographical location on the main sea lane between east and west, PTP was virtually starting from scratch. It had to resort to business acumen to exploit the opportunities lying in the global trends in shipping and port development that were taking place in the 1990s. This it did when it formed a strategic partnership with Maersk Sealand in 2000. With Maersk Sealand as its partner, some of the global trends could be further exploited to help transform itself into a major transhipment hub. It was like pulling itself up with its own bootstraps, albeit with the help of a strong arm from an established global player.

Though not impossible, it would have been difficult for PTP to exploit the trends in containerisation, transhipment, route configuration, fleet expansion, vessel size increase, and port privatisation on its own. The opportunities lay in the trends and PTP had to go along with the trends. This included attracting big ships to the port, attracting feeder lines, and putting together the complex set of activities that could support global logistics and shipping operations at the port. On its own, it could undertake dredging, berth construction, facilities installation, in particular, super post-panamax cranes for big ships, and the like. Adequate financing would have helped settle these issues. But what was needed for PTP to be a hub port was more than infrastructure construction. It needed strategic partners.

9.3   What it took for PTP to be a hub

The more difficult part was putting together the set of ingredients that could ensure the success of PTP as a transhipment hub port, and these would be the greatest challenges to PTP. These ingredients were essentially those factors which have contributed to the success of such hub ports as Singapore, Hong Kong, Rotterdam, Dubai and the like, and they included:[4]

- A thriving hinterland of economic activities – manufacturing, export and import – which helped to generate a sizeable base cargo;
- The presence of major international companies, in particular, shipping-related and logistics companies;
- The presence of a dense transportation network and a high level of connectivity to other ports, together with facilities for intermodal transportation;
- Efficient port services, especially reliability and rapid handling and turnaround for ships;
- Efficient administrative procedures, especially customs;
- Adequate and good landside facilities, such as yards, warehouses and storage and logistics facilities; and, finally,
- Attractive tariffs.

Beginning as a brand-new green-field port, all these ingredients had to be created. The road connecting PTP to the North–South Highway, i.e. the national highway network, and linking it to the Malaysia–Singapore Second Crossing had to be built. There was also no rail connection yet, and road connections to the nearest airport, Senai Airport, had to be improved. Contemplating the moves PTP had to make to foster a hub-like environment, one quickly gets into a chicken or egg dilemma. Where to begin and which hub ingredient should come first, knowing that each of these would take time to develop? The strategic move that PTP eventually took was focused on generating cargo and ship calls in the shortest possible time, rather than first establishing the essential ingredients of a hub. See Table 9.2 and Figure 9.4 for a sense of the sudden rise in cargo and ship calls.

With hindsight, this approach was the most feasible way for a new port to break into the world of transhipment hubs. The cargo and ship calls would form the chicken and egg that would in turn catalyse and expedite the development of the hub ingredients listed above. For ports which have few of the ingredients to begin with, this might be the only option. The challenge then became one of finding the right strategic partner to bring about the necessary level of cargo and ship calls. If cargo and ship calls were the principal launching pad for hub development, the move by PTP to enter into a partnership with Maersk Sealand as well as with A. P. Moller-Maersk and APM Terminals would be both logical and correct.[5] Other forms of alliance, such as one with a global

Table 9.2: Ship calls and container throughput in the Port of Tanjung Pelepas (TEU), 1999–2004

	1999	2000	2001	2002	2003	2004
Throughput TEU	20,696	423,710	2,049,487	2,668,512	3,487,320	4,020,421
Ship calls	124	1,221	3,388	3,957	6,535	

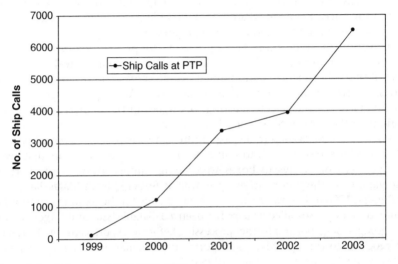

Figure 9.4: Ship calls at PTP, 1999–2004
Source: Table 9.2.

port operator which was strictly in the port business, would not have generated cargo and ship calls as instantaneously. A port-with-port alliance strategy would be one geared towards developing the hub ingredients in order to attract cargo and ship calls. A port–shipping line alliance strategy, on the other hand, would bring cargo and ship calls to bear on the port, necessitating the development of the hub ingredients. The alliance PTP forged with Maersk Sealand and APM Terminals, notwithstanding the actual equity ownership structure which saw APM Terminals taking a 30 per cent equity stake in PTP, is interpreted here as a port–shipping line alliance, given the prominent role of Maersk Sealand in the alliance. This was a demand-driven strategy, while a port-with-port operator alliance would be a supply-driven strategy. Both strategies would have their own risks and uncertainties, but for PTP to have some level of cargo and ship calls to start with, while infrastructures were being developed, would be a lesser risk. This experience provided a framework for future hub development elsewhere.

9.4   A national agenda

Even though a port–shipping line alliance strategy was better at initiating cargo and ship calls than a port–port alliance or a do-it-alone strategy, it served only as a catalyst. Eventually, all the hub ingredients have to be in place and investments made to create these ingredients. Infrastructure development in anticipation of future demand would be very expensive. The owners of PTP, or any private sector organisation, would be hard pressed to make such investments, or even raise the necessary capital on their own given that this was a brand-new port. Any forecast of demand and revenue would be speculative; since the project cost amounted to billions of ringgit, government support was needed.

Government support for PTP – a private sector project – has to be justified on national grounds.[6] The links to national interests could be real or tenuous yet, if properly concocted and framed, would serve as a powerful argument to elicit government support. An important reason for supporting the development of PTP was the perceived leakage of cargoes and containers of Malaysian origin to the Port of Singapore. It has been variously reported that about 65 per cent of Malaysian trade passed through Singapore (*Asia Inc. Magazine*, 1999). When translated into container boxes, PTP could claim that over 30 per cent of Malaysian boxes were being shipped through the Port of Singapore via the Johor causeway as well as feedered from Malaysian ports (*The Star*, 1998a). This was seen as a loss of revenue for the nation even though the extent of the so-called leakage has been a debatable issue and cargoes could be going to Singapore for further processing before re-export. Getting Malaysian cargoes to go through Malaysian ports, in particular, PTP, was viewed as a 'nationalistic mission' (*The Star*, 1998a).

Another argument often heard in industry and government policy-making circles was the desire of Malaysia to promote itself as a maritime and trading nation. Malaysia is a major trading nation, being the thirteenth largest exporter in the world in recent years. The west coast of the Malaysian peninsula is located on a major shipping lane – the Straits of Malacca. To develop ports was therefore a natural thing to do. This argument, of course, applied to any port in Malaysia and not just PTP, but the fact that it could provide a rationale for government support would not have escaped the proponents of PTP, in the same way that it has not been missed by proponents of other ports in the country.

The creation of a transhipment hub was in line with the desire of the nation to develop international logistics businesses and attract global players to set up their logistics operations in Malaysia to serve the region, such as global and regional procurement and distribution centres and regional headquarters. The landside portion of PTP could be developed for this purpose. Being a large-scale project, PTP would be a catalyst for further growth in the southern part of the country and could serve as the southern gateway for international trade.

Under the regime of Prime Minister Mahathir, it had become customary for ambitious undertakings to view themselves as a demonstration of the ability of Malaysian companies and individuals, symbolising the country and people as a whole, to compete and excel internationally, to break into a world hitherto dominated by foreign players. Beginning with a vision and mission to compete internationally was sufficient demonstration of this Malaysian willpower and ability. As a project which could show this so-called 'Malaysia Boleh' (roughly translated as 'Malaysia Can Do It') audacity, PTP warranted government support, especially when its game plan included outperforming Singapore, which has been recognised many times as the best performing port in the world. Whether explicitly stated or not, national ambition and the 'Malaysia Boleh' syndrome provided blessings to proponents of the project when seeking government support.

Privatisation and government support for private sector projects were also in vogue under the Malaysia Inc. concept. The Northport terminal of Port Klang has long been privatised. The development of the Westport terminal of Port Klang was by a new private sector group. Most of the federal ports have already been privatised and received government support, so it was only natural that PTP be given similar treatment. The commitment of the government was substantial. On 24 March 1995, the government and the Johor Port Authority awarded a 66-year concession to Seaport Terminal (Johor) (Seaport) to plan, design, construct, operate and maintain the port (*New Straits Times*, 1998a; *IEM Magazine*, 1999). Seaport also owned Johor Port which was located in Pasir Gudang. During the Asian financial crisis of 1997–8 when PTP was facing financial difficulty, Khazanah Nasional, an investment arm of the government, came to the rescue and invested in PTP[7] (*Malaysian Business*, 1999). The government also encouraged a syndicate of Malaysian banks to provide a RM2 billion loan to the project (Renkema and Kinlan, 2000).

The cost of developing PTP was substantial. Phase one would cost RM2.8 billion (*New Straits Times*, 1998b; *The Star*, 1998b). The development proceeded in phases. Phase one was completed in January 2000, involving the building of six container berths and the dredging of an access channel with a draft of 14 metres that could cater to post-panamax vessels (Renkema and Kinlan, 2000). Before this, the port was opened for a three-month trial run beginning in October 1999 (Baltic Asia-Pacific Shipping, 2003). Altogether, there would be five phases of development till 2020. With the completion of phase one, PTP has a handling capacity of 4.5–5.0 million TEUs per annum.

Phase two involved additional dredging, land reclamation and channel widening and deepening with the plan to add eight berths. As of February 2005, two of the berths in phase two were completed, giving a total of eight linear berths of 360 metres each and a linear quay length of 2.88 km (Port of Tanjung Pelepas website). By then, the port was equipped with 14 super post-panamax quayside cranes with 18 box outreach and 10 with 22 box outreach. The container yard behind the berths has a storage capacity of 110,000 TEUs which is one of the largest in the region. PTP could then handle up to 6 million TEUs a year (see PTP website).

It was public knowledge that the Malaysian government was backing PTP. The Minister of Transport announced that 'the Government has shown its commitment to the port by acquiring an 810 hectare site for its site' (*The Star*, 1999a). The government also built a 6 km stretch of road linking PTP to the North–South Highway and the Second Link Expressway to Singapore (*The Star*, 1998a). The government granted PTP free-zone status which allowed it to develop its 161 hectares of land reserve for district park and logistics activities, such as warehousing, international procurement and regional distribution[8] (Baltic Asia-Pacific Shipping, 2003). The government would also support, through the national rail company, Keretapi Tanah Melayu Berhad (KTMB), the construction of a 30.5 km rail link from PTP to Kempas to connect to the national rail network at an estimated cost of RM476 million (*The Star*, 1999b; *Straits Shipper*, 1997). With this, PTP would be connected to the national rail network which served the peninsula and all the way to Thailand. The rail connection would effectively help to enlarge the land-based hinterland for PTP, putting it on a par with Penang port and Port Klang which were also connected by rail to the same hinterland.

Other forms of government support included public endorsements of the project and periodic pronouncements in the media encouraging Malaysian industries and ports to support PTP. The then Prime Minister, Datuk Seri Dr Mahathir Mohamad, who officially opened the port on 13 March 2000, publicly urged local manufacturers to use PTP. Espousing the national agenda of PTP and the support it deserved, he declared that 'the people of Malaysia owned the Port of Tanjung Pelepas directly or indirectly as they would be the ones who would enjoy the spin-offs from the port's successful operations' (Bernama Online, 13 March 2000). In the same media report, the Prime Minister reiterated that 'in the government's commitment to ensure the port's success, it had spent more than RM100 million to build roads and about RM600 million to construct railway lines' (Bernama Online, 13 March 2000). The government has also helped to allay anxieties by reassuring port operators that PTP was not in violation of the National Load Centre policy which favoured Port Klang as the focal point for transhipment of cargo feedered from other Malaysian ports. PTP also received the support and approval of the regulator authority, the Ministry of Transport, to establish a competitive and attractive tariff structure which, in the words of the Minister, 'can draw international lines' (*Business Times*, 1999). Even Tenaga Nasional Berhad, the national electricity supplier and a government-linked company, assured PTP of uninterrupted supply (*Shipping Times*, 29 October 1999). In January 2001, the Ministry of Finance removed a levy on container trucks bringing containers from the Port of Tanjung Pelepas to Singapore and vice versa, to encourage Singapore exporters and importers to go through PTP (Dow Jones, 2001; *Fairplay*, 2001). This would help truck operators to save RM200 per trip which was the cost of the levy, and this tax exemption was for PTP only and not any other Malaysian port. The support given to PTP, a private sector project, was all but comprehensive.

9.5   Confounding or complementing national port policy

The surrealistic national status of PTP confounded existing national port strategies and policies, in particular, the policy of designating Port Klang as the National Load Centre. The National Load Centre policy was intended to help Port Klang develop itself into a major regional hub and transhipment port as well as ensuring that Malaysian cargo did not divert to ports in neighbouring countries. The process could hardly be considered complete when PTP came into the picture. Regional transhipment was only picking up in Port Klang, and the port still had a long way to go, although it was making steady progress. Whether intended or not, creating PTP would require a readjustment of national policy. However much one would like to deny it, PTP would compete with Port Klang, not only for regional cargo, but eventually national cargo also.

The endeavours of PTP not only challenged the status of Port Klang as the premier national port but upset the national framework that there should be a hierarchy of ports in the country (see Figure 9.5) This has been more or less the operating framework accepted by policy-makers, planners, port authorities and industry players. Perhaps it was time to review the national policy itself and related national port strategies. Since the emergence of PTP, policy-makers, planners and government think-tanks have been toiling with how to accommodate PTP within the National Load Centre framework. It would not be acceptable to forsake Port Klang. After all, Port Klang has proven its own worth by achieving steady growth in throughput over the years.

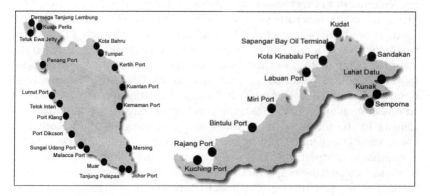

Figure 9.5:   Location of Malaysian ports
Source: http://www.portsworld.com/main/ports.htm.

Officially, Port Klang consisted of three entities – Northport, Southport and Westport. Westport itself was privatised around the same time as PTP. At times, Westport competed with Northport. Northport was itself a successful case of privatisation and was owned by a national investment company called Perbadanan Nasional Berhad (PNB). Administratively, the three ports formed Port Klang. The premier status of Port Klang in the hierarchy of ports in the country can be appreciated from its share of total national cargo (Table 9.3). From 1995 to 2003, container throughput at Port Klang grew from slightly more than 1 million TEUs to about 4.8 million TEUs, achieving an average annual growth rate of 20 per cent. In terms of the share of total container traffic for the country, the share of Port Klang increased from 53 per cent in 1995 to 61 per cent in 2000 when PTP came on stream (Table 9.4). The share of Johor port was steady whereas Penang port experienced a decline, in part due to the diversion of traffic to Port Klang in accordance with the National Load Centre policy. It can also be seen from Table 9.5 that more ships had called on Port Klang than any of the other major ports.

As of 2000, Port Klang was clearly the premier port, unrivalled by any other port in the nation. In world ranking, Port Klang moved from 57th position in 1980 to 35th in 1990 and 12th in 2003 (News & Ripples Statistics, undated). Port Klang has become a major world port, situated on the major shipping lane for east–west trade. Although its cargo came largely from the Malaysian hinterland, Port Klang also has a sizeable transhipment cargo and was connected to about 500 ports worldwide (Wong, 2002). Transhipment traffic has grown steadily and cargo has been coming from as far away as ports in the Bay of Bengal. By 2002, Port Klang could claim that 50 per cent of its cargo was transhipment cargo (Wong, 2002). Yet, PTP was challenging its national status. After PTP began operation in late 1999 and early 2000, Port Klang continued to grow and deserved recognition as the principal national port, but its share of total national traffic began to drop drastically (Table 9.4). The phenomenal rise of PTP was obviously not due to traffic being diverted from Port Klang, at least in these early years. It would also be naive to think that the PTP traffic could have been captured by Port Klang in its absence. PTP grew in parallel with Port Klang, but as its share of total national traffic reached the alarming figure of 34 per cent in 2003 and the share of Port Klang dropped to 47 per cent, its performance could not but challenge the National Load Centre policy which singled out Port Klang as the national port of choice. Port administration might have to face the possibility of having two National Load Centres in the future – which would be a confusing situation. Both Port Klang and PTP expanded, adding berths and, in the case of Port Klang, added a terminal in Westport which began operations in 1996. Both invested in facilities and increased their capacities, especially to service larger vessels, with Port Klang having a far larger capacity than PTP. In 2003, Port Klang had 13 berths totalling about 3.8 km compared to 6 berths and 2.16 km in PTP. As Table 9.3 shows, both ports experienced healthy growth in throughput throughout

Table 9.3: Throughput in major Malaysian ports, 1995–2003 (TEUs)

	1995	1996	1997	1998	1999	2000	2001	2002	2003	Average annual growth rate (1995–2003)
Port Klang	1,133,811	1,409,594	1,684,508	1,820,018	2,550,419	3,206,753	3,759,512	4,533,212	4,841,235	19.9%
Johor port	302,898	377,890	429,448	439,661	558,056	659,181	638,718	683,816	750,466	12.0%
PTP	0	0	0	0	20,696	423,710	2,049,487	2,668,512	3,487,320	260.3%
Penang port	433,474	454,765	506,863	510,307	566,409	635,780	604,294	634,042	688,171	5.9%
Other ports	265,301	322,056	393,678	294,085	305,131	356,782	453,627	540,740	456,546	7.0%
National total for all ports (TEUs)	2,135,484	2,564,305	3,014,497	3,064,071	4,000,711	5,282,206	7,506,638	9,060,322	10,223,738	21.6%

Source: Data collected from port authorities in Malaysia.

Table 9.4: Percentage share of national total container throughput by major Malaysian ports, 1995–2003 (TEUs)

	1995	1996	1997	1998	1999	2000	2001	2002	2003
Port Klang	53.1	55.0	55.9	59.4	63.7	60.7	50.1	50.0	47.4
Johor port	14.2	14.7	14.2	14.3	13.9	12.5	8.5	7.5	7.3
PTP	0.0	0.0	0.0	0.0	0.5	8.0	27.3	29.5	34.1
Penang port	20.3	17.7	16.8	16.7	14.2	12.0	8.1	7.0	6.7
Other ports	12.4	12.6	13.1	9.6	7.6	6.8	6.0	6.0	4.5
National total for all ports (TEUs)	100.0	100.0	100.0	100.0	100.0	100.0	100.0	100.0	100.0

Source: Computed from Table 9.3.

Table 9.5: Total number of ships calling by ports, Malaysia, 1994–2003

	1994	1995	1996	1997	1998	1999	2000	2001	2002	2003
Port Klang	7,286	7,870	9,533	10,984	10,764	11,439	12,416	14,207	15,313	16,251
Penang port	6,219	6,465	6,556	7,071	8,166	7,341	7,263	8,906	7,328	6,419
Johor port	4,138	5,481	5,887	6,089	6,051	6,001	6,485	6,242	6,631	6,877
Kuantan port	1,324	1,357	1,536	1,643	1,419	1,516	1,677	1,855	2,067	2,280
Port of Tanjung Pelepas	–	–	–	–	–	124	1,221	3,388	3,957	6,535
National total	45,418	50,053	57,156	59,214	51,183	51,003	53,224	57,985	60,064	65,973

Source: Data collected from port authorities in Malaysia.

the late 1990s till 2005. The government directed that Port Klang be the National Load Centre as early as 1993, seven years before PTP started operation. The support given to Port Klang was clearly outlined in the Seventh Malaysia Plan (1996–2000).

> More concerted efforts will be undertaken to promote Port Klang as a hub port. Cargo from all other Malaysian ports which act as feeder ports will be consolidated where possible through Port Klang where shipping services are more frequent and expedient. In this regard, close linkages with regional ports, as well as those ports in Sabah and Sarawak, will be established through the provision of feeder services at competitive rates. In addition, the supply of efficient support facilities and the gazetting of a free commercial zone at West Port of Port Klang will be implemented. Other promotional strategies to enhance the attractiveness of Port Klang as a transhipment centre, such as rebates, tariff restructuring, maximum back-up equipment facilities, volume discounts as well as allowing foreign equity participation in the Terminal Dedicated Berth Scheme, will be considered. (Government of Malaysia, 1996: 372)

Following this, the government also relaxed its cabotage policy to allow international main lines to carry cargo from Malaysian ports, especially Penang port, to Port Klang. With such commitment given to Port Klang, port authorities and the Ministry of Transport have to find ways to reconcile the National Load Centre policy with the strategy of PTP to become a transhipment hub. The Ministry of Transport went to the extent of commissioning a study to find ways to resolve the dilemma (*New Straits Times*, 2001).

The administrative quagmire has only produced innocuous statements from the Ministry and port authorities which helped to make the authorities appear fair and neutral, and supportive of both ports, but giving no real policy solutions. There were talks that competition for shipping lines and cargo between Port Klang and PTP was a sort of sibling rivalry, that the two could complement each other. Little has been spelt out regarding the nature of the complementarity. Another view, which was more convincing, was that the two ports could play separate roles: one as a National Load Centre and the other as a regional transhipment hub (*The Star Maritime*, 2001). The two could somehow segment the markets and, therefore, avoid competing directly with one another. National hinterland cargo would go through Port Klang while cargo from the region would go through PTP. Such views in the end were intended more to appease national policy than face reality.

PTP, however, dared to admit that business decisions of shipping lines and cargo owners were often beyond the control of ports, and ports have to go by the realities of market competition. Its executive vice chairman, Datuk Mohd Taufik Abdullah, could not rule out 'the possibility that some main line operators (MLOs) which are calling at Port Klang may decide to move to PTP'

(*The Star*, 1998a). In the same media report, he noted that the first target of PTP was the regional transhipment market, hence, entering into a head-on competition with Singapore. Besides this, PTP would focus on attracting Malaysian cargos which were still using Singapore, especially those from Sabah and Sarawak. Having achieved these targets, Datuk Mohd Taufik noted that 'we cannot turn away containers which are feedered to existing ports with direct calls', obviously referring to traffic hitherto going to Port Klang. 'These are the ones we cannot control as we cannot say no to them.'

9.6   Port administration and its limitations

In order to understand the difficulty of co-ordinating and regulating cargo flow through Malaysian ports, especially in trying to avoid competition between Malaysian ports and make them complement one another, one has to look at the system of port administration and the orientation of the various port authorities, as well as the bases of decision-making of shippers, transporters of all modes, and shipping lines. Port administration in Malaysia has evolved over the years into a decentralised structure yet retaining sufficient mechanisms for centralised co-ordination and control (see Figure 9.6). The various local port authorities regulated their respective ports and were collectively linked to the highest level of decision-making in the Ministry, namely the Secretary-General and Minister. For example, Penang port was under the Penang Port Commission, Port Klang was under the Port Klang Authority, and Johor port and the Port of Tanjung Pelepas were under the Johor Port Authority, but they all reported to the highest level of decision-making in the Ministry. The task of co-ordinating port strategies to meet national objectives would therefore be done at the highest level in the Ministry under this organisational structure.

Under this decentralised and dispersed structure, the respective port authorities would be trying as much as possible to carry out their regulatory functions in accordance with national policies and guidelines. To this end, the various port authorities would try to influence the ports under them to abide by the National Load Centre policy. However, besides regulating their respective ports, the port authorities would also play a role in promoting the ports under their jurisdiction, such as attracting cargo and ship calls to their ports. Each port authority would want cargo from its immediate industrial hinterland to go through its port. This dual role of the local port authorities – promotion of the port under its jurisdiction and regulating it to meet national policy objectives – made it difficult for them to be fully dedicated to co-ordinating and directing traffic to the National Load Centre port. When it came to port survival and revenue generation, for instance, a particular local port authority might not be so insistent that traffic had to be feedered to Port Klang, especially if feedering would mean losing the shipment entirely. The Penang Port Commission, for instance, would not be entirely happy with the National Load Centre policy as it also would want to promote the transhipment business of Penang

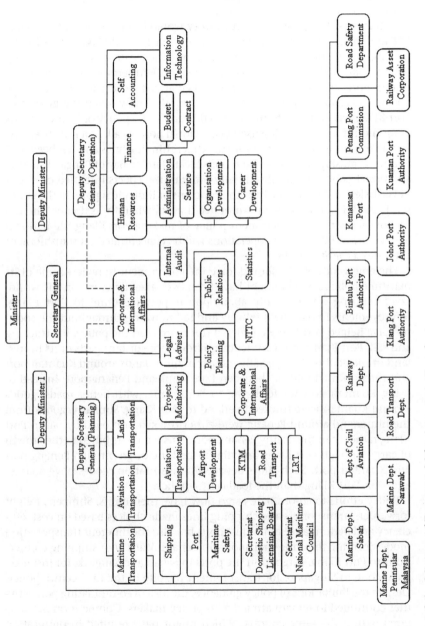

Figure 9.6: Ministry of Transport, Malaysia: organisation chart

port. When the performance of ports and their respective port authorities was measured in terms of cargo throughput it would be difficult for port authorities not to want to favour their own ports.

In this regard, the Johor Port Authority would be encumbered to support PTP and Johor port. Likewise, Port Klang Authority would favour Port Klang, leading to difficulty in co-ordination despite the existence of co-ordinating mechanisms within the Ministry of Transport. Furthermore, with privatisation of ports and liberalisation of port regulations, ports were freer to make business decisions. In this context, one wonders how much the growth of Port Klang has been due to the National Load Centre policy or its own efforts of promoting and marketing itself as a regional port of call. As a private entity, Port Klang has invested in facilities to attract shipping lines and has been able to attract transhipment cargo from ports located in the Bay of Bengal. Whether a national policy could substantially produce the effects intended or not, it nevertheless weighed heavily in the concerns of individual ports in the country. Even PTP had to publicly announce that for what it was doing: 'There is no conflict with the Government policy of making Port Klang the national load centre as 80% of PTP's operations will be concentrated on transhipment activities' (*The Star*, 1998a).

The emergence of PTP should force the government to review some of its maritime policies which might have been overtaken by events in the world. Load centring was not only about port-to-port feedering to Port Klang. Improvements in national highway and rail networks throughout the country have helped Port Klang equally, if not more than the policy. Via trucking and rail, Port Klang could attract cargo from more distant parts of its hinterland in the peninsula, especially industrial hinterlands around Kuantan port and those located midway between Port Klang and Penang port; instead of using Kuantan port for feedering to Port Klang, with better roads, goods around Kuantan were trucked overland to Port Klang. Similarly, goods from the hinterland around Penang were either trucked or moved by rail to Port Klang rather than the nearby Penang port. This has contributed to the growth of cargo through Port Klang and diminished the cargo through Penang port and Kuantan port. Such shifts between transportation modes have a larger effect on Port Klang than the load centre policy.

Policy efforts to co-ordinate cargo flow have their limits. Shippers, freight forwarders, transporters and shipping lines made choices based on cost, efficiency and performance of not just ports but also the different transportation modes forming the entire transportation chain. With poor shipping connections to Port Klang, cargo from the ports in Sabah and Sarawak, for instance, have gone to Singapore for transhipment in spite of the load centre policy. Despite the limitations of policy guidance, the idea of co-ordinating port activities continued to remain attractive to policy-makers. Competition between ports within the same country, which might have resulted in duplication of investments, tariff discounts which could have been avoided, and low profits, were viewed as a blight and a burden to the country. Complementing one another was the preferred framework, besides being a mark of national unity for policy-makers who were looking at things from a national holistic perspective. The National Load Centre policy was one of complementarity.

So off and on the government toyed with the idea of setting up a centralised national port authority to improve co-ordination. In February 2004, the Minister of Transport announced that: 'All the seven federal ports and 27 smaller ports in peninsular Malaysia will be under the jurisdiction of the proposed Malaysia Ports Commission once it is approved by the Parliament' (*The Star*, 20 February 2004).[9] However, the above analysis shows that the setting up of such a central commission should be undertaken with caution as there was a limitation on the ability of policies to co-ordinate cargo flow between ports. The various local port authorities have played a vital role in promoting their respective ports, and putting this role in the hands of a centralised authority would remove the element of competition that has driven the individual port authorities.

The dispersed form of port administration has its merits. It allowed individual ports to innovate based on their own situations. One needs to wonder if the idea of a brand-new PTP would ever have materialised had there been a centralised port commission deciding on investments and port strategies. The effort to co-ordinate port activities would have leaned towards conservatism, thus curtailing innovations. A central port commission would be more appropriate if the objective was to rationalise existing port investments in a mature setting, but for a developing country embarking on development projects, what was needed was an administrative structure which allowed for innovations and local initiatives. PTP as an innovative idea seemed to have worked under a decentralised administrative structure, albeit receiving substantial help from the central government.

9.7   The transhipment strategy of PTP

Given the limitations in what a government can do to assist port development using policy instruments, much of the development of PTP, and Port Klang, for that matter, has to depend on their own strategies and undertakings. Government policies can only facilitate and remove administrative obstacles hindering the strategies chosen by the ports. Privatisation of ports helped in both cases. It is interesting therefore to look at the strategy taken by PTP – why it chose the strategy and how it went about realising it.

The decision to turn PTP into a transhipment hub port was made while it was being constructed in the late 1990s. When Johor port was privatised to Seaport Terminal in 1995 the proposal included the building of a brand-new port and not just an expansion of the existing facilities at Pasir Gudang. It was estimated very early on that the land area around Pasir Gudang would not be sufficient to cater for future growth in cargo traffic through Johor port and it would encounter capacity problems by 2000. Another port in another location had to complement the existing Johor port at Pasir Gudang. The site for PTP would be at the estuary of the Pulai River close to the Second Crossing Expressway to Singapore (Renkema and Kinlan, 2000). The original concept, however, was a gateway port to serve the southern hinterland on the peninsula. Converting a gateway port to a regional transhipment port was a radical change in strategy, driven by circumstances which were probably not envisaged in 1995.

As PTP was undergoing construction at the mouth of the Pulai River, the transhipment strategy began to take root and eventually constituted its sole preoccupation.[10] Proponents of the PTP project began to realise that the port could not survive merely as an extension of Pasir Gudang. It was too close to Singapore, being only 2 kilometres away, and would be easily overshadowed by the second busiest container port in the world. In order to compete, it had to be of significant size and have a stature that could be compared to Singapore. The Johor hinterland was too small and limited to support a global port. The only way was for it to be a regional transhipment port serving cargo of the region. To be a regional transhipment port, it has to be of a reasonable size and equipped with modern equipment and facilities (*The Star*, 1999c). Equipped with state-of-the-art facilities, it might be able to attract mainline operators.

It was a decision which required heavy investment and financing. Being a green-field port helped as it was free to explore opportunities which would not be possible for old ports. Ultimately, the strength of PTP, which had no track record whatsoever, was its great strategic geographical location on the Straits of Malacca. About half of the world's merchant fleet capacity passes through the Straits of Malacca annually (Noer, 1996).[11] Being next door to Singapore meant that its location, from the perspective of international shipping, could not be wrong. PTP could literally see the ships sailing into Singapore. But being next door to Singapore also meant that it had to be of equal standing to be taken seriously by international shipping lines. Finally, PTP was assured of government backing.[12] Financial support from the government was forthcoming, especially during the period of the Asian financial crisis of 1997/8. With this, PTP could embark on its transhipment strategy and attempt to capture some of the business which had been the monopoly of the Port of Singapore. The strategy became one of both emulating Singapore and being an alternative to it.

At the same time, increases in ship size and the push for greater economies of scale would result in more hub-and-spoke operations, especially by the dominant shipping lines (see UNESCAP, 2001). These shipping lines would be looking for suitable ports to carry out their hub-and-spoke transhipment operations. The increase in vessel size could lead to either a greater concentration of transhipment in a small number of existing hubs or an increase in the number of hubs on existing mainline routes. The latter trend would favour PTP. Mainline operators and alliances which have their own feeder networks might be inclined to seek new green-field hubs to improve operations, hence producing a more fragmented system. Given the scenario of greater transhipment, PTP would not be hard-pressed to find a partner for its strategy. Wooing the right partner, however, was not an easy matter. It had to be done quietly, without stirring the giant next door. Already, the fast-paced construction of PTP had evoked quick responses from Singapore. Singapore made some pre-emptive moves to tighten its control over shipping lines, setting stringent contractual terms which were meant to forestall any possible switch over to PTP when the port came on stream in 2000.[13] Unfortunately, tightening the noose on its customers did not quite work, especially for large shipping lines, when PTP was appearing on the horizon with offers which were more flexible and less costly. Pulling in the rope too tightly ended up snapping it. PTP capitalised on the push factors.

According to Mohd Sidik of PTP:

> We offer a flexibility in how our users wish to do business in our premises. We offer them various options – they may want to operate the terminal on their own, hire a third party international operator or use us. This is because we are new and we can customise to their needs very early. (*The Star*, 1999c)

Eventually, PTP found a partner in Maersk Sealand, which became a highly publicised event. Initially, PTP approached Hutchison Port Holdings (HPH), a leading global port operator to be a partner (see Table 9.6).[14] The pursuit did not succeed. By then, PTP had also come to realise that an alliance with a global port operator would not suit its strategy to be a major transhipment

Table 9.6:   Market share of global port operators, 2001

Operator	Estimated TEU (m)	Share (%)
Hutchison Port Holdings	27	11
PSA Corp	19	7.7
APM Terminals	16	6.5
P&O Ports/P&ONL	9.8	4.0
Eurogate	8.6	3.5
DPA	4.7	1.9
MTL	4.3	1.8
NOL/APL	4.2	1.7
SSA	3.9	1.6
Cosco	3.9	1.6
Other carriers	24.9	10.2
Other private/public facilities	118.4	48.4
Total	235.1	100.0

Source: Fossey (2002).

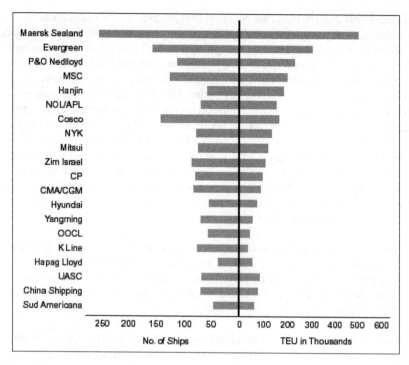

Figure 9.7:   Top 20 container carriers (as at September 1999)
Source: *Containerization International* (1999) (quoted in World Bank, 2002).

hub. Choosing a global port operator as partner would be more appropriate for gateway ports with existing hinterland cargo which needed an injection of efficiency in the management and operations. PTP needed to generate cargo and ship calls as much as ensuring port efficiency.[15] It needed to partner with a major shipping line to jump-start. Maersk Sealand, together with its sister company, A. P. Moller, provided the best option for PTP. At the time, Maersk Sealand was the biggest container shipping line, having the largest fleet in the world (Figure 9.7).

The pursuit of mainline operators (MLOs) was carried out as the port was being constructed. This latter culminated in a full-blown transhipment strategy. PTP did not concentrate its efforts on developing and attracting hinterland base cargo which would have been a gateway port strategy. The transhipment strategy was a conscious decision made even before the port was ready. In 1990, Mohd Sidik of PTP declared that:

> The focus until the port begins operations is on marketing efforts in both the overseas and local markets. Our plans here are largely to attract Main Line Operators (MLOs) and we are confident of success. (*The Star*, 1999c)

The transhipment strategy focusing on attracting MLOs which in turn would bring cargo to PTP required building facilities that suited the needs of such shipping lines. It made sense that marketing and negotiations with MLOs took place during construction. Words and promises were not enough though. MLOs needed to be convinced. There was a period of trial runs in late 1999 before the port officially opened in 2000. During this time, MLOs began testing the port, and this must have stirred concerns in Singapore.

The first mother vessel to call at PTP on 22 October 1999 was the 4,000 TEU Maersk Sealand line ship, *Maersk Munkebo* (*New Straits Times*, 1999). Maersk Sealand continued to make calls at PTP throughout the trial-run period. By December 1999, Maersk Sealand had made it public that it would consider investing in PTP (*Shipping Times Singapore Online*, 1999). At the same time, Maersk Sealand was negotiating with Singapore and weighing the offerings of PTP against that of Singapore.[16] Maersk Sealand wanted to operate its own dedicated terminals in the Port of Singapore which was not acceptable to the Port of Singapore Authority (PSA) (*Straits Times Singapore*, 2000). Evaluation of PTP went on throughout the trial period as more Maersk Sealand ships moored at PTP. On 4 January 2000, the world's then-largest vessel, the 6,600 TEU *Skagen Maersk*, with a length of 347 metres and draft of 15 metres, called at PTP (*The Sun*, 2000). Maersk Sealand was not only testing its mainline strings but also feeder vessel strings at PTP. Six months after the October maiden call at PTP, Maersk Sealand was more convinced yet still undecided. It was reported in May 2000 that:

'We have tested the port and found it to be in good working condition in terms of water depth, berth length and productivity ratios,' said a Maersk Sealand official. 'We are certainly looking at alternatives to Singapore but have made no definite decisions on whether to call at the port or on what strings.' (*Liner Shipping Network*, 2000a)

In June 2000, the wait was over, the pursuit of Maersk Sealand accomplished. Maersk Sealand signed a long-term user contract to make regular weekly calls at PTP for its mainline services to and from the United States, Northern Europe and the Middle East (*Lloyd's List Maritime Asia*, 2005; *Liner Shipping Network*, 2000b). Maersk Sealand would take a 30 per cent stake in PTP and move all its line-haul services over from Singapore. It would also move its operations in Westport to PTP, suggesting consolidation of its Southeast Asian operations at PTP.

Throughout 2000, the single-minded quest for MLOs bore fruit for PTP. PTP secured Japan's Mitsui OSK Line in April 2000. This was followed by Maersk Sealand, Yang Ming Line and its feeder service, Advanced Container Lines, as well as APL which was owned by Singapore's national carrier, Neptune Orient Lines (NOL). NOL-APL was one of the biggest customers of the Port of Singapore.[17] Others which called at PTP included the Japanese carrier,

K-Line, and Hub Line which was a feeder service. More importantly, in 2002, PTP struck mother load again, successfully enticing Taiwan's Evergreen Marine Corp., the second largest container shipping line in the world, away from Singapore to PTP, bringing with it about 1.2 million TEUs a year[18] (*Fairplay Shipping Weekly*, 2002).

The strategy of pursuing MLOs had paid off. According to Datuk Mohd Sidik, PTP first targeted shipping lines which were not part of alliances.[19] Approaching alliance lines was more difficult as negotiations have to be done quietly with each shipping line in the alliance. It would be difficult to maintain secrecy in the negotiations. Shipping lines would also need the agreement of others in the alliance to enter into contracts with PTP. Unable to negotiate quietly meant that it would be easier for the Port of Singapore to pre-empt overtures to alliance lines, which it did.

The increase in ship calls to PTP happened without any significant change in the volume of domestic base cargo.[20] In 2004, PTP recorded a throughput of 4.02 million TEUs (PTP's website, http://www.ptp.com.my/). About 96 per cent of the cargo was transhipment cargo (*New Straits Times*, 2005). By then, it had exceeded its initial modest target of achieving 10 per cent of Singapore's annual throughput. PTP had to continue to expand its infrastructure as the first phase facilities could only accommodate 3.8 million TEUs. It added two berths and additional cranes.

By and large, PTP embarked on a demand-driven strategy. The first-phase facilities were fully utilised in a fairly short time. Later facilities were added in pace with growth in demand. Perhaps the shipping business cycle was working in favour of PTP. Constructing the port at the time of the Asian financial crisis of 1997/8 helped to trim excesses. Construction was also cheaper and faster as contractors had fewer jobs in the region. By the time the port was complete, the Asian economy had revived and international trade was on the upswing. Even the Port of Singapore experienced increases in throughput after 2001 despite losing Maersk Sealand and Evergreen to PTP.

PTP built on its success in securing major lines, almost one at a time. Passing the tests of the major lines during the trial period was absolutely crucial. Success bred further success, and reaffirmed PTP's strategy of pursuing MLOs. It was more than just skilful negotiations. It involved knowing what the MLOs wanted and going all out to satisfy their needs. Ironically, this strategy of offering what investors wanted has all along been the essence of Singapore's Economic Development Board investment promotion strategy. PSA went against this time-honoured strategy and instead tried to tighten its hold on its customers, with the effect of sending them across the straits to PTP. At the time of economic crisis, the Malaysian government had to be liberal on foreign investments and went along with the tide of liberalisation of port ownership that was going on in most of Southeast Asia, except Singapore. PSA, of course, was a world player and cash rich, and so did not need any foreign help. The ports of Laem Chabang and Jakarta were attracting foreign investments and equity ownership of their terminals. P&O and HPH invested in Laem Chabang and HPH in Jakarta. PTP was not doing anything different. HPH was also investing in Westport with government approval around the same time. Selling a stake of PTP to APM Terminals to secure Maersk Sealand would not be objected to by the Malaysian government. In return, Maersk Sealand got what it could not get from PSA.

9.8 Following up on the transhipment strategy

The challenge has not ended for PTP after securing Maersk Sealand, Evergreen and other lines. In the early period, especially the trial runs, shipping lines were using PTP for repositioning empty containers for the region. Though there was revenue in empties, the port has to progress to handling laden containers. The reliance on transhipping empties was risky as shipping lines have increasingly sent their empties to ports in China given the demand there. After transhipping empties, mainlines would naturally bring laden containers for transhipment at PTP as connectivity to more ports in the region increased and more feeder vessels called on PTP. This, however, did not mean that PTP could sit and wait for things to develop naturally. Another way to generate laden container traffic was to have greater economic activities in the immediate hinterland of PTP. In particular, PTP was able to link its sea freight operations to air freight after the port received an airport code from the International Air Transport Association (IATA) (*Business Times*, 2003).

With the IATA code, documentation was reduced, and cargo offloaded from ships at PTP could be immediately trucked to the Kuala Lumpur International Airport (KLIA) to be air-freighted to final destinations. MASKargo, the air cargo division of Malaysian Airlines (MAS), which has been a pioneer in promoting this sea-air intermodal concept, was able to help bring cargo to PTP for sea-air moves. This sea-air intermodal move could reduce the journey time from the Far East to Europe from three weeks to four days (*The Star*, 2003). With the acquisition of Senai Airport in Johor by PTP's affiliate company, Senai Airport Terminal Services (SATS), PTP gained more ground to attract companies involved in intermodal operations. As with its transhipment strategy, the approach was to woo companies which would bring in the air cargo, rather than pursuing the cargo. Likewise SATS would go after air cargo operators, especially integrators, to establish or relocate their regional operations in Senai Airport. It still remained to be seen whether SATS could emulate the success of PTP in securing major air cargo operators.

Another activity which also remained to be seen was whether PTP could attract value-adding activities to its distri-park. Ideally, a fully-fledged transhipment hub would have the whole range of value-adding activities, from transportation to logistics, assembling, processing, manufacturing etc., as found in Singapore, Dubai and Rotterdam, for example. Pursuing companies involved in these would require more resources out of PTP. At the time of this research, PTP remained fairly focused, concentrating on attracting shipping lines, regional distribution companies, and air cargo operators, as parts of a moderately expanded transhipment port strategy.

9.9   Conclusion

This chapter has examined the transhipment strategy of the Port of Tanjung Pelepas and showed why it was conceived and how it developed. The core of the strategy lay in forging a port–shipping line alliance to bring in cargo and ship calls. PTP was highly focused in its quest for mainline operators until it managed to secure Maersk Sealand and Evergreen. It was also a demand-driven strategy, especially after the first phase of port construction. Facilities were added to with increases in transhipment activities. Getting shipping lines was not easy and did not simply rest on promises. The port was tested by the shipping lines over a trial-run period of close to nine months. Customers have to be convinced, and only success could breed further successes.

The support of the national government was crucial. Fortunately, the strategy of PTP squared nicely with national ambitions. Yet, it still has to be reconciled with existing national port policy and strategies, in particular, the National Load Centre policy which has favoured another port. This chapter also showed that PTP could forge ahead with its transhipment strategy even though it was never fully reconciled with the national policy. Under the current form of port administration in Malaysia, it would be difficult to reconcile the National Load Centre policy with PTP's strategy. Creating a centralised port administration to co-ordinate the activities of ports in the country would not work. It would end up smothering the efforts of local port authorities to assist their own ports. Making port authorities compete with one another would be a better policy approach than amalgamating all under one roof.

Privatisation and foreign participation in the PTP project helped. It would be impossible for a local port authority to have done it on its own, especially in a global environment of stiff competition and greater bargaining power of shipping lines vis-à-vis ports. In this regard, it is important to be flexible and offer as much as possible of what the strategic partners want to get for their business. It is to be hoped that the transhipment strategy of PTP can provide some useful lessons to national governments, port authorities and port operators on how to successfully develop and promote new ports and revamp old ones. Success and failure depends a great deal on the strategy chosen, and the right strategy is about understanding global trends in shipping and port development and not bucking these trends.

There are many scholars who have looked at competition and co-operation between ports located close to one another. See, for example, Barzdukas et al. (2000) on the ports of Tacoma and Seattle, Kleywegt et al. (2000) on the ports of Singapore and Malaysia, and Wang and Slack (2000) on the Pearl River Delta ports. Scholars recognised that amidst the competition ports are interdependent of one another. This study shows that in order for a port to survive and be an active part of a regional system of ports, it has to compete aggressively for cargo and ship calls. It would be difficult for ports to co-operate fully, even within the same country, let alone if they belong to two separate countries, as in the case of PTP and the Port of Singapore.

Notes

1. See Renkema and Kinlan (2000).
2. UNESCAP (2001).
3. The summary of these trends is derived from an earlier study by the author as part of the National Transport Policy Study presented to the National Economic Action Council of the Government of Malaysia and supplemented by more current thoughts on the topic culled from a large number of printed as well as internet sources.
4. Some of the factors listed here which contribute to the success of hub ports have been compiled in an earlier study by the author and presented as part of the National Transport Policy Study submitted to the National Economic Action Council of the Government of Malaysia.
5. The partnership with Maersk Sealand was further reinforced by the sister company of Maersk Sealand, APM Terminals, owning a stake in PTP. APM Terminals was a leading global port operator. Maersk Sealand and APM Terminals are part of the A. P. Moller-Maersk Group of companies. PTP's link to APM Terminals is highly visible on the websites of APM Terminals, suggesting close co-operation between PTP and APM Terminals.
6. In discussions the author had with industry experts, government officials and consultants, PTP has invariably been assessed on national terms. The debates concerning the extent of government involvement in PTP were about its cost and contributions to the nation. It was certainly thought of, and deliberated upon, as a national endeavour.
7. Later Khazanah Nasional sold off its stake when the economy recovered and when PTP found a new partner in APM Terminals. Khazanah Nasional made a profit off this investment. (Information provided by Datuk Mohd Sidik, CEO of PTP, in an interview, 7 March 2005.)
8. The exact size of the land available varied from time to time as more land was being acquired throughout its development.
9. The details of the responsibilities of this Port Commission were not available.
10. The information on the development of the transhipment strategy was largely provided by Datuk Mohd Sidik, CEO of PTP, through an interview on 7 March 2005.
11. The importance of the Straits of Malacca to shipping could be seen from the number of periodic conferences held to discuss its importance. See for example, Lim, Teck Ee, Deputy Director (Policy), Maritime Authority, Singapore (undated), 'Straits of Malacca and Singapore: Past, Present and Future Cooperation'; retrieved 16 March 2005, from http://www.mima.gov.my/mima/htmls/conferences/som04/papers/lim.pdf.
12. At a time when the relationship between the Malaysian and Singapore governments was at a low point, embarking on a strategy which competed directly with Singapore would naturally receive Malaysian government blessing if not direct support.
13. Datuk Mohd Sidik, the CEO of PTP, provided some of the information regarding the competition between Singapore and PTP for mainline operators through an interview on 7 March 2005.

14. Information provided by Datuk Mohd Sidik.
15. HPH eventually invested in Westport.
16. The author understood from industry sources that such multiple negotiations between shipping lines and ports were routine.
17. Information on the customers of PTP can be obtained from PTP's website.
18. The possibility of switching to PTP had been in the news in 2001 when Evergreen was negotiating with PSA on its terminal usage in the Port of Singapore (*Shipping Times*, 2001).
19. Interview with Datuk Mohd Sidik, the CEO of PTP, on 7 March 2005.
20. In this regard, PTP is radically different from the Port of Shenzhen or Shanghai.

References

Asia Inc. Magazine (1999) 'Straits of Excitement', 1 May.

Baltic Asia-Pacific Shipping (2003) http://www.stroudgate.net/aps/articles/053.html).

Barzdukas, D., Devore, J., Gamble, H. and Kopp, J. (2000) *Competition and Cooperation as Trade Policy: Past Lessons and Future Opportunities for the Port of Tacoma and Port of Seattle*, Nan Huai Chin Scholarship and University of Washington Global Trade, Transportation, and Logistics Studies. Available from: <http://depts.washington.edu/gttl/StudentPapersAbstracts/2000/port.competition.trade.policy.pdf>.

Bernama Online (2000) 'Dr M: Port of Tanjung Pelepas will be a Catalyst for Economic Growth', 13 March.

Business Times (1999) 'Ministry to Study Proposed Tariffs by Tg Pelepas Port', 31 July.

Business Times (2003) 'PTP Scores a First with Airport Status Fiven by IATA', 27 May.

Dow Jones (2001) 'Malaysia's MOF: No Tax on Singapore Container Trucks', 16 January.

Fairplay (2001) 'Malaysia Reinforces Pelepas', 16 January.

Fairplay Shipping Weekly (2002) 'Pelepas Snatches Evergreen', 11 April.

Fossey, J. (2002) 'A Global Outlook of Future Trends in Container Shipping and Port Development', paper presented at Ports and Logistics 2002 Conference in Johor Bahru, Malaysia, 24–25 September.

Government of Malaysia (1996) *Seventh Malaysia Plan 1996–2000*, Kuala Lumpur: Government Printers.

IEM Magazine (1999) 'Tanjung Pelepas Port', Johor, April.

Kleywegt, A., Goh, M. L., Wu, G. and Zhang, H. (2000) *Competition Between the Ports of Singapore and Malaysia*, the Logistics Institute, Georgia Tech, and the Logistics Institute – Asia Pacific, National University of Singapore. Available from: http://www.isye.gatech.edu/research/files/kley-2002-02.pdf.

Liner Shipping Network (2000a) 'Maersk Sealand Evaluates PTP', 2 May.

Liner Shipping Network (2000b) 'Maersk Sealand Signs Up for PTP', 5 June.

Lloyd's List Maritime Asia (2005) 'Maersk Sealand Chooses Tanjung Pelepas', 4 June.

Malaysian Business (1999) 'Counting on Containers', 16 June.

New Straits Times (1998a) 'Berthing Soon: a Global Maritime Hub Right in the Hub of South East Asia', 18 April.

New Straits Times (1998b) 'Tanjung Pelepas is Set to be Port of the 21st Century', 13 February.

New Straits Times (1999) 'First Mother Vessel Calls at Tanjung Pelepas', 23 October.

New Straits Times (2001) 'Defining the Roles of PTP, Port Klang', 12 February.

New Straits Times (2005) 'Port of Tanjung Pelepas Emerges as No. 1 Terminal in the Country', 24 January.

News & Ripples Statistics (undated) Port Klang Ranking.

Noer, J. H. (1996) *Southeast Asian Chokepoints: Keeping Sea Lines of Communication Open*, Institute for National Strategic Studies – Strategic Forum, No. 98; December, http://www.ndu.edu/inss/strforum/SF_98/forum98.html.

Port of Tanjung Pelepas Website (2005) http://www.ptp.com.my/

Renkema, A. and Kinlan, D. (2000) *Tanjung Pelepas Port: From Jungle to Malaysia's Newest Container Port*, September, Terra et Aqua No. 80.

Shipping Times (1999) 'PTP Assured of Uninterrupted Power Supply', 29 October.

Shipping Times (2001) 'PTP Set to be Busiest Port after Tie-up with Evergreen', 25 October.

Shipping Times Singapore Online (1999) 'Maersk May Consider Investing in Tanjung Pelepas', 28 December.

Straits Shipper (1997) 'Rail Link KTMB', 9 March.

Straits Times Singapore (2000) 'Maersk to Channel 85% of Box Cargo to Johor', 19 August.

The Star (1998a) 'PTP to Compete', 15 June.

The Star (1998b) 'Pelabuhan Tanjung Pelepas to Open in 1999', 13 March.

The Star (1999a) 'First Privatised Port Poised to be the Best', 31 July.

The Star (1999b) 'PTP to be Linked to National Rail Grid', 13 September.

The Star (1999c) 'Tanjung Pelepas – the Singapore Alternative', 17 May.

The Star (2003) 'PTP Part of MASKargo Sea-air Link Service', 28 April.

The Star (2004) 'Commission to Oversee all Ports', 20 February.

The Star Maritime (2001) 'PTP as Transhipment Hub', 26 February.

The Sun (2000) 'World's Largest Vessel Calls at Tanjung Pelepas', 5 January.

UNESCAP (2001) *Maritime Policy Planning Model (MPPM): Regional Shipping and Port Development Strategies Under a Changing Maritime Environment*, Transport and Tourism Division, UNESCAP, Bangkok.

Wang, J. J. and Slack, B. (2000) 'The Evolution of a Regional Container Port System: the Pearl River Delta', *Journal of Transport Geography*, 8(4): 263–75.

Wong, H. W. (2002) *Developing Malaysian Ports into Regional Hubs*. Available from: <http://www.mima.gov.my/mima/htmls/papers/pdf/whw/whw_port-dev.pdf>.

World Bank (2002) *Port Reform Toolkit: Overview*. Available from: <http://www.worldbank.org/transport/ports/toolkit/overview.pdf>.

Part V

Competition and Co-operation

10
Shanghai and Ningbo: In Search of an Identity for the Changjiang Delta Region

James Wang and Daniel Olivier

10.1 Introduction: dual hub systems

Early analysts of containerisation anticipated concentration of maritime traffic in single regional mega-hubs surrounded by peripheral competitors (Rimmer, 1967; Hayuth, 1981). While this was true during the earlier stages of the containerisation process, few port systems have neatly conformed to the ideal single-hub logic of concentration dictated by scale economies. Rather, of late, several regional port systems display a *dual hub* structure: Los Angeles–Long Beach, New York–New Jersey, Hong Kong–Yantian, Busan–Gwangyang, Singapore–Tanjung Pelepas, Kobe–Osaka, Tokyo–Yokohama are notorious cases in point. The sheer magnitude of such port complexes are such that they have 'outgrown' their host cities to adopt a cross-jurisdictional spatial logic, rendering traditional ideas of competition and co-operation fuzzy or obsolete: an idea recently encapsulated by Song's (2002) notion of port 'co-opetition'.

While single-hub systems have been theorised as assuming isoplanar market environments, recent studies suggest political and regulatory environments remain strong 'distortion' forces in shaping regional port systems (Wang, 1998; Slack and Wang, 2003). Although governments worldwide have adopted a generally sympathetic attitude to foreign participation in their port industry in the past decade, regulatory environments remain spatially variegated. Several governments have now turned their policy towards a logistics offensive. For example, the spectacular rise of Yantian and Tanjung Pelepas are the result of aggressive government policies aiming to enhance national logistical systems in Malaysia and China respectively, while simultaneously destabilising the established spatial monopolies of Hong Kong and Singapore. In both cases, private interests have been quick to capitalise on green-field opportunities opened up by aggressive state policies. In these cases, cargo demand is such that it can sustain organic growth at more than one hub. In other instances, dual hub structures emerge out of rational central planning; the green-field container terminals at Gwangyang are the direct result of the Korean government's attempt to relieve congestion at the main hub of Busan. Dual hub systems have emerged essentially from the capacity of governments to channel private capital to serve national interests. In sum, while private firms now occupy the forefront of port development, state-motivated investment opportunities remain important underlying forces in the emergence of such regional systems.

It is therefore worthwhile, not to say essential, to investigate the institutional dynamics underlying such systems. Although in its early stages, the Shanghai–Ningbo complex displays features of a dual hub system, more specifically, we wish to set analysis of this dual hub framework within the transitory logic proper to China's national port system. Questions concerning jurisdictional competence, restructuring of power, and competition–co-operation will be addressed.

As discussed in Chapter 2 of this book, since the 1990s Shanghai, as the dragon-head of China, has gone to great lengths to re-establish itself as the international shipping centre in Eastern China. Although premised on port growth, the term Shanghai International Shipping Centre (SISC) in fact reaches far beyond the port itself. It includes all the ports located in China's most dynamic and promising region – the Changjiang Delta Region (CDR) – from the city of Nanjing in the north to the city of Ningbo in the south. Among these ports, Ningbo is the second largest port and the only one that may challenge Shanghai's hub position in the range. In fact, as Table 10.1 suggests these two ports are clearly operating in a league of their own relative to other regional ports. We wish to show how the concept of regional co-operation is a necessary condition to the realisation of the SISC, yet at the same time remains a perceived hindrance to competing local ambitions. The following section is a brief account of the functional relationships linking Shanghai to Ningbo, based on

Table 10.1:   Container port throughputs in the CDR, 2003

Rank	Port		Throughput (000 TEU)	Growth vs. 2002 (%)
1	Shanghai		11,285	31.02
2	Ningbo		2,772	49.14
3	Nanjing		405	32.2
5	Nantong		247	21.1
		Total	346	12.4
4	Suzhou	*Zhangjiagang*	247	16.9
		Taicang	50	0.42
		Changshu	49	19.9
6	Wenzhou		181	20.53
7	Yangzhou		136	37.4
8	Zhenjiang		133	30.4
9	Zhoushan		34	n/a
10	Jiangyin		33	33.9
11	Taizhou		18	84.1
12	Jiaxing		8	964.3
Total			15,597	–

Source: www.portcontainer.com

familiar measurements. Section 10.3 analyses the intricacies of the institutional environment underlying regional dynamics, while section 10.4 digs deeper into the implications of the institutional context for the Shanghai–Ningbo link. The chapter concludes on the necessity to frame China's port development around broader issues of FDI and inter-urban competition.

10.2 Shanghai–Ningbo: distant neighbours?

Although located only 200 km (or 130 nautical miles) apart (Figure 10.1), both ports have very different geographical endowments. The Port of Ningbo possesses the following characteristics:

- Better water conditions for deep-sea terminals (entrance channels at 18.2 m).
- A history as a bulk cargo hub designated by the central government for Shanghai and the CDR.

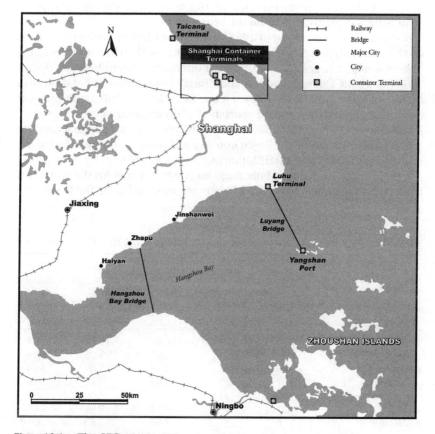

Figure 10.1: The CDR port system
Source: HKU Geography cartographic unit.

- Relatively weak and distant urban support.
- Distant from northern CDR hinterland (mainly Jiangsu Province).
- Lower administrative level in Chinese national port/city system.

Shanghai's severe draft constraints at its traditional terminals on the Huangpu River (8.5 m) were partially alleviated by the completion in 2003 of new container terminals on the Changjiang River (Yangtze) at Waigaoqiao, near the new Pudong district. This development increased draft capacity to 12.5 m, but conditional upon tidal movements. However, water conditions are made worse by the high level of siltation of the Changjiang River which requires periodic expensive dredging programmes. Consequently, local authorities saw Waigaoqiao as only a temporary measure and the local planning philosophy believed that if Shanghai is to become a truly continental hub it must permanently resolve its draft issue. Meanwhile, Ningbo's naturally sheltered harbours do not suffer any draft problems with an 18.2 m entrance channel and up to 50 m berth side, with little or no tidal constraints.

Historically, both ports played different roles in the region. Shanghai has been an all-round hub port for decades in serving both the Shanghai manufacturing base as well as a necessary transhipment intersection point between destinations along the Changjiang River and China's coastal cities. It has dealt with cargoes of every kind (Table 10.2), but due to its limited draft depth, the port cannot accommodate the latest generation of ocean-going vessels. This physical disadvantage became apparent when Shanghai-based Shanghai Baoshan Iron & Steel Corporation, the largest iron and steel complex in China, had to rely on Ningbo's facilities as a transhipment port for its ore imports. Meanwhile, Ningbo earned the status of bulk cargo transhipment hub for the entire East China region as designated by the Ministry of Communication (MOC) in 1989

Table 10.2:   Profile of non-containerised cargo terminals at the Port of Shanghai, 2003

Terminal type	No. of berths in operation		Design capacity (mil T)	Actual throughput (mil T)	Growth vs. 2002 (%)
	Total	10,000 T or above			
Bulk	514	43	11.69	12.30	15 4
Coal	34	7	3.97	3.05	11.6
Oil	60	16	2.84	2.09	26.3
Crude oil	7	5	0.83	0.78	19.0
Petroleum products & LNG	41	4	1.13	0.94	24.5
Metal ores	6	5	2.88	1.83	6.10

Source: Shanghai Port Administrative Bureau.

for handling metal and non-metal ores, coal, and crops. Its privileged status attracted port-related industries and power-generating industries, notably power plants locating near the port in order to maximise the usage of its outstanding water conditions.

Things changed drastically in the early 1990s when Shanghai, along with key coastal areas of China, began capturing substantial inflows of FDI and when major international shipping lines began integrating Shanghai into their networks, serving world destinations for containerised trade. Following a spectacular take-off boom at the Port of Shanghai, planners were soon faced with strategic decisions on how to accommodate sustained yearly growth rates in the order of 25 per cent (Table 10.3). Shanghai planners and the MOC were faced with two strategic paths: (1) a regional co-operative strategy based on exploiting the natural conditions at Ningbo as a complementary back-up facility or (2) adopt a go-it-alone strategy to assert Shanghai's national supremacy.

To consolidate its hub status, planners saw themselves needing to address its prime growth hindrance: a limited water draft which could not accommodate fourth and fifth generation container vessels. However, since candidate sites within Shanghai's jurisdiction failed to meet requirements, local authorities began looking beyond city boundaries for feasible options. Meanwhile, spectacular growth rates at the Port of Ningbo (Table 10.3) proved insufficient to warrant its own future: the port saw 85 per cent of the cargo from its own province of Zhejiang (i.e. its natural hinterland) being routed to Shanghai due largely to its very limited international calls and connectivity. This is in spite of the port's superior physical conditions for large-sized ocean-going vessels. In attempting to redress this imbalance based on Ningbo's poor inland

Table 10.3: Container annual throughput growth in Shanghai and Ningbo, 1990–2003

Year	Shanghai (000 TEU)	Annual growth rate (%)	Ningbo	Annual growth rate (%)
1990	456	–	22	
1991	577	26.5	36	47.2
1992	731	26.7	53	49.1
1993	935	27.9	79	58.2
1994	1,199	28.2	125	28.0
1995	1,527	27.4	160	26.3
1996	1,971	29.1	202	27.2
1997	2,527	28.2	257	37.4
1998	3,066	21.3	353	70.3
1999	4,215	37.5	601	50.1
2000	5,612	33.1	902	34.5
2001	6,340	13.0	1,213	53.3
2002	8,612	35.8	1,859	49.1
2003	11,282	31.0	2,772	63.6

Source: China Shipping Gazette at http://www.snet.com.cn/infomarket/

connectivity, the Zhejiang government is now building the Hangzhou Bay
Bridge (Figure 10.1), the magnitude of which easily rivals Shanghai's ambitions.
Eventually, Shanghai opted for the second option and rallied a powerful lobby
in Beijing to support its case, in turn compromising the fragile integrity of the
regional SISC concept. Shanghai proposed to develop a deep-sea harbour on
the offshore islands of Yangshan, a set of islands under the jurisdiction of the
municipality of Zhoushan, Zhejiang. After years of effort in persuading the State
Council, it finally achieved approval in the spring of 2002 to kick-start the
mega-project under an RMB 15.7 billion (or US$2 billion) initial investment
covering Phase 1 of Yangshan port plus the controversial 31 km Shanghai–
Yangshan Bridge to be built by the end of 2005. Phase 1 of Yangshan port was
planned to be equipped with five deep-sea berths with a minimum length of
350 metres, each to meet the current and near future requirements of the largest
vessels, with an overall design capacity of 2.5 million TEU (Wang and Slack,
2004). Phase 1 was planned in such a way that further enlargement to a total of
nine berths (and a capacity of 4 million TEU) may be accommodated.

Table 10.4: Comparative outbound call patterns of Shanghai and Ningbo ports,
March 2004

Destination	Number of calls in March 2004		Number of calls at both ports (3)	(3)/(2) (%)
	Shanghai (1)	Ningbo (2)		
Mid East	45	74	12	16
Japan	182	104	17	16
Taiwan	44	16	11	69
Korea	69	82	7	9
India	0	8	0	0
Mediterranean & Black Sea	37	48	5	10
Africa, Red Sea	19	26	0	0
Russia	9	18	4	22
South America	2	14	0	0
North America	126	128	24	19
Hong Kong	21	18	4	22
Australia and New Zealand	12	18	6	33
Southeast Asia	85	66	15	23
Europe	59	88	10	13
Ocean-going	288	378	51	19
Short sea	422	330	64	13
International total	710	708	115	18

Source: Compiled by authors from unpublished official port data.

Shanghai's growth has too often overshadowed Ningbo's spectacular strides. Table 10.4 compares recent port call patterns of the two competing ports. The data suggest that Ningbo is developing an identity of its own in that it is serving different markets than Shanghai. The compiled ratio (last column) demonstrates the degree of overlapping calls affecting Ningbo. While both Ningbo and Shanghai display significant overlap in serving the Taiwan market, only 18 per cent of port calls at Ningbo on average coincide with Shanghai. Ningbo has attempted to catch up at a striking rate. Beyond their absolute capacity to sustain spectacular growth, fundamental questions remain: why Shanghai and Ningbo do not co-operate or, alternatively, in what situation may they co-operate? The following sections address some of the reasons.

10.3 City-ports or port-cities? Intricacies of the institutional environment

In addition to becoming a critical means of engaging with the global economy, ports in China are also seen as a strategic apparatus for boosting a city's profile and competitiveness. Ports compete against each other but so do rival cities. Municipal rivalries add to existing port competition to create complex dynamics of functional and jurisdictional competition/co-operation. City-based competition has two implications for the CDR port complex: (1) port infrastructure provision is embedded in broader schemes of municipal competitiveness enhancements and (2) recent waves of decentralisation have provided municipalities with new tools to enhance their status. The tremendous growth at the Port of Shanghai must be placed within the context of a broader and ambitious infrastructural programme put forward by the Shanghainese government some ten years ago, of which elements have now become showcase symbols of development: Pudong new financial district, Pudong Airport, MagLev airport express train connection, its subway enhancement plan, the Nanpu and Yangpu bridges, etc. Developments at the Port of Shanghai therefore only reflect broader development ambitions embraced by municipal leaders. For instance, as early as 1995 investment in infrastructural projects had already reached a quarter of total investments in municipal assets, or some Yuan 250 million annually (STPI, 2004).

Administratively speaking, the difficulty for the two ports in China to co-operate today is no less than between a French port and a Dutch port in the European Union. Since 1984 China embarked on a gradual programme of decentralisation of power in the port sector (Wang et al., 2004). The first ten years (1984–1993) were marked by a period of 'dual leadership': the ports were directly under both local municipal governments and the MOC, the former responsible for infrastructure maintenance and daily management and operation, while the latter assumed planning duties. The MOC subsequently passed its financial responsibilities to the local governments through various models, most notably through allowing the entry of international terminal operators that would lease and invest in terminals. Such a 'dual leadership' led to a 'dual track' system in the following areas of management and operation:

- dual pricing;
- separate channels of finance.

It was gradually recognised that such a dual track system brought positive changes, notably in increasing the conformity of the port sector with market principles through such means as the introduction of FDI into the port business. On the other hand, unforeseen consequences have resulted in a fuzzy vertical distribution of powers, essentially an ambiguous share of responsibilities and accountability between central and local authorities. Therefore, following another ten years the authorities were compelled to clarify key components of port development with China's first Port Law entering into effect on 1 January 2004. The new law helps clarify the responsibilities of each party involved in a port:

- Port authorities remain the sole body under the command of local governments, which implies that all staff of port authorities are now detached from the MOC salary payroll, and it is up to local (often municipal) governments to decide how and to what extent a port should be privatised or remain under public holdings of one form or another (such as the 'Shanghai Port Group')
- The local government and port authorities are responsible for managing and planning their ports, and port master plans require MOC approval. Among other dimensions in these plans, the most important to be scrutinised by the MOC is the resource of the deep-water shore. It remains the MOC's duty and right to decide which part of the coast is considered as 'deep-water', with any change necessitating its approval.
- Provincial governments are responsible for co-ordinating port development within their own jurisdiction, as well as retaining stamps of approval for port master plans before they are submitted to the MOC.
- The MOC is responsible for national port allocation planning.

From these new measures, Chinese ports have thus come a long way from the old regime of central planning, and municipal governments have never had such an exciting incentive to develop their 'own' ports as a mean of city competition (rather than in a pure port competition mindset). Consequently, the recent decentralisation of administrative powers has enhanced the status of municipalities: the power of individual cities has become more important in China's port relationships and development. In this regard, one may understand better the difficulty for Shanghai to co-operate with Ningbo: the former is a province-level autonomous city (a 'city-province'), while the latter is a regional-level city under the jurisdiction of Zhejiang Province. The two cities

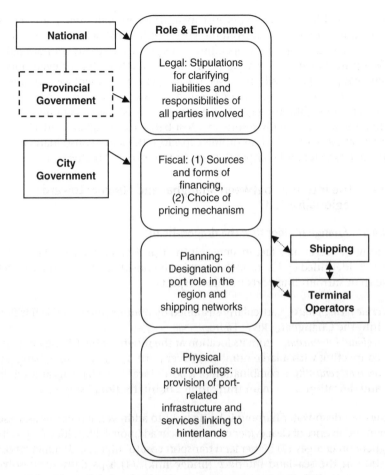

Figure 10.2: The institutional environment of port operations in China
Source: Derived from Wang and Slack (2004).

are therefore not on an equal footing regarding China's vertical urban hierarchy, not to mention the fact that Shanghai ranks first among China's provincial-level administrative units in terms of its economic contribution (GDP) to the country. Figure 10.2 summarises the institutional context described above. In sum, the introduction of market forces within a centrally planned system has ironically made port development more politically motivated than ever.

In addition, organisational reforms have accompanied redistributions of power among the various stakeholders: new bodies were established ad hoc to illustrate the government's commitment in separating administration from operation (Wang et al., 2004). Both Shanghai and Ningbo have adhered to this practice by establishing an independent and market-compliant 'Port Group Co.', namely a publicly owned enterprise assuming corporate-style management of operations independent from the Port Administrative Bureau, the official regulatory body. Such port operating enterprises are legally empowered to develop new or merge existing berths or terminals within or even outside their own port. Practically, however, the market environment for carrying out such practices is far from mature because any acquisition from an enterprise owned by a neighbouring city is not as welcome as, say, foreign investment. While the former usually results in a lost battle to a neighbouring city (in a statistical sense of its FDI-absorbing capacity), the latter consolidates a city's 'global' character and competitiveness in terms of city performance.

10.4   The interplay between Shanghai and Ningbo: towards regionalisation?

10.4.1   Shanghai's identity: the dragon-head

Among the seven key factors determining the competitiveness of container ports as identified by Jun (2004), Shanghai is considered to be more competitive than surrounding ports in three respects:

1. *critical cargo mass,* particularly sustained by manufacturing-led FDI inflows into the Changjiang River Delta;
2. *regional intermediacy* from its location at the mouth of the Changjiang River connecting with a large number of river ports along the Changjiang; and
3. *regional centrality,* a combination of a port's local cargo base, its accessibility and deviation from main trunk routes of international shipping.

Yangshan deep-water harbour is being built to address the port's weaknesses, but in the absence of clear evidence it may incur additional difficulties: (1) possibly higher port charges, (2) higher land transport cost to shippers, (3) punctual congestion at the sea–land interface (bridge link), (4) a partially (un)resolved managerial/administrative situation as the harbour falls in the territory of Zhoushan (a municipality of Zhejiang Province), and (5) some concerns expressed by potential investors over the bridge's capacity to weather typhoons and deal with the delays incurred. The project is the first of its kind through which a port authority builds a container terminal outside its own boundaries on 'borrowed' (leased) land. Exactly how the two neighbouring governments co-ordinate the financial arrangements concerning land leasing and taxation of terminal operation remains to be seen. Technically, the province of Zhejiang retains the right to reclaim land around the port on its own island of Yangshan in its own potential attempt to reap benefits from the port project, for instance, by setting up a port-related logistics park. Were such a move to turn into concrete action, it would threaten the potential benefits of Shanghai's building of a new town at Luchao, the southern tip of Shanghai to be linked by a 31 km bridge to the Yangshan container terminals.

None of these problems can be handled at the port authority level. As a result, the Shanghai municipal government has done the following:

- To reduce the land transport cost for shippers, the city government has decided to assume the cost of the bridge between Shanghai and Yangshan harbour as part of the 'urban infrastructure', paid for fully by the government and free to all users.
- To reduce the port charges of Yangshan deep-water port, Phase 1 is contracted out exclusively to Shanghai Port Group Co. and its subsidiary (Shanghai International Port Group) so that the cost-price ratio and cost-recovery scheme for the first five berths becomes hidden.
- To overcome administrative difficulties, Shanghai has negotiated with Zhoushan City over three key issues about Yangshan port: (1) Shanghai Port Administrative Bureau will take over the responsibility of port administration; (2) Zhoushan will be responsible for ancillary services such as pilotage; and (3) tax revenues from port operations shall be remitted to Zhoushan.

Shanghai is demonstrating strong leadership in consolidating its status as China's dragon-head as the achievement of the SISC concept is not limited to building and developing container terminals. Its functions and ambitions stretch across a wide range of maritime activities: establishing itself as a regional/international ship registration centre, becoming the largest shipbuilding centre in China, developing a world-class container port, etc.

10.4.2 Ningbo's multiple identities: low cost multi-functional option

Among all major ports in China, Ningbo has the best deep-water coastal conditions and vast coastal land available for port development (over 120 km of exploitable coastline). Ningbo is essentially a multi-functional port surrounded by vast industrial complexes. The Port of Ningbo is composed of five harbour areas, namely Beilun, Zhenhai, Ningbo, Daxie and Chuanshan. As the recent facilities at Beilun attest, its 27 deep-water berths and substantially lower deep-water infrastructure costs have allowed for more spatially extensive container and bulk facilities to be built. As of 2003, there were a total of 35 deep-water berths of over 10,000 DWT capacity, including one 100,000 DWT, and one 200,000 DWT, ore transhipment berths, a crude oil berth for tankers up to 200,000 DWT, and one LPG berth.

The Beilun Harbour area was first developed in the 1970s for receiving ores from Australia serving the Shanghai Baoshan Iron & Steel Complex. Subsequently, harbour facilities served the electricity-generating industry and the Zhenhai Petrochemical Co. – key projects behind the erection of local port-related heavy industrial complexes. Beilun Harbour retains enormous future potential as the port claims as many as 152 deep-water berths could be accommodated in the future (Ningbo Today, 2006). The figure highlights a stark contrast with Shanghai's capacity constraints.

Coinciding with the gradual decentralisation of powers in the early 1990s, local authorities began their engagement in various incentives to build a free-trade zone (FTZ) and economic development zones (EDZs) near the port as well as building new container terminals. The joint venture between Hutchison Port Holdings (HPH) and Ningbo Port Authority in 2001 helped consolidate Beilun port's credibility as a serious regional contender by securing the presence of a world-class port operator. Leading regional port investors, such as China Merchants Holdings International (CMHI, Hong Kong) and CITIC, have also taken stakes in recent projects at Daxie Island. By May 2004, the port had already established 708 international routes, with 570 international ports connected, covering some 90 countries. Total container throughput increased tenfold over a seven-year period, from 0.26 million TEU in 1997 to 2.77 million TEU in 2003.

As for its cargo base, the majority of its boxes are from two main sources: the export-processing industries in the EDZ and FTZ near the port site, and cargo from the province of Zhejiang, the majority of which was formerly routed to Shanghai. In fact, Zhejiang (along with Jiangsu) is one of the two overlapping hinterland provinces over which both ports are competing. In an attempt to stretch its outreach into Jiangsu (northwest of Shanghai), Zhejiang province is currently completing the Hangzhou Bay Bridge (anticipated opening 2006) which should cut the existing distance from Jiangsu to Ningbo by half (Figure 10.1). By the year 2010, there should be two distinct yet parallel network systems in place feeding into the two major deep-sea regional harbours: Beilun and Yangshan. Although stakeholders for the Yangshan project are yet to be officially revealed, different private interests are expected to run the two competing facilities. Concerning future handling capacity, Shanghai and Ningbo plan to add 13.5 million TEU and 12.5 million TEU respectively of capacity by 2020 (*Jiaotong Shibao*, 2003).

10.4.3   The role of private participation

As if the dynamics of competition–co-operation were not complex enough, private participation further complicates the general picture. While rivalry revolves around the dual hubs, smaller regional ports are staking growth aspirations. One such port is Suzhou which has recently secured participation from Hong Kong-listed operator COSCO Pacific (part of PRC-based COSCO Shipping Group) at its Taicang and Zhangjiagang container terminals (Figure 10.1). The Taicang BOT (build-operate-transfer) scheme also involves Modern Terminals Ltd., another leading Hong Kong-based operator. While HPH and COSCO Group interests retain forefront positions with investments in several regional operations,[1] other private interests are taking stakes in smaller facilities to redraw the competitive landscape of the CDR.

Naturally, the EDZ and FTZ play a critical part in attracting FDI. Ningbo's Daxie EDZ was established in 1991 with special permission from the central government (following a Hong Kong-style model of planning) and was invested in a few years later by CITIC and more recently by CMHI, both Hong Kong-listed arms of PRC-based financial groups. Being located further east of the Beilun area, Daxie has built two deep-water berths for super large oil tankers, and more berths for containers and coal transhipment are under construction. Although the throughputs of these berth operations are counted into Ningbo port statistics, the development and management of these terminals are not under the direct control of Ningbo Port Authority.

The Zhoushan Islands have also been successful in attracting private capital. They are located east of Ningbo within Zhoushan City and are host to sizeable port operations. Currently a city of Zhejiang Province today, this municipality has been formerly under Shanghai's administrative control for three periods since the establishment of the People's Republic of China. In terms of total annual throughput volumes of bulk cargo, Zhoushan ranks number two among all mainland Chinese ports, largely due to its new purpose-built deep-water ore terminals in Majishan serving the Shanghai Baoshan Iron & Steel Co. (the largest in China) but also to its crude oil transhipment facilities in Aoshan Island (one berth for 250,000 ton oil tankers, at a capacity of 15 million tons p.a.) operated by China Shipping Group in partnership with Sinopec. Fearing potential over-capacity and infrastructural redundancies among the two ports and municipalities, the Zhejiang provincial government has devised a rational allocation plan between the two facilities. Ningbo is developing its core function into container handling while Zhoushan seeks to exploit its offshore outlying island location to concentrate on bulk cargo handling. An expensive bridge to link Zhoushan with Ningbo is to be built by 2010, aiming to enhance physical integration between the two cities. However, uncertainty remains over how far the two municipalities can further functionally and administratively integrate over common goals. Or alternatively, uncertainty surrounds possible closer ties between Zhoushan and Shanghai based on their close history but also following Shanghai's bullish offshore territorial expansion scheme.

10.5 Conclusion: dual hub, dual identity

The CDR port system is embedded in two overlapping logics of competition. The first one sees municipalities using ports as instruments to enhance their positions within China and, eventually, the global economy. Port competition is perceived as a part, and a means of, city competition. Pressures and requirements are essentially exogenous and FDI-driven. Sophisticated EDZs are now commonplace among the coastal landscapes of China (Wang and Olivier, 2003). While regional complementarities drawing on Ningbo's low costs and favourable water conditions appear as a rationally compelling solution for the CDR, these complementarities are overshadowed by Shanghai's infra-structural ambitions and its desire to position itself in command of the SISC.

Following recent waves of power decentralisation, municipalities are now better endowed to compete and gain control over their identity and destiny. Against Shanghai's strong regional leadership, Ningbo municipality is teaming up with neighbouring Zhoushan, under the guidance of the provincial government, to erect a competitive and integrated port facility. City-based partnerships, however, remain fragile and ambiguous given this new competitive spirit.

The second factor is a restructuring of logic proper for China's port sector, but also one that shares structural features with parallel industries undergoing a profound market-driven transition. This reconfiguration of governance demands a qualitative understanding of the internal political dynamics of China's maritime industry (Wang et al., 2004). Consistent with the central argument put forward in this chapter, evidence surrounding the Yangshan case emphasises the strength of localism as an inherent feature of China's infrastructural development process.

Both logics interact in a way specific to the CDR as a dual hub system in-the-making. Additional factors superimpose to increase the complexity of the competition–co-operation landscape: (1) differentials in container cargo and bulk shipping and locational requirements, (2) private participation and (3) a new legal framework imposed by the central government in 2004. As the most lucrative of port sectors, container facilities have attracted private interests and forced a necessary and rapid enlargement of stakeholder communities. As such, private entrants' strategies also render port rivalries politically sensitive, through the presence of single operators at a *priori* competing ports. However, so long as the regional cargo base can grow at rates sustaining both ports, the cost-led advantage of Ningbo may not be evident against the grandiose projects of Shanghai. Meanwhile, high degrees of specialisation in bulk facilities, with cases such as the Majishan ore terminal and the Aoshan oil terminal, offer 'ready-made', yet highly place-specific, private investment opportunities as they present possibilities of vertical integration along the supply chain in bulk cargo transport. It was shown how other parties – private (CITIC, MTL, CMHI, HPH, etc.) and non-private (e.g. the province of Zhejiang) – may re-steer the Shanghai–Ningbo relationship by adding new possibilities of port development, notably in Daxie and Zhoushan, and eventually redraw the regional map. While Shanghai's draft limitations fuelled its *inferiority* complex and originally gave it impetus for expansion, its new identity is being quickly transformed into a *superiority* complex. A regional identity is in the making: can the CDR strive for a common identity?

Note

1. HPH is in Shanghai-Waigaoqiao, Shanghai-Huangpu (SCT), and Ningbo-Beilun; COSCO Pacific is in Shanghai-Waigaoqiao, Shanghai-Huangpu (SCT) as well as Suzhou-Taicang, Suzhou-Zhangjiagang and is also involved in the Port of Yangzhou (Jiangsu Province).

References

Hayuth, Y. (1981) 'Containerisation and the Load Centre Concept', *Economic Geography*, 57: 160–76.

Jiaotong Shibao (2003) 'The Integration of Ningbo and Zhoushan Ports to Make a World Super Port', Transport Bureau of Zhejiang Province, www.zjt.gov.cn/node90/200311/con105708.htm.

Jun, I.-S. (2004) 'Comparative Analysis of Capacity and Competitiveness of Seaports in Northeast Asia', NEAEF/KOTI Conference, Honolulu, 19–20 August.

Ningbo Today (2006) 'Port of Ningbo – Beilun Harbour Area', http://www.cnnb.com.cn/gb/node2/node48/node44980/node44983/node44995/userobject7ai1120986.html.

Rimmer, P. J. (1967) 'The Search for Spatial Regularities in the Development of Australian Seaports 1861–1961/2', *Geografiska Annaler*, 49(1): 42–54.

Shanghai Transportation Planning Institute (2004) official website, www.scctpi.gov.cn.

Slack, B. and Wang, J. J. (2003) 'The Challenge of Peripheral Ports: an Asian Perspective', *Geoforum*, 56(2): 159–66.

Song, D.-W. (2002) 'Regional Container Port Competition and Co-operation: the Case of Hong Kong and South China', *Journal of Transport Geography*, 10: 99–110.

Wang, J. J. (1998) 'A Container Load Centre with a Developing Hinterland: a Case Study of Hong Kong', *Journal of Transport Geography*, 6(3): 187–201.

Wang, J. J., Ng, A. K.-Y. and Olivier, D. (2004) 'Port Governance in China: a Review of Policies in an Era of Internationalizing Port Management Practices', *Transport Policy*, 11(3): 237–50.

Wang, J. J. and Olivier, D. (2003) 'La Gouvernance des ports et la relation ville-port en Chine', *Cahiers Scientifiques du Transport*, 44: 25–54.

Wang, J. J. and Slack, B. (2004) 'Regional Governance of Port Development in China: a Case Study of Shanghai International Shipping Centre', *Maritime Policy and Management*, 31(4): 1–17.

11
Hong Kong and Shenzhen: the Nexus in South China

James Wang and Daniel Olivier

11.1   Introduction

Success at Shenzhen port has been so astonishing in recent years that the phenomenon has at times acquired the allure of a tabloid scoop. Shenzhen came out of nowhere to top the world container port league in less than a decade, ranking number four in 2003 behind Hong Kong, Singapore and Shanghai respectively. Its close location and shared geographical features with leading neighbour Hong Kong has fuelled recent speculation about an eventual overtaking. This dual hub system has reached a spatial magnitude and a functional complexity that have allowed a fundamental requestioning of traditional issues of competition and co-operation as well as aspects of jurisdictional competence over mega-port structures endowed with regional vocations. The idea was suggested by Song (2002) who observed how the overlapping of private capital among *a priori* competing ports creates new *de facto* co-operative bonds between regional competitors.

Such a close relationship allows unique opportunities for research into the dynamics of regional governance. What is the future of this system? Is Hong Kong really under threat? What are the dominant discourses? More importantly, in an alleged growing climate of co-operation how should competitive endowments be interpreted? At a shallow level of analysis, the Shenzhen threat to Hong Kong has been mainly reported in quantitative terms, backed by its sheer growth and massive throughput surges. Quantitative analysis alone has tended to either hide the real qualitative issues or mislead the debate, however. This chapter seeks to clarify the ongoing and dynamic relationship between the two neighbouring ports. First, we wish to set port development within an adequate time–space framework. Second, the Hong Kong–Shenzhen nexus is analysed in terms of functional linkages by identifying persisting sources of differentiation among them. Third, we wish to open up the analysis through an evaluation of governance structures and future prospects for a pan-regional co-operative effort. Reflections on the lessons learned from the Pearl River Delta (PRD) will conclude the chapter.

11.2   Background and geographical relationship

From its modest origins as little more than a small town of 100,000 population, Shenzhen's phenomenal growth as a city may be attributable to its status as China's very first Special Economic Zone (SEZ) in 1980. After two decades of very fast development and urbanisation, its population has now reached the seven million mark, bringing it within the top tier of China's urban hierarchy as the third largest city in the southern China region behind Hong Kong and Guangzhou (Canton). Since the 1980s, Hong Kong has maintained tightly-knit relationships with its northern neighbour, the former as a source of capital and management know-how, the latter as a low-cost land and labour pool. But most recently, it is Shenzhen's port ambition that has drawn attention. The pace and magnitude of its port development became the more obvious when in 2001 the municipal authorities decided to regroup its three port facilities of Chiwan, Shekou and Yantian under a single statistical unit (previously counted separately), thereby propelling it to the top ranks of the world container port traffic league.

The source of competition between the two ports has a strong geographical rationale as: (1) they serve a roughly identical hinterland, namely the Pearl River Delta manufacturing basin, to which each port's intermodal access differs; (2) they constitute an essential call on continental deep-sea routes to and from the Far East by the leading mega-carriers; (3) Yantian and Hong Kong both have prime deep-water conditions for deep-sea shipping. Where they differ most geographically, however, is in their *in situ* back-up land reserves, with Yantian having a net advantage as a green-field port. The resulting port system may be conceived as a triangle formed by the upper tips of the Shenzhen east and west port facilities and lower Hong Kong tip (Figure 11.1).

Shenzhen's port success is made the more spectacular given that its history is remarkably young and theoretically atypical in the sense that it has not followed a gradual and historically driven spatial evolution as described in conventional port theory (Bird, 1963; Robinson, 1985). Unlike several world port-cities which have undergone a long process of port-city evolution from a fish ferry to conventional break-bulk port and then to specialised container facilities, Shenzhen became a port-city out of aggressive developmental state policies when it erected its first container terminals almost simultaneously in Shekou and Yantian in the early 1990s. Fed by an ever-growing manufacturing base and a favourable geographical location in its capacity to intercept Hong Kong-bound cargo flows, the story of Shenzhen's catching-up with Hong Kong is now well known. Figure 11.2 illustrates the closing gap between both ports in terms of container throughput.

While Hong Kong began securing its position as a world-class container port in the early 1970s, in Shenzhen massive infrastructural investments arose out of the necessity of satisfying the SEZ's rapidly emerging export-led manufacturing identity. As a result, Hong Kong and Shenzhen share similarities in the structural features of their cargo base, such that both ports target the container market as their core market and dominant sector of operation (Tables 11.1 and 11.2).

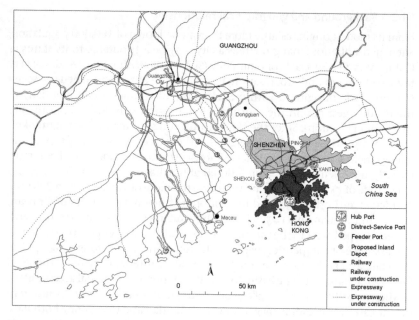

Figure 11.1:   The Pearl River Delta regional port system
Source: Copyright rests with the authors.

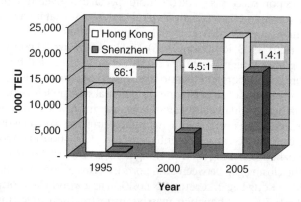

Figure 11.2:   Annual container throughput Hong Kong vs. Shenzhen
Source: Compiled with data from (1) website of Hong Kong Port Development Council,
(2) the *2005 Report on Shenzhen Municipal Port & Shipping Development*, Shenzhen Port
Administrative Bureau.

Table 11.1: Shenzhen port throughput by cargo type, 2002

Type of cargo	Throughput ('000 tons)	% of port total
Containerised cargo	52,693	60.1
Coal	2958	3.4
Oil and petrol products	7819	8.9
Iron and steel	4670	5.3
Construction materials	3680	4.2
Crops and cereals	8230	9.4
Cements	1864	2.1
Timber	1173	1.3
Ores	194	0.2
Fertilizers	3109	3.5
Others	1270	1.4
Total	*87,660*	*100*

Source: Shenzhen Port Authority (2003).

Table 11.2: Vessel arrivals by ship type at the Port of Hong Kong, 2002

Ship type	Number		Capacity	
	'000 NRT	(%)	'000 NRT	(%)
Chemical carrier/tanker	1,000	0.46	1,442	0.39
Conventional cargo vessel	56,080	25.67	28,632	7.69
Cruise/ferry	66,040	30.23	37,559	10.09
Dry bulk carrier	1,260	0.58	13,569	3.64
Fishing/fish processing vessel*	350	0.16	53	0.01
Fully cellular container vessel	55,490	25.40	237,835	63.86
Gas carrier/tanker	420	0.19	830	0.22
Lighter/barge/cargo junk#	21,500	9.84	38,731	10.40
Oil tanker	2,870	1.31	8,725	2.34
Pleasure vessel*	90	0.04	2	0.00
Roll on/roll off	360	0.16	2,524	0.68
Semi-container vessel	1,870	0.86	982	0.26
Tug	10,890	4.98	690	0.19
Others	290	0.13	843	0.23
Total	218,490	100.00	372,415	100.00

Notes:
The number of vessels is rounded to the nearest 10.
* Excluding figures on pleasure vessels and fishing vessels plying exclusively within the river trade limits.
# The figures for August 2001 onwards include the trip records of 'Lighter/barge/cargo junk' carrying out dredging of marine sand outside the river trade limits in connection with the reclamation in Penny's Bay, Lantau Island.
Source: Hong Kong Shipping Statistics, Hong Kong SAR Government.

11.3 Functional relationship and sources of competitiveness

In general terms, much of the (highly hyped and mediatised) speculation over Shenzhen's capacity to eventually overtake Hong Kong's port rests on debates over what constitute the 'real issues', or qualitative aspects, behind the ports' differentiation as well as their adequate quantification. For instance, controversy over the media's impartiality in dealing with the sensitive issue of Terminal Handling Charges (THC) in recent years has motivated passionate reactions from the entire port and shipping communities (Giron-Urquiola, 2004). The following points are key considerations shaping the Hong Kong–Shenzhen dynamic.

11.3.1 The politics of statistics

A first and shallow aspect of competition relates to the actual representation of a port's competitive features: the *discourses* shaping the issues. As mentioned previously, Shenzhen authorities have statistically merged the three container facilities to be represented under a single statistical unit. If individually represented, Yantian, Chiwan and Shekou facilities would have ranked as 14th, 63rd and 74th respectively in the world traffic league in 2002. Together, they occupied the 6th rank. Aggregate throughputs provide a stronger rationale for municipal-level governments to approach higher-tier government levels in accessing infrastructural funds under a volume-leadership discourse. Commenting on this, a leading Hong Kong-based operator underlines that 'understandably, league tables make good press ... When the focus is misplaced on quantity, rather than quality, the issue becomes political. Then you have overinvestment in unnecessary facilities. This is a growing trend evident throughout Asia' (*Shippers Today*, 2004: 3). At a higher level of analysis, this highlights the need to factor-in value-adding capabilities, quality of services, capacity to sustain shareholder value, etc. in the overall competitiveness of port operations. Volume-based competition has too often taken centre-stage in constructing the Shenzhen threat discourse. In addition, throughput calculation may not follow standard practices. For instance, the Port of Hong Kong double-counts containers handled by river trade, meaning that a single container is recorded twice in official statistics if it is handled by river barge. By contrast, if a container is handled by truck, it is counted only once. Under this logic, a modal shift from road to river could dramatically enhance Hong Kong's throughput statistics.

11.3.2 Cost-based differentiation

A more profound and widespread concern over Hong Kong's long-term attractiveness is its capacity to control costs. While from a port operator's point of view, cost control may represent a major challenge, from a shipper's point of view regional cost differentiation among ports (or terminals) makes for a healthy and competitive regional port system. Arguments usually revolve around the alleged fact that cost-conscious shippers will eventually re-route their cargo to cheaper, more cost-efficient solutions. While in theory this makes good sense, in practice we know shippers still value time-sensitive efficiency, value-adding options, reliability, customer service, etc. (Song and Yeo, 2004) in addition to selecting an ocean carrier prior to selecting a specific port (Tongzon, 2002). Such elements constitute and remain the core of Hong Kong's competitive advantage, as one senior Hong Kong industry expert puts it:

> Of course, the shipper will look at the cost of shipping out the goods. But on the other hand, you don't get the facilities that we have in Hong Kong for reliability of the vessels, and for quicker Customs clearance which is one thing they don't have in China. In Hong Kong, if you miss one vessel on Tuesday, you can get it the next day whereas in China, it may not be so flexible . . . Actually, I've been told by shipping lines that it costs them more to operate the same vessel in China versus Hong Kong. (Giron-Urquiola, 2004: 14)

The above raises the critical issue of costs related to flexibility. Our interviews with port community representatives in Shenzhen and Hong Kong revealed that when PRC shippers shipping via Shenzhen facilities miss their sailing, they are charged 'storage costs' in a third-party warehouse outside the terminal area until their cargo can reach the next sailing.

But trucking costs remain at the forefront of cost differentials between the two ports. A recent study released by McKinsey & Co. (2004) reveals that the total difference in terms of monetary cost for shipping a 40 ft container from Dongguan (a PRD city north of Shenzhen; see Figure 11.1) to the west coast of North America *ex* Hong Kong against *ex* Yantian is US$300. Of this total, a $100 difference is attributable to port charges (THC), while the rest ($200) is due to differentials arising from inland trucking by more expensive Hong Kong drivers moving boxes cross-border over a longer distance. The cost argument thus needs to be refined: facts indicate that (1) the major cost difference is not intrinsically linked to the port itself, and (2) cross-border trucking remains the single most critical variable in total transport cost, beyond efficiencies at the port itself. Here, Hong Kong's disadvantage is real so long as the majority of its cargo remains road-based and the SAR government does not address serious labour cost differentials in truckers' wages. Finally, an often-forgotten fact is that an average 40 per cent of Hong Kong's total containerised traffic is handled mid-stream; Hong Kong's very own low-cost alternative. This segment of operation is under monopoly in Hong Kong, which *a priori* suggests further cost competitiveness may be achieved.

11.3.3   Customs clearance and cross-border issues

The McKinsey study identifies three hindrances relating to current trucking practice and its related low frequency of trips per truck. First, the so-called

'4-up-4-down' rule requires the driver to stay with the container, the trailer and the truck during its return trip to Guangdong. The ultimate outcome is the superfluous generation of empty container cross-border movements. Such regulations translate into substantial cost savings for those PRC shippers using Hong Kong port who can command a return trip within the same day. The time-sensitivity of this practice in turn translates into daily synchronised waves of cross-border congestion. The second is the '1-truck-1-driver' rule which is enforced by the Guangdong Public Security Bureau and requires a truck to be registered to a single driver. Also, current regulations state that a Hong Kong trucker entering China through a given border crossing must re-enter the SAR using the same border crossing. The rule is a major offset in asset optimisation. Given that an average 20,000 container trucks cross the border daily, such practices do not ease congestion concerns. Third, the study identifies long waiting times as an important concern for competitiveness. This point, however, is more subject to debate given the recent efforts by the SAR government in this direction. According to a recent government survey, 90 per cent of border crossing times have been reduced on average to under an hour (Giron-Urquiola, 2004). Nevertheless, in spite of infrastructural adjustments and technical improvements, the problem remains for the most part at the regulatory level.

Meanwhile, customs reforms are under way on the mainland side. Yantian has been chosen since February 2004 for the pilot-testing of a comprehensive reform programme intended by the PRC government. The Dapeng Customs' Sea Port Customs Reform Team was purposely established to look at ways to speed-up clearance and collect views from port users. While reforms remain slow by industry standards, the PRC government's commitment to change is real. The critical question for Hong Kong is knowing how deep reforms may go, knowing its free port status and smooth customs clearance remain a strong comparative advantage in Hong Kong's favour.

11.3.4 Intermodal endowments and hinterland access

Rail connectivity differs among terminals of the same port (west vs. east Shenzhen) and terminals of competing ports (Shenzhen vs. Hong Kong). Yantian enjoys arguably the best intermodal rail connections with the new 23 km Pingyan Railway which connects the marine terminals to inland collection depots at Pinghu (Figure 11.1). April 2004 coincided with the launch of another rail line: the Chengdu–Shenzhen Express Railway (Rongshen Railway). The new line connects at Pinghu and is anticipated to stretch the hinterland outreach of Yantian as the one-way transit from Sichuan takes 91 hours.

Intermodal competitiveness of each port has been looked after primarily by private-led initiatives. In Shenzhen, HPH has begun operation of its Guanlan inland container depot (near Pinghu) in 1999 under a joint venture agreement with majority interests (71 per cent). In Hong Kong, Kwai Chung terminals only benefit from rail access indirectly, as containers wishing to move through rail must tranship at the Hung Hom Kowloon-Canton Railway

(KCR) facility. However, it must be remembered that intermodal endowments remain dictated by inland/hinterland conditions. Statistics show that up to 2003, none of the rail-accessible container ports in China has any significant volume (Yantian: <1 per cent, Shanghai: 0.76 per cent, of their total container throughput respectively, for example). Consequently, although differentials in intermodal endowments may appear considerable, in reality their net effect remains minor due to China's weaker inland intermodal environment.

In Hong Kong, an early response to competitive threats came through the creation of the River Trade Terminal (RTT) at Tuen Mun in 1998. Inland barging was early seen as a strategic response to maintain cost-effective access to the hinterland. However, although technically and legally the RTT was designed for handling river barges, controversy emerged over rumours that Kwai Chung operators were redirecting deep-sea traffic to the river facility because the RTT was invested by common investors already present at Kwai Chung. Companies involved neither at the equity nor operational level in the RTT, such as Modern Terminals Ltd. (MTL), have put forward initiatives of their own in recent years. In 2002, MTL set up express river barge shuttle services connecting key inland feeder ports of the PRD to secure Hong Kong traffic. MTL runs this new integrated feeder service under the banner of MTL Inland Gate.

11.3.5 Future capacity and expansion schemes

Hong Kong's surprising ability to accommodate new capacity during long delays surrounding the completion of CT9 has seriously questioned the need for additional facilities planned on Lantau Island. Scepticism about the need for additional capacity in Hong Kong is only reinforced by Shenzhen's aggressive growth. The common discourse regarding this issue is that the PRD cargo basin is sufficiently large to sustain growth at both ports over the short-to-medium term. Official estimates of the PRD's containerised cargo-generating capacity stood at about 20 million TEU in 2002. Exactly how the pie may be divided between the rival ports becomes a central concern of local media as well as the two city governments.

The question of building additional container facilities in Hong Kong must be also placed within the context of the growing involvement of leading private Hong Kong-based operators and investors in Shenzhen operations. Early developments at Shenzhen ports were often ironically heralded as 'Hong Kong's CT9', due to delays experienced at CT9 combined with the overlapping involvement of private operators at both ports (Airriess, 2001). Since traditionally the private sector has assumed the bulk of capital investments in Hong Kong's port infrastructure, their recent cross-border involvement may cool down enthusiasm for local ambitions. Adding to this slowdown are important differentials in environmental considerations surrounding large infrastructure projects. Following the experience of Western (i.e. democratic) port-cities, Hong Kong's 'democratic advantage' and greater public environmental sensitivity may be turned into a relative disadvantage in lengthening the approval process.

11.3.6 The spatiality of private capital

A unique feature of the PRD port system is that the private entrepreneurs who have secured the reputation of Hong Kong port in terms of efficiency and quality are also behind the rise of the Shenzhen ports. There is indeed a great deal of overlap among leading private investors' interests between the two ports. This creates a unique split-benefit effect. On the one hand, public opinion is being shaped and influenced by the potency of a volume-leadership rhetoric, whereby Shenzhen's spectacular throughput figures are too often presented as the sole source of threat. Rarely are deeper issues taken into the public debate, such as value-adding capacity, labour quality differentials, regulatory practices, etc. On the other hand, the dual involvement of Hong Kong's largest port-related conglomerates is perceived within a broader pattern of leaking capital from Hong Kong out to mainland China. After all, transport demand is a derived demand which follows market principles, remarks a senior manager at Hutchison Port Holdings (HPH): 'In line with the forces of a free market, Hong Kong operators have followed the migration of manufacturers into China. We simply follow the market' (*Shippers Today*, 2004: 20). The duality is the following: what is good for the private sector is yet to be proven beneficial for the public interest of Hong Kong at large. Concerns are founded on Hong Kong's liberal tax system which does not levy taxes on corporations' overseas operations. However, earnings across the border may be partially repatriated depending on corporate strategy and may indirectly benefit Hong Kong by way of various forms of reinvestment schemes into R&D or IT, which remain strongly concentrated in Hong Kong.

Hong Kong and Shenzhen as two major competing port-cities in South China have a unique organisational relationship. Figure 11.3 illustrates the complex web of common shareholding between the two competing ports. Leading Hong Kong-based conglomerates with strong maritime interests now have a considerable overlapping presence. HPH, COSCO Pacific, China Merchant Holdings International (CMHI), Wharf Holdings and Swire Pacific are leading enterprises that hold major shares in both ports. Some other multinationals such as Singapore Port Group (PSA) and Dubai Port International (DPI) have just joined the game in 2005, making the Hong Kong side more global. The major difference between the two ports is that on the mainland side, state-owned listed firms such as the Yantian Port Group Co. were formed to represent the Shenzhen government at the equity level, thereby linking operations to municipal government interests. By contrast, in Hong Kong, equity (i.e. shareholding) and operation remains under the full aegis of the private sector, while the government takes on a back-up role in the provision of supporting infrastructure and land tenure.

By shedding light on cross-border cross-shareholding intricacies, Figure 11.3 helps better understand the complexity of the competition and co-operation dynamics between the two ports. At the terminal level, one will find that since HPH is the dominant player in both ports, the relationship between their

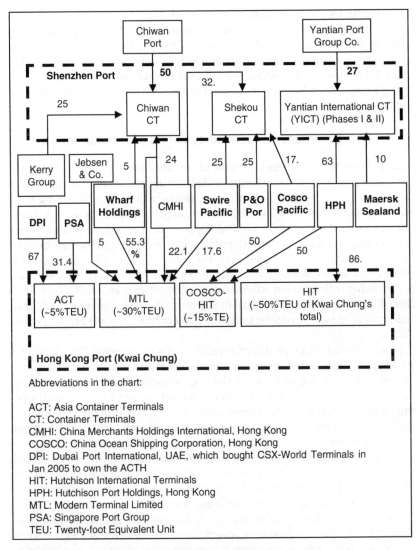

Figure 11.3: The ownership web between Hong Kong and Shenzhen ports, as in February 2005
Source: Compiled by authors from the websites of related firms.

own terminals in Yantian and Kwai Chung is becoming a matter internal to the corporation and, consequently, increasingly difficult to regulate. Terminal-level analysis also helps to clarify port–port relations. Indeed, internal competition exists between east (Yantian) and west (Shekou and Chiwan) since the two parts of Shenzhen port are operated by two distinct and competing groups of firms.

By displacing the analysis at a territorial (statistical unit) standpoint, however, a different picture emerges. The mainland side has been investing heavily and continuously in port infrastructure in its attempt to sustain industrial growth in Shenzhen. Financial issues revolving around government-backed capital have also caused increased political pressure on the government of Hong Kong, which leads us to another dimension of this relationship: port governance.

11.4   Port governance issues and dynamics of regionalisation

Recent years have witnessed profound institutional changes marking the container port industry. Ports worldwide have been generally sympathetic to private entrants on the basis of efficiency gains and FDI spin-offs. Hong Kong has long been regarded as a model for private participation-induced performance through the notorious 'landlord approach' (i.e. private terminal operations based on a lease system with public regulation and land ownership) since *laissez-faire* principles prevailed from the early origins of the port's commitment to containerisation in the early 1970s. The situation across the border is somewhat different. But when compared to other ports in China, there is little doubt that Shenzhen's spatial proximity and interaction with Hong Kong has translated into Shenzhen's attempts to emulate its southern neighbour (Wang et al., 2004).

Indeed, Shenzhen adopted similar yet distinct arrangements. The underlying guiding principle is that of separating administration from commercial operations, in accordance with one of the core objectives stated by the Ministry of Communications (MOC). To this end, several ports in China have adopted organisational reforms which consisted in the dual creation of a commercial stock-listed corporation to take interests in operations, which are in turn overseen by a purposely established Port Bureau. Organisational reforms were adopted in an ad hoc fashion and have created varying governance models throughout China's ports (Wang et al., 2004). In Shenzhen, minor shares of the major container terminals are held indirectly by the local government through corporate subsidiaries listed on the local stock market, while the Shenzhen Port Administrative Bureau (SPAB) assumes regulatory functions. Figure 11.4 illustrates the resulting governance structure at the Port of Shenzhen.

The two respective governmental authorities in charge of port business, namely the SPAB and the Hong Kong Port Development Council (created in 2003 from the Port and Maritime Board), assume the role of planning and executing port development within their territory. However, they differ in their relationship with the higher administrative hierarchy: while Hong Kong's PDC enjoys greater independence in the overall decision-making process pertaining to port planning matters, the SPAB requires master plan approval from both the province of Guangdong and the MOC in accordance with the new Port Law, in effect from January 2004 (for more on this see Chapter 10).

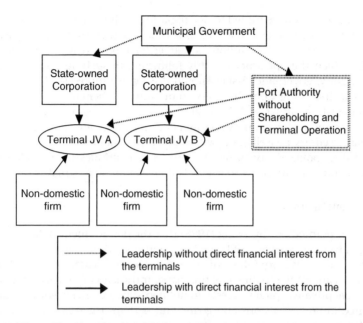

Figure 11.4: The Shenzhen model of port governance

These added bureaucratic layers have not, however, translated directly into a more passive approach to port planning, as Shenzhen's capacity to achieve its port ambitions has been most impressive (and aggressive) given the time-frame of its development. For instance, the next phase of Shekou port is about to begin, which will add 5 million TEU capacity to its existing West Shenzhen facilities, while Phase 3 of Yantian will also add another 5 million TEU capacity to the east. Expansions at both sites together should double the current handling capacity of Shenzhen port to at least 20 million TEU by 2010. In other words, within a five- to ten-year horizon, it is likely that Shenzhen will handle more containers than Hong Kong. HPH's recent downsize of its stakes in Yantian are rumoured to be the result of Beijing's attempts to slow down the company's China ambitions (Gilley, 2002).

The government of Hong Kong, however, assumes a relatively more passive role and in recent years has redeployed its resources towards such things as emerging environmental concerns over marine infrastructure development. Its port planning approach is based on a 'trigger point' mechanism: subsequent phases of development are initiated only once current traffic reaches a capacity utilisation threshold set at 80 per cent. Past experience surrounding delays at CT9 forcing *in situ* capacity increases by operators has, however, illustrated the port's impressive resilience against capacity constraints. Furthermore, as we have noted earlier, *in situ* expansion becomes suddenly blurred by the fact that local operators have turned to neighbouring facilities to exploit commercial growth opportunities and at the same time ease their own local capacity concerns – a situation that follows a market logic of northward migration of cargo which the operators are only following. In such an environment of uncertainty, governance issues should distinguish more clearly between benefits to the Hong Kong business community *vs.* benefits to the Hong Kong population at large. In the absence of a pan-regional governance body overseeing regional infrastructure allocation, it is our view that while co-operative efforts are well under way, competitive ambitions remain strongly embedded in political discourses. This dialectic continues to be addressed through a formula unique to Southern China: economic pragmatism.

11.5   Conclusions

It has been pointed out by Wang (1998) that the development of Shenzhen port is, in fact, an extension of Hong Kong port operation in peripheral locations beyond its territory following migrating trends in cargo sourcing. This chapter has attempted to illustrate the spatial intricacies of modern port systems where private capital interests do not necessarily coincide with socially consented long-term visions and goals. And perhaps there lies the crux of Hong Kong's concerns: its failure to empower itself with visionary and strategic goals due to its persisting universal belief in neo-liberal market principles as an end solution (Yeung, 2000). As the PRD port system demonstrates, the true visionaries are the corporations.

The term 'co-opetition' fares well in encapsulating the complex webs of competition and co-operation. However, closer scrutiny of competing dynamics, as well as regional migration trends in private capital, indicate that the co-operation side of 'co-opetition' remains precarious: co-operative efforts remain essentially private-led initiatives. While this reality accurately reflects *laissez-faire* principles dear to Hong Kong, there remains a number of impeding regulatory and discursive barriers which suggest that the elaboration of a broader public-led pan-regional dialogue may be stretched further. Private sector strategies translate into a 'lock-in effect' where policies of *a priori* competing ports are forced to converge in compliance with overlapping private interests. Pan-regional resolutions stretching beyond mere accommodation of private interests become increasingly difficult and sensitive, as the trucking issue demonstrates. Regulatory practices imposed by the mainland put Hong Kong at a disadvantage and it seems the only way out of this conundrum lies in the enlargement of sustainable regional dialogues and of governance structures – this, in light of increasing public distrust over the true intentions behind northward capital leakages. Any inter-port relationship must also be understood within a broader logic of fierce inter-urban competition over FDI which also puts genuine co-operative efforts at risk. This, again, makes more problematic the co-operative aspects of 'co-opetition' simply because Hong Kong is a *source* of FDI while Shenzhen is a *recipient*.

Nevertheless, the case of the Hong Kong–Shenzhen port relation still demonstrates how geographical penetration of capital and management at the sub-port (i.e. terminal) level towards nearby ports consolidates the conceptual validity of 'co-opetition': ports *should* co-operate while terminals *must* compete. Moreover, the formation of regional port 'co-opetition' seems *a priori* to be more cost-effective in matching market needs. Ironically, such trends also demonstrate how terminal-level entry may undermine port-level policies aiming to achieve regional cohesion by creating a lock-in effect. While such an effect could only be resolved through a philosophical contest between private and public interests in other parts of the world, it is accommodated in Southern China by an economic pragmatism. The strong leadership of private interests in Hong Kong means that Hong Kong operators have been allowed to dis-invest locally and refocus on a regional corporate strategy. The dominating entry of Hong Kong operators (some with mainland China backgrounds such as COSCO Pacific and CMHI) did not encounter much resistance for three principal reasons: (1) China's commitment to its 'One Country Two Systems' economic pragmatism policy which allows economic synergies, in line with the fact that Shenzhen's economy has historically relied on Hong Kong capital and management know-how; (2) a time-sensitive window of opportunities that saw a northward migration trend of cargo coincide with substantial capital requirements to develop transport infrastructure in Shenzhen and Guangdong under private initiatives; and (3) the very short history of Shenzhen as a port-city.

Also, while the port relationship between Hong Kong and Shenzhen differs from that of ports in other parts of China such as between Shanghai and Ningbo (see Chapter 10 of this book) on the basis of regional idiosyncrasies, the PRD port system highlights similar dynamics of competition created by institutional change. Any given interport relationship within mainland China remains deeply affected by similar hierarchical port administrative structure, management, ownership and the role of local governments. Whether such a development model may be applicable to other regions depends on a regional environment of governance within and beyond the ports.

References

Airriess, C. A. (2001) 'The Regionalization of Hutchison Port Holdings in Mainland China', *Journal of Transport Geography*, 94(4): 267–78.

Bird, J. H. (1963) *The Major Seaports of the United Kingdom*, London: Hutchinson.

Gilley, B. (2002) 'Deep Water', *Far Eastern Economic Review*, 26, November.

Giron-Urquiola, G. (2004) 'Hong Kong Port: Dealing with the Issues', *Shippers Today*, 27(3): 12–17.

McKinsey & Co. (2004) 'Shoring Up Hong Kong's Port', *The McKinsey Quarterly*, 3.

Robinson, R. (1985) 'Industrial Strategies and Port Development in Developing Countries: the Asian Case', *Tijdschrift voor economische en sociale geografie*, 76: 33–143.

Shenzhen Port Authority (2003) *Shenzhen Municipal Port & Shipping 2002*, Shenzhen, China.

Shippers Today (2004) 'View from the Top', *Shippers Today*, 27(3): 18–22.

Song, D.-W. (2002) 'Regional Container Port Competition and Co-operation: the Case of Hong Kong and South China', *Journal of Transport Geography*, 10: 99–110.

Song, D.-W. and Yeo, K.-T. (2004) 'A Competitive Analysis of Chinese Container Ports using the Analytic Hierarchy Process', *Maritime Economics & Logistics*, 6: 34–52.

Tongzon, J. (2002) 'Port Choice Determinants in a Competitive Environment', *IAME Panama 2002 Conference Proceedings*, electronic format: http://www.eclac.cl/Transporte/perfil/iame_papers/papers.asp, 22p.

Wang, J. J. (1998) 'A Container Load Centre with a Developing Hinterland: a Case Study of Hong Kong', *Journal of Transport Geography*, 6(3): 187–201.

Wang, J. J., Ng, A., K.-Y. and Olivier, D. (2004) 'Port Governance in China: a Review of Policies in an Era of Internationalising Port Management Practices', *Transport Policy*, 11(3): 237–50.

Yeung, H. W.-C. (2000) 'Neoliberalism, *Laissez-faire* Capitalism and Economic Crisis: the Political Economy of Deindustrialisation in Hong Kong', *Competition & Change*, 4: 121–69.

12

Singapore and Tanjung Pelepas: Co-operation or Competition?

Jose Tongzon

12.1 Introduction

Recent developments in the shipping industry such as shipping alliances and the use of very large ships by shipping lines in major international trade routes and advances in transport technology such as containerisation and the possibility for intermodalism and door-to-door transport services are well documented. These developments in the shipping sector have intensified inter-port competition with major implications for ports. Under this increasingly competitive business environment, ports have constantly made an effort to upgrade their port facilities and develop competitive strategies to remain relevant to their port users and to stay ahead in the competition. The ports in Southeast Asia in particular are accelerating the process of indigenous port development, and some of them are even promoting themselves as hub ports in the region. With particular emphasis placed upon the Ports of Singapore and Tanjung Pelepas, this chapter will review port development trends, infrastructural plans and strategies adopted by the major container ports in Southeast Asia in dealing with the increasing inter-port competition.

12.2 Port development trends and strategies

Some of the major container ports in Southeast Asia have over the years built up a significant container cargo base, mainly as a result of the surge in international trade in the region buoyed up by the remarkable trade-oriented growth of the economies they have served particularly in the latter half of the 1980s and throughout the 1990s and despite the Asian crisis of 1997/8. As can be gleaned from Table 12.1, the volume of cargo through the major container ports in Southeast Asia continued to grow for the period 1990–2002 despite the economic crisis. In particular, the Ports of Singapore, Manila and Tanjung Priok have emerged over the years amongst the top ten ports in the world. The Port of Bangkok was also one of the top ten ports in 1990, but since then has been surpassed by other ports in Asia due to its policy of cargo diversion.

214

Table 12.1a: Ten largest container ports in Asia, 1990–1998

Rank	1990	TEUs	1995	TEUs	1997	TEUs	1998	TEUs
1	Singapore	5,223,500	Hong Kong	12,549,746	Hong Kong	14,567,231	Singapore	15,100,000
2	Hong Kong	5,100,637	Singapore	10,800,300	Singapore	14,135,300	Hong Kong	14,582,000
3	Kaohsiung	3,494,631	Kaohsiung	5,232,000	Kaohsiung	5,693,339	Kaohsiung	6,271,053
4	Kobe	2,595,940	Busan	4,502,596	Busan	5,233,880	Busan	5,945,614
5	Busan	2,348,475	Yokohama	2,756,811	Shanghai	2,520,000	Shanghai	3,066,000
6	Keelung	1,807,271	Tokyo	2,177,407	Yokohama	2,347,635	Manila	2,690,000
7	Yokohama	1,647,891	Keelung	2,169,893	Tokyo	2,322,000	Tokyo	2,168,543
8	Tokyo	1,555,140	Manila	1,687,743	Manila	2,121,074	Tanjung Priok	2,130,979
9	Bangkok	1,018,290	Shanghai	1,527,000	Tanjung Priok	2,091,402	Yokohama	2,091,420
10	Manila	1,014,396	Nagoya	1,477,359	Kobe	1,944,147	Kobe	1,900,737

Source: Containerisation International Yearbook, various issues (1992–2000).

Table 12.1b: Ten largest container ports: 1995–2002

Rank	1995	TEUs	1997	TEUs	1998	TEUs	2002	TEUs
1	Hong Kong	12,549,746	Hong Kong	14,567,231	Singapore	15,100,000	Hong Kong	19,140,000
2	Singapore	10,800,300	Singapore	14,135,300	Hong Kong	14,582,000	Singapore	16,800,000
3	Kaohsiung	5,232,000	Kaohsiung	5,693,339	Kaohsiung	6,271,053	Busan	9,436,307
4	Busan	4,502,596	Busan	5,233,880	Busan	5,945,614	Shanghai	8,610,000
5	Yokohama	2,756,811	Shanghai	2,520,000	Shanghai	3,066,000	Kaohsiung	8,493,000
6	Tokyo	2,177,407	Yokohama	2,347,635	Manila	2,690,000	Shenzhen	7,613,754
7	Keelung	2,169,893	Tokyo	2,322,000	Tokyo	2,168,543	Rotterdam	6,515,449
8	Manila	1,687,743	Manila	2,121,074	Tanjung Priok	2,130,979	Los Angeles	6,105,863
9	Shanghai	1,527,000	Tanjung Priok	2,091,402	Yokohama	2,091,420	Hamburg	5,373,999
10	Nagoya	1,477,359	Kobe	1,944,147	Kobe	1,900,737	Antwerp	4,533,212
11							Klang (12)	4,533,212
22							Pelepas (26)	2,660,000

Port authorities and operators in these major container ports in Southeast Asia have attempted to upgrade their ports and improve their efficiency with the aim of attracting more local and international cargoes to their ports. Economic considerations and political factors have motivated this trend. Some nearby and emerging ports, such as the Ports of Klang in West Malaysia, Laem Chabang in Thailand, and Tanjung Pelepas on the southern tip of Malaysia are also aspiring to be hub ports in the region. Malaysia in particular has been attempting to reduce their volume of cargoes transhipped through the Port of Singapore by lowering their port charges, improving their infrastructure and efficiency, and adopting punitive measures including the imposition of additional levies for cargoes coming out of and entering into Singapore. An investment of S$2.6 billion in port development has been committed for the last five years (*The Straits Times*, 1996a). Tanjung Pelepas is a newly opened port in Johor Baru, Malaysia, that commenced operation in 2000, despite the Malaysian government's drive to promote the Port of Klang as a hub port in the region and the world. In 1994 none of the cargo from Penang, Malaysia was shipped through the Port of Klang. In the first nine months of 1996 60,000 TEUs from Penang were shipped through the Port of Klang, reducing the cargo shipped through the Port of Singapore to 57 per cent (*The Shipping Times*, 1996).

The Thai transport ministry has also announced plans to cut its dependency on other ports for transhipment. In 2000, the Port of Bangkok launched a modernisation programme aimed at improving the port's operational efficiency by simplifying wharf procedures and reducing their container handling operations (*The Straits Times*, 1998). One proposal being considered was for master vessels to be offered lower handling charges in return for loading their cargoes directly at the Port of Laem Chabang in eastern Thailand (*Lloyd's List Maritime Asia*, 1996).

The Philippines has been seriously marketing the strategic location, excellent infrastructure and natural harbours of Subic Bay (a former US naval base, the biggest outside the US) as a regional hub port since the expiry of the lease agreement between the US and the Philippines. Indonesia has planned to develop its port in Batam (*The Straits Times*, 1996b). Although the Asian financial crisis has put this plan on hold due to financial difficulties, once Indonesia is back on the road to economic recovery, it is likely that this plan will be implemented.

Although these ports are relatively undeveloped in terms of throughput and infrastructure, they are, however, well located geographically to service Asia. With adequate investments in technology and infrastructure, it may just be a matter of time before they can become a real threat to other transhipment ports.

Other considerations have been responsible for the trend towards indigenous port development and aggressive modernisation plans in the region. Firstly, the inadequacy of port infrastructure to accommodate the rapid increase in cargo flows, especially in containerised traffic, has resulted in severe port congestion. These countries have experienced trade-oriented rapid growth rates for the past decades, and this economic dynamism has stretched their port infrastructure to its limits. Another consideration is the growing deficit in their services sector, particularly for Malaysia, which has traditionally been using the Port of Singapore as a transhipment port for a great bulk of its inward and outward-bound cargo. Estimates have placed the amount of Malaysia's cargo going through Singapore within the range of one-quarter to more than one-half of Malaysia's foreign trade, which totalled 374.4 billion ringgit in 1995 (*Far Eastern Economic Review*, 1996). The use of foreign-registered ships has also contributed to the outflow of foreign exchange. Port development has also become an integral part of their national development strategy to maintain and improve their international competitiveness. Realising the importance of port development to their overall national development plans, the respective governments of these countries have launched an aggressive drive to promote their ports as hub ports to attract cargoes and global carriers.

12.3   Singapore vs. Tanjung Pelepas

This section will now attempt to discuss in detail the infrastructural plans and strategies adopted by the Ports of Singapore and Tanjung Pelepas. The choice of these two ports is justified by the fact that the Port of Singapore holds the position as the premier hub port in Southeast Asia – a position which it has held for several years – while the Port of Tanjung Pelepas – a newly built port possessing a similarly good locational advantage – with its recent remarkable performance and ambitious plans, has posed the most immediate threat to the hub port status of Singapore. As can be gleaned from Figure 12.1, the Ports of Tanjung Pelepas and Laem Chabang have over the years registered one of the highest growth rates in terms of container throughput. The Port of Tanjung Pelepas in particular has surpassed the Port of Singapore in terms of growth rate since it commenced operation in 2000. The decision by Maersk Sealand and Evergreen to transfer their base for transhipment operations from the Port of Singapore to the Port of Tanjung Pelepas has further signalled to Singapore the potential threat this new port can pose to Singapore's premier position as the major transhipment port in Southeast Asia. As a result of this move by Maersk in 2000, the Port of Tanjung Pelepas captured more than 10 per cent (1.8 million TEUs) of Singapore's total containers handled in 1999.

12.3.1   Port of Tanjung Pelepas (PTP)

One significant port development in the region was the construction of a new port on the southwestern tip of the Malaysia Peninsula, adjacent to the Second Link connecting Malaysia and Singapore across the Johor Straits. It has been in operation since January 2000. The construction began after the signing of the build-operate-transfer (BOT) privatisation agreement between the Malaysian government and Seaport Terminal (Johore) Sdn Bhd which relegated its rights and obligations to its wholly-owned subsidiary, Pelabuhan

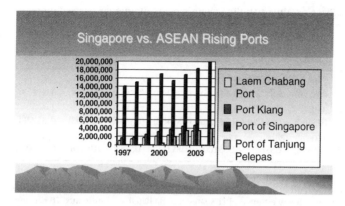

Figure 12.1: Comparison of selected ports' container handling 1997–2004 (TEUs)
Source: Computed from figures taken off official websites, newspapers and *Fairplay Port Guide* (1999/2000).

Tanjung Pelepas Sdn Bhd. The concession period for the BOT project is 60 years.

The development of this port has five phases up to 2020, worth 10 billion Malaysian ringgit. The first phase, which was completed in June 2001, provides 6 berths along 2.16 km of linear container berth with a capacity to handle 3.8 million TEUs. The first two berths were scheduled to open in late 1999, the next two in 2000 and the remaining ones by June 2001. With the completion of the first phase, the port is now equipped with 18 super-post and post-panamax quay cranes with a lifting capacity of 40 tonnes and an outreach of 53 metres, capable of serving the biggest containership, and 58 rubber-tyred gantry (yard) cranes. PTP is linked to national road and rail networks that puts all of the Malaysian Peninsula and Thailand within reach. A new rail link is expected to start block train services between major seaports and inland ports in Malaysia.

This port possesses some characteristics, which could make it an alternative port of call for mainline operators. First, it is well located. It is just 45 minutes from the region's international shipping lanes – the Straits of Malacca – and thus offers ships only a small deviation from the trade lanes it serves. Although it is not as close to the main shipping routes as the Port of Singapore, it is certainly close enough so as not to become a serious obstacle for ships to call. Like Singapore, it also has a natural deep-water harbour with a draft of 15 metres supported by a 12.6 km approach channel of 250 metres width and a 600-metre turning basin which allows for a two-way passage of vessels and a quick turn-around of vessels' transit time. It has a sheltered bay, which makes it protected from any possible natural disturbances.

Second, it enjoys competitive charges and lower labour costs, as Table 12.2 shows. There is a 30 per cent reduction in port charges for shipping lines by

Table 12.2:   Container handling charges per container for selected ports

	Port Klang		Port of Singapore		Laem Chabang 20 ft	Chabang 40 ft	PTP* 20 ft	PTP* 40 ft
	20 ft	40 ft	20 ft	40 ft				
FCL	190 (US$50)	285 (US$75)	270 (US$155)	382 (US$220)	972 (US$23)	1,462 (US$34)	189 (US$109)	267 (US$154)
LCL	330 (US$87)	490 (US$129)	565 (US$325)	786 (US$452)	2,500 (US$58)	3,995 (US$93)	395 (US$227)	550 (US$316)
Tran-shipment	160 (US$42)	240 (US$63)	174 (US$100)	252 (US$145)	462 (US$11)	697 (US$16)	121 (US$70)	176 (US$101)

Notes: Exchange rates used are US$1 = S$1.74, US$1 = RM3.8 and US$1 = THB42.8.
Port Klang: RM, Port of Singapore S$, Laem Chabang THB, PTP S$ (Port of Tanjung Pelepas).
* According to industry estimates, PTP's rates are calculated at an estimated 70 per cent of
Singapore's rates.
Source: *Fairplay Port Guide* (various issues).

using the Port of Tanjung Pelepas rather than Singapore. Third, it is close to the
local market, which can provide a base and a potential hedge in the event
that market forces and other factors compel shifts in transhipment patterns.
Unlike a hub port entirely dependent on discretionary transhipment cargo,
PTP would have sufficient internal cargo as a result of its proximity to the
domestic market. It has a wide back-up area and covers a spacious 1,935 acres of
land for port-related industries. The area around the port has been earmarked
for maritime and port-related activities. An area of 903 acres has been identified
for commercial and industrial activities of which a distri-park covering an area
of 290 acres would be developed for warehousing and distribution, while the
remaining 613 acres are available for port-related industrial activities. There is a
large land bank covering an area of more than 5,000 acres for subsequent
development. Because of its huge land area, the Port of Tanjung Pelepas can
offer dedicated berths to more customers.

It uses state-of-the-art information technology and equipment, which gives
every port user instant access to the port's purpose-designed integrated terminal
and port management information system (ITPMIS). By synergising all the
port's operations and communication centres, the ITPMIS facilitates a free
flow of updated information and provides near paperless transactions between
port personnel, shipping lines, marine services and freight forwarders. Gate systems, berth allocation, ship planning and yard planning have also been fully
computerised for smooth flow and reduced waiting times. On-line container
status inquiry and history and a container tracking system can track cargoes
from the time they arrive.

The new port is reportedly moving aggressively to achieve its goal of securing
a position as Southeast Asia's premier transhipment hub. Like the Port of
Singapore, transhipments make up the bulk of its business, with transhipped
containers accounting for 85 per cent of its total throughput for the year

2000. To achieve this goal, the management has focused on securing mainliners as well as feeder operators to call at the port by offering incentives: dedicated berths to certain customers and the same level of service and efficiency as PSA, but at 30 per cent lower costs (*The Shipping Times*, 2000). Compared to Singapore, Malaysia can offer lower rates due to its cheaper labour costs, availability of land and government incentives. As a result, it has already gained some 2 million TEUs a year from Maersk Sealand and a growing number of feeder operators have expressed their keen interest (*The Shipping Times Online*, 2000). Since starting operations in 2000, it has already attracted four major shipping lines, including Maersk Sealand, APL-NOL, K-Line and Mitsui OSK Lines, to call at its port. The relocation of Maersk Sealand, the word's biggest container shipping line, and Taiwan-based Evergreen from the Port of Singapore to this port has provided a big boost to the port's transhipment status.

In a bid to increase port throughput, the Malaysian Ministry of Finance has lifted a levy on container trucks ferrying goods from Singapore to Tanjung Pelepas, as well as on trucks transporting goods that arrive at Tanjung Pelepas bound for Singapore. Raising the levy on trucks ferrying containers to Singapore is currently under consideration. It is estimated that more than 2,000 trucks move goods from Johore to Singapore daily, carrying almost 1 million TEUs a year to Singapore. Malaysia hopes to plug this leak (*Journal of Commerce*, 2001). The Malaysian government has also made it easier for cargoes to be channelled from the Port of Pasir Gudang to the Port of Tanjung Pelepas by doing away with detailed customs procedures and other documentary requirements, when cargoes are transported from Pasir Gudang in eastern Johor to the Port of Tanjung Pelepas in the west for subsequent export (*The Shipping Times*, 2001).

Although the Port of Tanjung Pelepas has much lower container handling charges and its container handling efficiency is catching up with that of Singapore, the Port of Singapore still enjoys an edge over Tanjung Pelepas in terms of connectivity and frequency which could be more important to shippers. From the shipping lines' viewpoint, Singapore is also much better off in terms of cargo base, which is an important factor influencing the hub port choice of mainliners. Although the Port of Tanjung Pelepas does not pose any threat to Singapore's hub port position in the short and medium term, this possibility cannot be ruled out in the long run if the trend of an increasing cargo base at the Port of Tanjung Pelepas continues. Changes in the allocation of cargoes between the Ports of Singapore and Tanjung Pelepas do not, however, diminish the importance of Singapore as long as there is an overall increase in cargo throughputs at these ports.

12.4   Port of Singapore's response

The success of port development lies predominantly in the competitive strategies ports adopt as well as the competitive advantage they can capture and sustain (Robinson 1993: 85). To maintain its position as the region's hub port, the Port of Singapore has adopted two strategic approaches: one based on competition (or a confrontationist approach by capitalising on its areas of competitive advantage) and the other based on co-operation (by forging more co-operative alliances with other ports). The confrontationist approach has traditionally been Singapore's strategy with the aim of improving its infrastructure, level of efficiency and quality of service. Under this approach it tries to ensure that its port facilities are adequate to handle future increases in cargo traffic and ship visits in the region by investing in port expansion and upgrading. The completed development of the Pasir Panjang terminal, which opened in 1998 (after completion of the first phase of the project), has given an extra handling capacity of 18 million TEUs. In addition, the port's terminals are supported by a number of district parks, providing over half a million square metres of warehousing in total. A district park is a large covered warehouse, which provides automated storage facilities. Customers can process their documents, pack and unpack, mark, label and assemble their goods for distribution to other distribution centres.

The Port of Singapore (PSA) has constantly tried to maintain close relations with its clients, especially the shipping lines. By constantly conducting meetings with clients, PSA is kept up-to-date with their needs and complaints so as to provide them with more customised services. A Key Customer Manager (KCM) is in charge of looking after individual customers' needs and complaints and to work out solutions to fulfil their requirements with help from PSA. A series of cost reduction measures has been implemented as a result of these regular meetings. For example, a 20 per cent concession on port dues for container ships (except long-standing ships) was extended into 1998 and 1999 (*The Shipping Times*, 1997).

PSA has also embarked on the strategy of signing contracts with shipping lines to ensure their continued patronage in the near future. For example, the Virtual Terminal (VT) contract, which PSA signed with the Global Alliance[1] on 12 August 1996, guarantees PSA this alliance's shipping business for ten years. The VT contract is the world's first type of contract to cater to the different logistical requirements of shipping lines. It also promises reliability of service, greater customisation, price stability and cost effectiveness (press release, 12 August 1996).

The Port of Singapore has also been promoting itself as a total logistics centre where door-to-door services are available with state-of-the-art logistical facilities and which can add value to the activities of the shipping lines. It has done this by promoting its bunkering industry, ship registry and other marine-related activities including marine finance, insurance, brokerage and others that make up a one-stop centre. As a result, the Singapore Registry of Ships has grown rapidly in recent years and today ranks as the 7th largest in the world. To attract shipowners to set up a base in Singapore, since 1991 the Trade and Development Board has implemented an attractive incentives scheme called the Approved Shipping Enterprise Scheme (AIS). Companies under this scheme enjoy a tax exemption of up to ten years on income earned from qualifying shipping operations. To qualify for the scheme, 10 per cent of the company's fleet has to be registered with the Singapore flag. The scheme has proved a strong draw for some of the world's top shipping companies, with 36 AIS companies operating a total of more than 500 vessels using Singapore as a base.

Singapore now has a thriving ship financing community with shipping banks such as ING, Christiana Bank and MeesPierson joining the local player – the Development Bank of Singapore. Progress has also been made in building up the local insurance industry. Two P&I Clubs, the Standard Club and the UK Club, now have regional offices in Singapore. Lloyd's of London is continuing negotiations to set up an underwriting presence in the republic. Further, it endeavours to increase the profile of the port of Singapore internationally by actively participating in the activities of the International Maritime Organisation (IMO) to safeguard its strategic maritime interests and keep the sea safe and open to navigation, and by establishing links with other like-minded countries in the form of inviting certain prominent individuals to international advisory groups and as distinguished visitors.

The second strategy adopted by the Port of Singapore follows the policy of active engagement with other ports. There are a number of advantages that can be derived from this strategy. Firstly, apart from marketing its consultancy services internationally, particularly in information technology-based port operations and port terminal logistics management, the Port of Singapore has forged certain co-operative ventures with other ports even as far away as China, India and Africa, offering its capital and expertise in developing and managing state-of-the-art ports. Through these overseas ventures it hopes to build up stronger port linkages with other countries via hub-spoke networks.[2] In this way it can maintain its position as a hub by having greater influence on the supply of transhipment cargo from other ports in the region. These partnerships have so far shown positive results. For example, PSA's joint venture project with the Port of Dalian Authority in northeast China, has seen an increase of 11 per cent growth in 1998. In that year, PSA handled 1.5 million TEUs overseas and aimed to handle at least 10 million TEUs by the year 2007 and to earn at least a third of its revenue from overseas projects (*PSA Annual Report*, 1998).

Secondly, by forming these types of partnerships, PSA can reap economic benefits in terms of revenue. By forming partnerships with ports (those which have the potential of becoming hub ports), PSA is guaranteed a source of revenue. PSA's joint venture with the Middle East, for example, to construct Aden Container Terminal (ACT) in Yemen, which has the potential to become the region's most efficient and advanced container terminal hub, will guarantee PSA a viable source of revenue.

Thirdly, it is a form of diversification. Rather than simply relying on its own port, PSA now has the back-up of other ports. In the event that the Port of Singapore loses its competitiveness, PSA still has these overseas ports to fall back on.

Fourthly, it enhances PSA's partnerships with major shipping lines through co-operation in overseas port projects. This has helped PSA to breeze through the recent Asian crisis. The crisis has resulted in a considerable reduction in imports coming into Southeast Asian markets, leading to lesser containers coming in at a time when the demand for containers was high due to the surge in exports to the West. To salvage this situation, PSA used its joint efforts with various shipping lines to bring in more cargo from China, Australia/New Zealand and South Asia, and thus managed to secure double-digit growth for PSA (*PSA Annual Report*, 1998). The revenue gained from these overseas port joint ventures in turn enabled PSA to give out rebates and simplify its port tariffs for the benefit of its clients. By forming partnerships with overseas ports, PSA not only diversifies its investment, but also improves its competitiveness by giving out rebates and implementing other cost-reduction measures from the revenues earned through overseas investments. Even if PSA's charges were to be higher than those of regional ports, the shippers are compensated in the form of rebates and other cost-reduction measures. Furthermore, PSA has not only been involved in overseas projects but has also diversified into other business areas. It is now partnering with the Port of Dalian Authority to redevelop the eastern area of Dalian port into a modern waterfront leisure and business hub (*PSA Annual Report*, 1998).

12.5   Competition or co-operation?

The major ports in the region have adopted port development policies and strategies that are generally aimed at expanding and upgrading their port infra-structure. For most ports, access to state-of-the-art technology and management has been brought about through privatisation. However, in the development of their respective infrastructures, little attention has been given to the social aspects of infrastructure and to the need for co-operative endeavours among ports in the region.

It should be pointed out that greater inter-port competition is likely to bene-fit port users including both the shippers and the shipping lines, at the expense of lower profit margins for port operators. This is to be expected given that ship-ping lines have more choice in choosing their few ports of call. The trend towards load centring, as shipping lines try to rationalise their operations and cut costs, has made competing port authorities offer a number of incentives including lower port charges to major shipping lines. Thus, from the viewpoint of port operators, co-operation rather than competition between ports could be more beneficial. In the area of warehousing and distribution, for example, the Port of Tanjung Pelepas can perform the labour-intensive aspects of the oper-ation, such as the packing and unpacking of containers, while the Port of Singapore can look after the shipping and distribution parts of the operation. While there is definitely a strong case for some form of co-operation between ports in the region, it is difficult in practice to find the most appropriate basis for the allocation of functions. There is a natural tendency for ports to look after their national interests before regional interests. Specifically, each port would like to benefit more from co-operation than the other, and therefore, would like to perform the higher value-added functions or parts of the operation. This kind of attitude, in the context of an unequal distribution of gains and costs from co-operation, can pose a serious obstacle to establishing some form of co-operation among ports as much as among nations.

12.6   Conclusion

To combat increasing inter-port competition, major ports in the region have upgraded their infrastructure as well as developed more and more advanced services to improve their productivity and efficiency so as to lower port charges and increase their international competitiveness. Ports will have to be constantly on their toes to come up with appropriate policies and strategies to attract shippers and shipping lines. In this increasingly competitive environment some ports will succeed while others may fail, depending on their ability to understand and meet the needs and preferences of port users.

The Port of Singapore has adopted two approaches to deal with this increasingly competitive environment: one is 'confrontationist', while the other is seeking ways of co-operation. Given that any country with money or with the privatisation option can procure the latest and best technology to modernise its ports and investments to improve the quality of its workforce, the first line of approach (the 'confrontationist' approach) is no longer sufficient and sustainable. A judicious combination of both strategies with more emphasis on forging business alliances and joint ventures with other ports is suggested. However, the right form of alliance and co-operation it should take is an issue that needs to be resolved.

Notes

1. This Global Alliance is the combination of American President Lines, Mitsui OSK Lines, Nedlloyd Lines and Orient Overseas Container Lines.
2. The Port of Singapore aims to achieve 20 per cent of its annual revenue derived from these overseas ventures, particularly from various strategic alliances and investments in the logistics business and port terminal development. It is currently involved in projects in China, India, Indonesia, Vietnam, South Korea, Hong Kong, Italy, Belgium and Brunei.

References

Central Intelligence Agency (2006) *Map of Southeast Asia,* http://www.cia.gov/cia/publications/factbook/reference_maps/southeast_asia.html
Containerisation International Yearbook (1992–2000).
Far Eastern Economic Review (1996) 'Battle on the High Seas', 6 June: 56–8.
Fairplay Port Guide (various issues).
Journal of Commerce (2001) 'New Malaysian Port Moves to Gain Singapore Business', 24 January.

Lloyd's List Maritime Asia (1996) Regional update, 4 January.

Map of Singapore and the Southern Part of Malaysia (2006) http://www.lonelyplanet.
com/mapshells/south_east_asia/singapore/singapore.htm)

PSA Annual Report (1998) PSA Ltd.

Robinson, R. (1993) 'The Changing Patterns of Commercial Shipping and Port Concentration in Asia', in R. Babbage and S. Bateman (eds), *Maritime Change: Issues for Asia*,
New South Wales: Allen & Unwin, 69–88.

The Shipping Times (1996) 'Port Klang's Promotion Drive Paying Off', 24 October, p. 1.

The Shipping Times (1997) 'PSA Adopting Cost Reductions', 5 August.

The Shipping Times (2000) 'Tanjung Pelepas Offers Similar Level of Services as PSA',
12 January.

The Shipping Times (2001) 'KL Gives Further Boost to Tanjung Pelepas Port', 13 February.

The Shipping Times Online (2000) 'PTP Shifts Focus to Securing More Common Feeder
Operators', 13 November.

The Straits Times (1996a) 'Staying on Top as the Top Port', 10 July, p. 28.

The Straits Times (1996b) 'KL to Spend S$2.6b on Port Development over Five Years',
26 June, p. 36.

The Straits Times (1998) 'Bangkok Upgrades Port to Stay Lean', 5 September 1998, p. 22.

13
Busan and Gwangyang: One Country, Two Port System

Gi-Tae Yeo and Sam-Hyun Cho

13.1   Introduction

There is no doubt that ports play a very significant role in logistics, since over 80 per cent of cargoes in world trade are handled in ports. In Korean ports the trade volume is increasing constantly with the growth of the Far East Asian economy generally and of the Korean economy specifically. In particular container volume is rising sharply. Since 99.7 per cent of trade volume is handled in ports, they constitute a major piece of infrastructure and have an essential role in the national economy (Kang, 2003).

During the last 20 years (1982–2002), container cargo volume has increased by 14 per cent per year on average. In 2002, a throughput of 11.89 million TEUs was recorded for Korean ports, at a growth rate that is 3.8 per cent higher than the 10.2 per cent growth rate for world container cargo volume. In 2002, this growth trend has caused 136 million tons of excess demand with only 79 per cent of total demand accounted for by available capacity. Hence, the Korean government has started constructing 30 berths in Busan New Port and 33 berths in Gwangyang (Han, 2002).

Since the late 1990s the Far East region has exhibited the most vigorous economic activity. The world's top six hub ports are located in that region and 16 out of the 30 biggest ports are also in the Far East. As a result, the competition among those ports is becoming severe (An, 2002). The two major ports in Korea, Busan and Gwangyang, are focusing on maximising profits under a simultaneous competitive and co-operative relationship with other hub ports in the Far East.

This chapter aims to examine the present situation of competition and co-operation between Busan and Gwangyang ports. In section 13.2, co-operation in port construction is dealt with. Competition in government investments is examined in section 13.3. Competition and co-operation in container terminal operation and port administration are examined in section 13.4 and regional and national port competition and co-operation in section 13.5. Finally conclusions are drawn from these discussions in section 13.6.

13.2   Co-operation in port construction

Before implementing a port development plan, a decision should be made as to whether a single heavy investment in a hub port or a diversified investment in two or more ports should be undertaken. In the case of container ports, it is essential to have economies of scale because if enough cargo volume is not guaranteed, it is impossible to obtain operational efficiency and connectivity, with an insufficient service frequency. Therefore, most countries invest heavily in developing a hub port with operational efficiency, aggressive marketing etc. (Lee and Park, 2003). However, the number of hub ports is limited in a particular area. In the case of Korea, the ports of Busan and Gwangyang have both been developed as hub ports for the region.

Most container cargo in Korea is sourced from Seoul and its surrounding area and from Busan, the biggest port city in the country, where the throughput volume has exceeded the port's capacity (Table 13.1). Thus, long service times and high logistics costs have caused Busan to lose its competitiveness. Moreover, Korean export products have become less price-competitive because of these two factors. As a result, in the early 1980s, the concept of the 'two ports system' was adopted and Gwangyang port was developed to resolve these problems (Figure 13.1).

The development of Gwangyang port means not only lifting a great burden from Busan port, but also a better balance in terms of Korea's geographical development. With the construction of a container port and an iron works, the Port of Gwangyang has grown to become the main port in the south of Korea (Ma, 2003). Both Busan and Gwangyang ports are located in the middle of the main trunk shipping route. In addition, following any future reunification, or the establishment of more friendly relations between North and South Korea, the two ports can be connected with China and Russia via railway. These facts mean that the two ports have the possibility of becoming the

Table 13.1:   The forecasting of supply and demand in Korean ports (unit: 1,000 tons, %)

	2000	2001	2002	2006	2011	2015	2020
Total cargo volume	833,579	886,373	935,126	1,182,235	1,512,894	1,734,737	2,089,117
Demand for facilities (A)	517,210	578,481	647,424	767,862	1,015,837	1,192,096	1,482,939
Supply of facilities (B)	417,561	430,437	511,572	527,969	527,969	572,969	572,969
Excess demand (B − A)	−99,649	−148,044	−135,852	−239,893	−487,868	−664,127	−954,970
Secured facilities ratio (B/A)	80.7	74.4	79.0	68.8	52.0	44.3	35.6

227

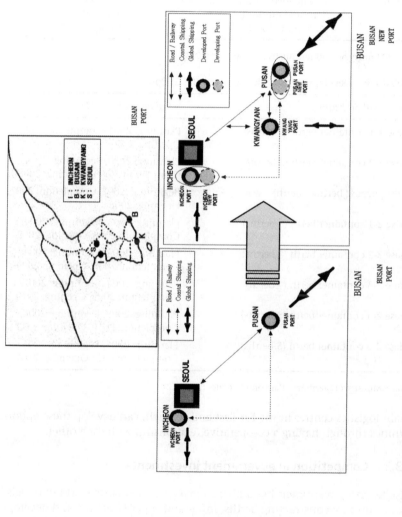

Figure 13.1: The concept of the two port system – Busan and Gwangyang

Table 13.2:   Development plans of container ports

	New Busan Port (1995–2011)	Gwangyang Port (1987–2011)
Berths	30	33
Capacity	8.04 million TEU	9.13 million TEU
Cost (US $)	8.5 billion	7.3 billion
Investors	Private sector, Korea Container Terminal Authority, government sector	Korea Container Terminal Authority, government sector

Source: Ministry of Maritime Affairs and Fisheries (2003).

Table 13.3:   Development schedule for New Busan Port

Items (total 30 berths)	Schedule (1995–2011)
Phase 1-1 container berth (6 berths)	Planning: 2001, Completion: 2006, Opening: 2007
Phase 1-2 container berth (3 berths)	Planning: 2000, Beginning: 2004, Completion: 2008, Opening: 2008
Multi-purpose berth (1 berth)	Beginning: 2002, Completion: 2007, Opening: 2008
Phase 2-1 container berth (3 berths)	Planning: 2003, Beginning: 2004, Completion: 2008, Opening: 2009
Phase 2-2 container berth (3 berths)	Planning: 2003, Beginning: 2004, Completion: 2008, Opening: 2009
Phase 2-3 container berth (4 berths)	Planning: 2004, Beginning: 2005, Completion: 2009, Opening: 2010
Phase 2-4 container berth (5 berths)	Planning: 2005, Beginning: 2006, Completion: 2010, Opening: 2011
Phase 2-5 container berth (5 berths)	Planning: 2005, Beginning: 2006, Completion: 2011 Opening: 2012

Source: Ministry of Maritime Affairs and Fisheries (2003: 12).

main logistics centres in the Far East and, as such, can develop these opportunities through having a co-operative relationship with each other.

13.3   Competition in government investments

The Korean government has a plan to make the two ports world hub logistics centres by constructing berths, infra- and super-structure, and developing the hinterlands etc. (Han, 2004) (Table 13.2).

In Busan port, under the title 'The Hub Port in the Pacific for the 21st Century', US$8.5 billion will be invested up until 2011 in constructing 30 container ship berths in Kadukdo, to the southwest of Busan (Port of Busan, 2006) (Table 13.3).

Table 13.4: Development schedule of New Gwangyang Port

Items (total 33 berths)	Schedule (1987–2011)
Phase 1 container berth (4 berths)	Planning: 1985, Completion: 1987, Opening: 1998
Phase 2-1 container berth (4 berths)	Planning: 1996, Completion: 2001, Opening: 2002
Phase 2-2 container berth (4 berths)	Planning: 1999, Completion: 2003, Opening: 2004
Phase 3-1 container berth (4 berths)	Planning: 2001, Beginning: 2002, Completion: 2006, Opening: 2007
Phase 3-2 container berth (3 berths)	Planning: 2002, Beginning: 2003, Completion: 2008, Opening: 2009
Phase 3-3 container berth (5 berths)	Planning: 2003, Beginning: 2004, Completion: 2009, Opening: 2010
Phase 3-4 container berth (5 berths)	Planning: 2004, Beginning: 2005, Completion: 2010, Opening: 2011
Phase 3-5 container berth (4 berths)	Planning: 2005, Beginning: 2006, Completion: 2011, Opening: 2012

Source: Ministry of Maritime Affairs and Fisheries (2003: 12).

In Gwangyang port, US$7.3 billion will be invested until 2011 in constructing 33 berths and related infrastructure (Port of Gwangyang, 2004) (Table 13.4).

It is estimated that US$38.1 billion will be invested in total port development, including developing the two mega hub ports. In the period 2002–11, US$27.3 billion from government and US$10.8 billion from the private sector will be needed. However, there is a budget shortage of US$10.2 billion in government and US$5.0 billion in the private sector (Korea Container Terminal Authority, 2004) (Table 13.5). As a result of this budgetary shortfall, one selected port shall receive the full investment amount first. This means that Busan and Gwangyang are facing a highly competitive relationship.

13.4 Co-operation and competition in port administration and terminal operation

Before the 1990s, Korean ports were owned and operated by the government since ports were recognised as public sector entities. Since the 1990s, however, with the inauguration of the Korea Container Terminal Authority (KCTA), a government-owned and privately operated port system has been adopted, with the objective of achieving a high level of operational efficiency and service levels (Kim, 1998). More recently, from 2004 both Busan and Incheon ports adopted a Port Authority System where both central and local government are

Table 13.5:   Budgetary shortages for port investments in Korea (US$ billion)

	Required investment (A)	Available investment (B)	Shortage of investment (A) − (B)
Total	38.1	22.9	15.2
Government sector	27.3	17.1	10.2
Private sector	10.8	5.8	5.0

Source: Korea Container Terminal Authority (2004).

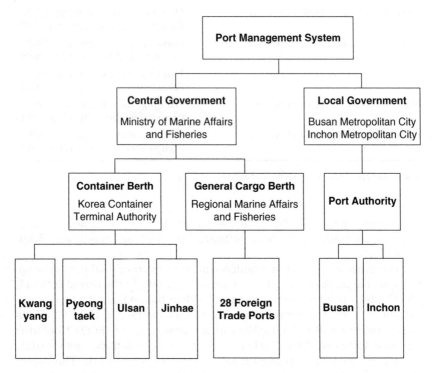

Figure 13.2:   Schematic diagram of port management system in Korea

in charge of operating ports. The purpose of this system is to resolve problems with central government ownership and operation. Such problems include, for example, ignoring regional characteristics, a lack of transparency and irrationality in making decisions (Sohn and Won, 2004). In Korea, the port operational system has developed as a three-step process characterised by: government-owned and operated ports, government-owned and private sector operated ports and, finally, government-owned and central and local government operated ports.

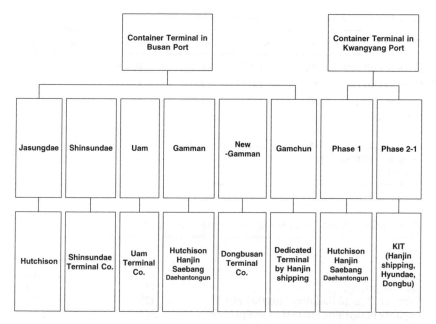

Figure 13.3:   Status of container terminals in Busan and Gwangyang ports

Figure 13.2 shows that Busan port is administered by a Port Authority which is operated in common by central, and Busan local, government. Meanwhile, the Port of Gwangyang is operated by the KCTA and supported by local government in marketing. Therefore, these two ports have similar aspects in their relationships with central government, but with respect to their relative locations and operation there are some differences. This means that the two ports have both a co-operative and competitive relationship.

Busan port has six terminals, Jasungdae, Shinsundae, Gamman, New-Gamman, Uam and Gamchun, and Gwangyang Port consists of a first phase and 2-1 phase terminal as shown in Figure 13.3. Table 13.6 shows each terminal's length, draft and alongside capacity.

Jasungdae Terminal is operated by Hutchison, Shinsundae terminal by Shinsundae Terminal company, Gamman by Hanjin/Hutchison/Saebang/Daehantongun, New-Gamman by Dongbusan Container Terminal company, and Uam terminal by Uam Terminal company. However, Gamchun Terminal is a dedicated terminal for Hanjin Shipping.

From the above, Hutchison operates two terminals – Jasungdae and Gamman – which are recognised for having a co-operative relationship with each other. These facts indicate that the terminals in Busan port are in a relationship that is both co-operative and competitive (Korea Container Terminal Authority, 2003).

Table 13.6a: Overview of Busan container terminals

Berth	Jasungdae	Shinsundae	Gamman	New-Gamman	Uam	Gamchun
Quay length (m)	1,447	1,200	1,400	826.5	500	600
Water depth (m)	12.5–15	14–15	15	12–15	11	13
Capacity of cargo handling (10,000 TEU)	120	120	120	65	27	34
Capacity of berthing (10,000 ton/ships)	5/4 1/1	5/4	5/4	5/2 5/1	2/1 0.5/2	5/2

Table 13.6b: Overview of Gwangyang container terminals

Berth	1 Phase	2-1 Phase
Quay length (m)	1,400	1,150
Water depth (m)	15	12–15
Capacity of cargo handling (10,000 TEU)	120	81
Capacity of berthing (10,000 ton/ships)	5/4	5/2 2/2

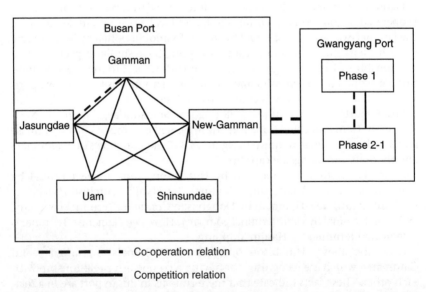

Figure 13.4:   Co-operation and competition relationship between Busan and Gwangyang ports

Gwangyang's first phase terminal is operated by Hanjin/Saebang/ Hutchison/Daehan tongun. This is exactly the same company that operates Gamman terminal in Busan port. The 2-1 phase terminal is operated by KIT (Korea International Terminal) which is invested in by Hanjin shipping, Hyundai Merchant Marine and the Dongbu company. An interesting fact is that Hanjin Shipping has invested in both Phase 1 and Phase 2-1 terminals. That is, co-operation and competition occur between two terminals within Gwangyang port.

Overall, considering both Busan and Gwangyang ports, Gamman terminal in Busan and the Phase 1 terminal in Gwangyang have a co-operative relationship. However, with other terminals in both ports competition prevails (Figure 13.4).

13.5   Regional and national port competition and co-operation

13.5.1   Regional and national competition

Competition between ports may be classified as international *vs.* domestic and regional *vs.* local. First, internationally, Busan, Kobe, Kaohsiung, Hong Kong and Singapore are in competition, as they have a similar hinterland and are located on the main shipping trunk route. Second, in the domestic arena, ports compete for the attraction of import and export cargoes (for instance, Hamburg and Bremen etc.). Third, on a regional basis, with a similar hinterland and function, competition also exists. Busan, Gwangyang, Shanghai, Kobe and Qingdao ports are located within 1,000 km of each other and compete for transhipment cargo from Korea, Japan and China. Finally, at the local level, Busan and Gwangyang ports compete with each other within the same country (Koh and Yeo, 2003).

Over the last 30 years (1970–2000), world container cargo handled in container ports has increased more than 37 times. In 2002, the volume recorded was 266 million TEU including transhipment and empty containers. This continuing trend is strongest in the Far East region. The containerised share of the world total cargo volume increased from 37.6 per cent to 46.4 per cent in 2002 (Lee, 2002). Regional predictions for 2010 and 2015 are shown in Table 13.7.

As cargo volumes increase, the competition among ports in the Far East region is becoming increasingly severe. In the twenty-first century, the current 20 top hub ports in the world will be reduced to a world top 10 mega-hub ports through competition. It is predicted that five of the top ten ranked ports will be in the Far East. In this region, Hong Kong and Singapore are already defined as mega-hub ports by having an annual container throughput of over 10 million TEU. However, Kaohsiung in Taiwan, Shanghai in China, Kobe, Tokyo and Yokohama in Japan, and Busan in Korea have to compete to survive as mega-hub ports. Moreover, Tianjin, Dalian and Qingdao in China, Osaka and Kitakyshu in Japan, and Gwangyang, Incheon and Pyeongtaek in Korea

Table 13.7:   Forecasting container cargo volumes in East Asia (unit: million TEU)

	2002	2005	2010	2015
Total	83.7	109.3–111.5	146.7–156.0	178.4–194.8
Korea	11.9	19.3	29.7	37.6
Japan	13.1	14.5–15.3	16.1–19.2	17.5–22.2
China	29.3	40.9–41.6	60.2–63.1	77.8–83.8
Northern China	7.2	10.6–10.9	16.6–17.7	23.0–25.4
Southern China	22.1	30.3–30.7	43.6–45.4	54.8–58.4
Hong Kong	18.7	21.5–22.0	24.8–27.2	27.2–31.2
Taiwan	11.2	13.1–13.3	15.9–16.8	18.3–20.0

Source: Ocean Shipping Consultants (2003).

have joined this competition with recent fast growth. Hence, the survival game is likely to become even more complicated.

Each country has its own port competition strategy. First, China is investing heavily in the 'top two box ports', Shanghai and Shenzhen. In particular, the government is promoting the Shanghai International Shipping Centre, especially with its investment in the Yangshan Islands Container Terminal Development Plan, whereby 52 berths with 16 metres draft will be built within the next 20 years. As a result, Shanghai is expected to have the capacity for an annual throughput of 30 million TEUs per year. Second, Japan has its Super Hub Port Development Plan, with Tokyo, Yokohama, Nagoya, Kobe, Osaka, Kitakyshu and Hakata ports as the first candidates. Third, in Taiwan, under the Asia Pacific Regional Operation Centre Plan, a concentrated development has been adopted in Kaohsiung port and a new port construction is considered in Taipei. These ports were designed for containerships of 15,000 TEU alongside. In addition, the labour supply and pay structure have been reformed and an Automatic Customs Clearance system (i.e. EDI) has been introduced. Fourth, Hong Kong aims to maintain its position as the world's top container port by expanding its hinterland and facilities.

Yeo et al. (2004) analysed the competitive advantages of the seven major ports in Korea and China that are predicted to face the severest competition – Busan, Gwangyang, Shanghai, Qingdao, Tianjin, Dalian and Kaohsiung. By applying factor analysis, the seven 'port competitiveness power' factors – port service, hinterland, availability, convenience, logistics cost, centrality and connectivity – were investigated. The results are given in Table 13.8 and Figures 13.5–13.7.

A Port Competitiveness Power Structure was developed and total competitive power was appraised by MDMG-HFP (Multi Decision Multi Group-Hierarchical Fuzzy Process). The result shows that the most competitive port is Shanghai (0.93660), with Busan (0.91426), Kaohsiung (0.88407), Qingdao (0.85600), Gwangyang (0.83377), Tianjin (0.81571) and Dalian (0.80740) following.

For the Port of Busan, convenience was superior to other ports, but hinterland and connectivity were relatively poor. In the case of Gwangyang, logistics cost

Table 13.8:   Port competitiveness factor values

	Port service	Hinterland	Availability	Convenience	Logistics cost	Centrality	Connectivity
Busan	0.99704	0.91426	0.98990	1.00000	1.00000	0.97222	0.96616
Gwangyang	0.95092	0.62955	0.97860	0.97276	0.99029	0.84444	0.83377
Shanghai	1.00000	1.00000	0.98986	0.93660	0.98693	1.00000	1.00000
Qingdao	0.94162	0.74041	0.97582	0.95216	0.97961	0.91667	0.88970
Tienjin	0.88715	0.70597	0.95508	0.94590	0.95783	0.86111	0.81571
Dalian	0.89069	0.62899	0.94639	0.92144	0.97304	0.84167	0.80740
Kaohsiung	0.97147	0.92023	1.00000	0.97053	0.98470	0.97500	0.88407

Source: Yeo et al. (2004).

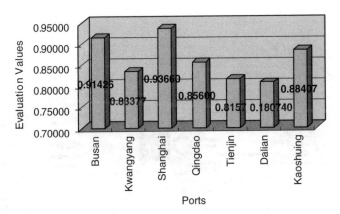

Figure 13.5:   Evaluation values of each port

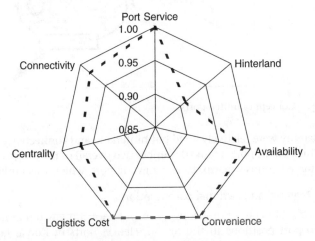

Figure 13.6:   Status of port competitiveness factors at Busan port

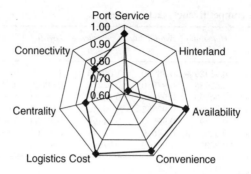

Figure 13.7:   Status of port competitiveness factors at Gwangyang port

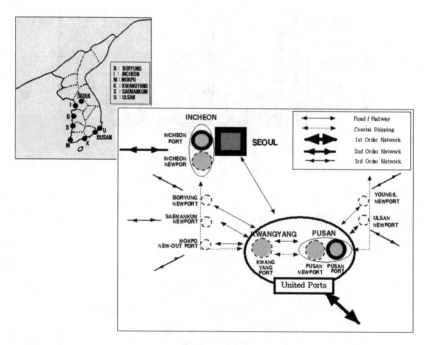

Figure 13.8:   Concept of united ports

and availability were relatively good but hinterland and connectivity were the lowest. Thus, Busan port is ranked number two overall of the target ports that were evaluated and is superior to Gwangyang port, which was ranked fifth.

13.5.2   Regional and national co-operation

It is foreseen that Hong Kong, Singapore and Kaohsiung will maintain their main hub port positions in the region. Hence, ports in Korea, Japan and

China will experience severe competition. As a counterplan and encompassing both Busan New Port and Gwangyang port, a 'united ports' approach (Figure 13.8) could prove to be a good plan (Park, 2003).

Indeed, for the 'united ports' approach to work between two ports, the integration of port logistics systems is necessary. For this, the connectivity between the two ports via road and rail should be available, and, if possible, the transport time between the two ports should be two or three hours. More specifically, a fast transport unit, for example a 40 knot vessel or express rail etc., will enhance the effectiveness of the 'united ports' concept. Finally, inspection, immigration and CIQ controls should be integrated and port facilities and agencies should be shared (Ma, 2004).

If the united ports concept expanded to encompass other ports in the western area of Korea, the united ports can become a 'transit centre' for the region as a whole. Thus, the competitive power of the ports involved will be greater.

13.6 Conclusions

During the last 20 years (1982–2002), Korean container cargo volumes have increased by 14 per cent per year on average. However, this trend has caused 135,850,000 tons of excess demand in 2002, for which only 79 per cent of capacity is available to handle the total volume. Therefore, in an effort to resolve this problem, Busan and Gwangyang are expanding through construction, irrespective of the fact that the regions where the two ports are located are two of the most competitive from the point of view of attracting rapidly increasing container volumes. The concept of the 'two port system' was initially aimed at releasing the burden on Busan port, but now the two ports are in both a co-operative and a competitive relationship.

This chapter's purpose was to examine the present situation of competition and co-operation between Busan and Gwangyang ports. The two ports have a competitive relationship due to limits on the availability of Korean government funds. In operational aspects, Busan port is owned by central and local government, while Gwangyang port is owned by central government alone. They are, therefore, in a relationship of simultaneous competition and co-operation. In the administration of container terminals, there are some cases where operating companies have invested in both ports. This point also indicates that the two ports are in a relationship of simultaneous competition and co-operation. In final conclusion, for developing competitive advantages and attracting greater cargo volumes, an approach based on the 'united ports system' can be very effective.

References

An, S.-Y. (2002) 'Financial Plans of Busan Port for Increasing Nation Competitiveness', *Maritime Korea*, 76–82.

Han, C.-H. (2002) 'Strategies of China and Japan's Ports', *Korea Maritime Institute Report*, 1–37.

Han, C.-H. (2004) 'Strategy of Global Terminal Operator', *Korea Maritime Institute Report*, 86–99.

Kang, B.-G. (2003) 'Developing a Financial Plan for Gwangyang Port', *Maritime Korea*, 100–113.

Kim, H.-S. (1998) 'Korean Port Management System', *Korea Maritime Institute Report*, 1–4.

Koh, Y.-K. and Yeo, T.-D. (2003) 'A Study of the Competition and Cooperation between Ports as an Industrial Logistics Policy: Past Lessons and Future Opportunities for the Ports of Busan & Gwangyang', *Korea Logistics Review*, 13(2): 139–60.

Korea Container Terminal Authority (2003) *Strategy for Korea as Logistics Hub*, Busan.

Korea Container Terminal Authority (2004) *Developing Impacts of Northern China Ports including Shanghai Port to Korea*, Busan.

Lee, S.-W. and Park, S.-H.(2003) 'Strategies for Korean Port Authority', *Korea Maritime Institute Report*, 25–40.

Lee, Y.-S. (2002) 'Efficient Using Method for Busan Container Terminal', *Maritime Korea*, 30–5.

Ma, M.-S. (2003) 'Developing and Activating Policy for Gwangyang Port', *Korea Maritime Institute Report*, 1–8.

Ma, M.-S. (2004) 'Issues of Developing Gwangyang Port: Human, Budget, Logistics', *Korea Maritime Institute Report*, 1–8.

Ministry of Maritime Affairs and Fisheries (2003) www.momaf.go.kr/eng/main/main.asp.

Ocean Shipping Consultants (2003) *World Container Port Outlook to 2015*, London: Ocean Shipping Consultants.

Park, C.-H. (2003) 'Strategy for Developing Gwangyang Port', *Maritime Korea*, 120–7.

Port of Busan (2006) 'Busan New Port', http//www.portbusan.or.kr/service?id=en_newport_02.

Port of Gwangyang (2004) http://www.portgy.com.

Sohn, A.-H. and Won, H.-Y. (2004) 'The Regional Economic Effects of the Establishment of the Busan Port Authority and Improvement Strategies', *Korean Association of Shipping and Logistics*, 40: 83–96.

Yeo, K.-T., Park, C.-H., Jeon, I.-S., Lee, H.-G. and Ryoo, H.-K. (2004) 'A Study on the Analysis of Competitiveness in Container Ports of Shanghai and North China & Korea Using MDMG-HFP Process & Inverse Relation of Fuzzy Evaluation', *Korean Association of Shipping and Logistics*, 42: 45–70.

Index